Content Management for E-Learning

Núria Ferran Ferrer • Julià Minguillón Alfonso
Editors

Content Management
for E-Learning

 Springer

Editors
Núria Ferran Ferrer
Universitat Oberta de Catalunya
Barcelona, Spain
nferranf@uoc.edu

Julià Minguillón Alfonso
Universitat Oberta de Catalunya
Barcelona, Spain
jminguillona@uoc.edu

ISBN 978-1-4419-6958-3   e-ISBN 978-1-4419-6959-0
DOI 10.1007/978-1-4419-6959-0
Springer New York Dordrecht Heidelberg London

Library of Congress Control Number: 2010937638

Printed on acid-free paper

Springer is part of Springer Science+Business Media (www.springer.com)

Foreword

This is a book about content management for technology-enhanced learning (TEL). Of course, learning is not *only* about content. If it was, as many have argued before, then we could have just sent students to the library in the predigital era and we could have asked them to come back for exams after 5 years or so.

However, content (or maybe the more general notion of resources) certainly is important in learning: learners manipulate content to figure things out, teachers (in more or less formal settings) use content to demonstrate or illustrate or provide background or detail, etc.

After the initial hype around "learning objects," learning content suffered from a "bad reputation" in TEL research circles. This may be the natural backlash of disappointment after initial expectations that were too high or that did not factor in the time it would take to reach some of the goals. Maybe the renewed interest in Open Educational Resources will make research on learning content more respectable and popular again. But then again, it will only be a matter of time before the hype cycle will take its downward dive again. Still, then the Next Big Thing will come along and content will be "hot" again...

Beyond the changing appreciation of the value of content for learning, on a more fundamental level, I am convinced that research on content management is a core topic for the TEL community and I am delighted to see how many of the more prominent researchers in our domain continue to focus on this topic, exploring issues ranging from theoretical perspectives, over pedagogical design and copyright to more technical aspects like interoperability and repositories. Even strategic management issues are explored in the concluding chapter of this book.

I also note with particular pleasure that the second part of this book focuses on case studies and practical issues – all the more relevant in a field like ours where too many people have too many opinions (not necessarily hindered by any knowledge of the domain or practical experience with trying things out in practice) and few dare to actually build prototypes or even production level systems, in order to observe what happens when these get deployed and learn from the experience in a more scientific way.

In short, this book addresses an important and enduring topic for TEL research: as such, it will be a valuable resource for many current and future researchers. But first and foremost, I do hope that this book will be of value to you, dear reader... Enjoy!

Leuven, Belgium   Erik Duval

Preface

The increasing growth in the use of e-learning environments, in which education is delivered and supported through information and communication technologies, has brought new challenges to academic institutions. E-learning through virtual environments could be defined as the use of the Internet to access learning resources, interacting with contents, instructors, and other learners, in order to obtain support during the learning process, with the aim of acquiring knowledge, constructing personal meaning, and growing from the learning experience. From all the current definitions of e-learning, it can be seen that learning contents are one of the key issues for a successful e-learning experience. This is the reason why there is a real need for academic staff, managers, and librarians to rethink the whole process of delivering courses, information resources, and information services.

E-learning systems involve, therefore, users, services, and contents. All these elements cannot be independently managed, as the learning process is a complex combination of all of them. With respect to contents, some authors point out that traditional content management systems applied to learning resources try to reproduce the traditional learning process where contents are transmitted (or, in this case, delivered) from teachers to learners, following a producer–consumer model (one-to-many). But the concept of learning itself has changed, shifting from a content-centered paradigm to a learner-centered one, where contents are no longer the most important element in the learning process. On the contrary, it is much more important to focus on the interaction between the learner and the contents (wherever and whatever they are). We live in an age of content abundance, so the problem now is not finding contents, but organizing them and selecting the most appropriate ones for a given learning objective. Recent initiatives such as Open Education Resources or OpenCourseWare are making quality contents publicly available, so contents are no longer confined to a single educational institution. In this sense, learning object repositories (as a specialization of digital libraries) are becoming a common element of educational institutions, allowing both teachers and learners to build true learning communities around a common subject or field of interest. Furthermore, the apparition of the web 2.0 has promoted a new create-remix-share model (many-to-many) where all users (experts and teachers but also learners) are potential authors of new kinds of contents. Therefore, the concept of content management applied to e-learning needs to be rethought.

Nowadays, the term content management has been widely accepted and commonly used, and there are hundreds of products that offer solutions for several areas of application, including education. For this reason, this book tries not to focus on specific product solutions but rather offering on the one hand, a conceptual framework that comprises what is content management and the relationship with knowledge management together with providing perspectives on how the semantic web could complement content management and also how to deal with copyright restrictions, and how to describe information competences and skills required and acquired by teachers and students in virtual environments. On the other hand, the book also provides case studies and practical solutions for designing a project for managing content, standards for content e-learning management, a review of existing experiences of learning repositories, and a survey of available platforms for delivering courses and providing access to information resources.

This book attempts to address content management in the elearning sector from mainly two approaches; one theoretical and the other, a more pragmatic one.

The 11 chapters explore the areas and issues that are highly important in relation with content management for e-learning. The chapters are organized in three parts. The first one includes the conceptual framework, the second outlines the case studies and pragmatic issues and the last one is a chapter with the perspectives and the conclusions.

The conceptual part of the book starts with a background on content management and the role of the content management systems and the social software, beyond the technological solutions, in the disciplines of knowledge management and e-learning. This chapter revises the idea of implementation of content management systems in relation with the context of e-learning and the different types of knowledge involved.

Chapter 2 sets out how the methodological changes imposed by the European Higher Education Area and the technological changes derived from Web 2.0 have modified the requirements of content management systems in educational institutions. This chapter also describes the learning process in virtual learning environments as something that is much more than just providing learners with digitized content. The chapter also explores the relationships of traditional content management systems and the broader scope of virtual learning environments, including aspects of metadata standards, content personalization, the use of semantic web techniques and ontologies, the use and annotation of learning resources and the possibilities offered by the use of web 2.0 technologies.

The concept of the learning object is deeply studied in Chap. 3. This chapter tries to establish basic definitions around the learning object with the aim of promoting findability and retrieval which are two basic requirements of any educational scenario dealing with learning objects. In order to do so, a list of assertions and implications related to learning objects are discussed, raising several important issues with respect to context of use, metadata, instructional design and automation. These assertions establish a minimum set of requirements that should be taken into account when designing any educational experience based on the use of learning objects.

The following chapter explores the relationship between pedagogical design and content management in the creation and use of online learning resources. A strong relationship between the two concepts is presented and in particular that the strategies and considerations around content management in e-Learning systems impose a number of constraints on the variety of pedagogical designs and methods that are available to teachers using these technologies. For instance, it exposes the problems that arose when changing from one Virtual Learning Environment (or Learning Management System) to another one. It also outlines the issue of reusability which is a crucial factor of many aspects of e-learning content management and pedagogy.

The aspect of the competences required for searching and using information for learning is addressed in Chap. 5. First of all, the chapter explains the concept of "information competence" and how important it is to develop such competence in the context of workplace skills required in a knowledge society, and specially, in an e-learning environment. Being competent in the use of information is a requirement for life-long learning. In that sense, the information competence development has been a controversial aspect since their implications on the learning and teaching process makes it difficult to see it as an isolated concept. The components of these competencies are explained, such as skills, attitudes, and all other aspects linked to information seeking and use process. Finally, some recommendations of the aspects of information competence are laid out and which must be taken in to account in order to design systems that help teachers and students to be more competent in their use.

The last chapter of the theoretical part of the book is about copyright as for a successful and peaceful production and exploitation of e-content, one needs to take into account any possible pitfalls that may exist under the legal systems and adopt the best contractual practices to avoid them. This chapter outlines the several legal issues involved in the production and exploitation of e-learning contents, copyright, and intellectual property, which deserve special attention not only because of their strategic and economic importance in any e-learning project, but mainly because of the intricacies that may result from the different national laws that may be affected as a result from the ubiquitous nature of the Internet. This chapter will identify these issues and examine the existing legal framework from an international perspective.

The second part of the book presents a more practical perspective and provides case studies to illustrate the issues presented.

The first chapter of this second part provides a more technical view provided through a review of the LCMS (Learning Content Management System) with regard to its functionality for content management, which is classified in four categories: creation, management, publication, and presentation. Content creation provides creators that do not have technical knowledge in building web pages with the necessary tools to focus on the contents. Content management puts at one's disposal the mechanisms to store all documents in a central database where the rest of the web page data, users, preferences, and structure are also stored, in order to facilitate the work flow and the communication among all the participants. Content publication provides the automated mechanisms so that an approved page can be presented, applying the established patterns, which once expired, can be filed for future reference. Finally, content presentation in a LCMS can manage automatically the accessibility of the web site, with the support of international rules like WAI, and adapt itself to the preferences or needs of each user.

In Chap. 8, an introduction to e-learning technical standards, where the principal actors in e-learning standardization efforts are presented, together with the main areas of standardization and the most important initiatives in progress is offered. This chapter describes the most relevant standards for content management within the e-learning context. The first part of this chapter is devoted to the concept of the Learning Object, which is presented and studied as a way of management learning content within e-learning environments. The final part describes the most popular content management standards and specifications, such as IEEE LOM (Learning Object Metadata), SCORM (Sharable Content Object Reference Model), and IMS Content specifications (IMS Content Packaging, IMS Question & Test Interoperability Specification and IMS Digital Repositories Specification).

Apart from the interoperability and reusability of the learning objects, one of the key issues in learning repository design is the quality of the content. Chapter 9 presents a peer evaluation process that was developed for and trialed on learning objects and funded by the LEARNet project in Hong Kong. The chapter begins with a discussion of learning objects and why there is a critical need for evaluation of them. It then outlines methods of evaluation, the rationale for choosing peer evaluation in the Hong Kong context, how the peer reviews were conducted, the obstacles faced, and the resulting recommendations for future evaluation.

There are many critical issues around quality, access and the costs of information and knowledge over the Internet, as well as the provision of content and learning material. As it becomes clearer that the growth of the Internet offers real opportunities for improving access and transfer of knowledge and information from universities and colleges to a wide range of users, there is an urgent need to clarify these issues with a special focus on Open Educational Resources initiatives. This is the aim of the last chapter of the section. This work addresses the need to define the technical and legal frameworks, as well as the business models, to sustain these initiatives. That is the background to the study which has aimed to map the scale and scope of OER initiatives in terms of their purpose, content, and funding.

Finally, the last part of the book, offers an e-learning management strategic perspective as a conclusion. Content management is not an issue most senior administrators in educational institutions will be familiar with. In this chapter, a strategic view of content management, especially for those institutions that have or are about to make a major commitment to the development and delivery of online teaching and learning materials.

Although content management is probably most likely to be implemented from the bottom up, through small projects initiated at a departmental or divisional basis, there will come a point at which the institution needs to look at content management as a whole. This chapter will not provide definitive answers to these questions since these answers will vary from institution to institution. However, the chapter will discuss some of these questions and suggest a process for dealing with the management of content.

Contents

Contributors

A.W. (Tony) Bates
President and CEO of Tony Bates Associates Ltd, a consultancy
company specialising in planning and managing e-learning
and distance education, Vancouver, BC, Canada
tony.bates@ubc.ca

Josep Maria Boneu
Professor of Computer Science at the Centre d'Estudis Politècnics. Barcelona,
Catalonia, Spain
jboneu@uoc.edu

Sandy Britain
Research consultant for the Ministry of Education in New Zealand, New Zealand
sandybritain@gmail.com

Núria Ferran
Professor at the Department of Information and Communication Sciences,
Universitat Oberta de Catalunya, Barcelona, Catalonia, Spain
nferranf@uoc.edu

Dirk Frosch-Wilke
Professor at the Faculty of Business Information Systems,
University of Applied Sciences Kiel, Germany

Jennifer Jones
Faculty of Education, The University of Wollongong,
Wollongong, NSW, Australia
jlj366@uow.edu.au

Brian Lamb
Manager of Emerging Technologies and Digital Content with the Office of
Learning Technology at The University of British Columbia, Vancouver, BC,
Canada

María Gertrudis López
Professor at the Central University of Venezuela, Caracas, Venezuela

Carmel McNaught
Centre for Learning Enhancement and Research (CLEAR),
The Chinese University of Hong Kong, Shatin, N.T, Hong Kong, China
carmel.mcnaught@cuhk.edu.hk

Julià Minguillón
Professor at the Computer Science, Multimedia and Telecommunication
Department, Universitat Oberta de Catalunya, Barcelona, Spain
jminguillona@uoc.edu

Mario Pérez-Montoro
Professor at the Department of Information Science, Universitat de Barcelona,
Barcelona, Catalonia, Spain
perez-montoro@ub.edu

Salvador Sánchez-Alonso
Lecturer at the Computer Science Department, University of Alcalá,
Alcalá de Henares, Spain
salvador.sanchez@uah.es

Niall Sclater
Director of Learning Innovation, Open University, Milton Keynes, UK
N.L.Sclater@open.ac.uk

Miguel-Angel Sicilia
Head of Information Engineering Unit at the Computer Science Department,
University of Alcalá, Alcalá de Henares, Spain

Sirje Virkus
Tallinn University, Institute of Information Studies, Lecturer and Erasmus
Mundus Digital Library Learning (DILL) Master Programme Coordinator

David Wiley
Instructional Psychology and Technology, Brigham Young University,
Provo 84602, UT, USA
david.wiley@gmail.com

Raquel Xalabarder
Professor of Intellectual Property Law, Universitat Oberta de Catalunga,
Barcelona, Catalonia, Spain
rxalabarder@uoc.edu

Part I
Conceptual Framework

Chapter 1
Theoretical Perspectives on Content Management

Mario Pérez-Montoro

Abstract In the last decade different software solutions have appeared in order to facilitate content management. These solutions make the life cycle of digital contents more comfortable and flexible so that it is possible to improve and to automate processes and make both more effective and efficient the communication via Internet. Nevertheless, there is a lack of a single standard that integrates all these products and applications. In this chapter we present a state-of-art of the different types of existing products, including Content management (CM), Web content management (WCM), Record management (RM), Document management (DM), Digital asset management (DAM), Enterprise content management (ECM) and Learning content management (LCM), and their characteristics are defined. We will also approach the different research lines associated with these solutions, showing a special attention to the application of these solutions in the knowledge management and e-leaning fields.

1.1 Introduction

In the last decade, different software solutions have appeared in order to facilitate content management. These solutions, Content Management Systems (CMS), make the life cycle of digital contents more convenient and flexible so that it is possible to improve and automate processes and make communication via the Internet both more effective and efficient. Nevertheless, there is a lack of a single standard that integrates all these products and applications.

This chapter has a dual purpose: on the one hand, to look at content management in a wide sense, and, on the other hand, to demonstrate the role played by the new CMS, beyond the technological component, in the disciplines of knowledge management and e-learning.

M. Pérez-Montoro (✉)
Department of Information Science, Universitat de Barcelona, Barcelona, Catalonia, Spain
e-mail: perez-montoro@ub.edu

N. Ferran and J. Minguillón (eds.), *Content Management for E-Learning*,
DOI 10.1007/978-1-4419-6959-0_1, © Springer Science+Business Media, LLC 2011

To achieve this aim, the following points will be developed. First, in Sect. 1.2, providing a description of the context in which they originate, with special emphasis on the needs that lead to their development will be discussed. Second, a characterisation and defining a special type of CMS will be made, i.e., social software. Following on from this, in Sect. 1.3, an examination of the different types of knowledge that might be found in a teaching–learning environment and within the context of an organisation will be made. Once this examination has been fully completed, we will then identify and analyse the critical operations that define both the disciplines of knowledge management and that of e-learning with regard to this cognitive typology. Thus, we will analyse the critical operations that would have to be implemented for the knowledge to fully achieve a central role within the organisational environment and to ensure that it is transferred correctly within an e-learning context. Finally, in Sect. 1.4, we will assess to what extent the technological solutions offered by CMS can help in the appropriate implementation of critical operations in these two different contexts.

1.2 Content Management

In recent years, there has been a proliferation in the number of different technological solutions geared towards facilitating and making the creation, management and use of web page content easier. All these solutions, with their individual peculiarities, offer a series of common features and properties that enable them to be identified as CMS.

The expression CMS has become a macro-label used to classify a broad and extensive set of existing technological products on the market, ranging from document management systems in the traditional sense to new solutions for the creation and diffusion of knowledge.

In financial terms, as quoted by certain sources (Shegda et al. 2006), these types of solutions[1] are widely established, generating a $2.3 billion software market in 2005, with an annual forecast growth of 12.8% up to the year 2010.

Yet it is not only in terms of the financial aspect that these types of solutions are beginning to become established. The theory, for example, has also inspired a significant amount of specialist literature. The important role that these types of tools may play has been studied with regard to different fields, from economics to education, but it must be stressed that in this particular case, practical development clearly preceded subsequent theorisation.

However, although rivers of ink have been written on the subject of CMS, characterising these types of solutions is no easy task. The problem does not lie in the complexity of the object analysed, but rather in the nature of it. Indeed, as some authors have said (Browning and Lowndes 2001, for example), CMS is more a new concept than a new technology.

---

[1]In the version known as Enterprise Content Management (ECM).

1.2.1 The Origin of Content Management Systems

In general terms, it can be said that CMS appear to meet the needs that result from a technological evolution and the use made of it.

If an approximate date has to be proposed, as some authors agree (Tramullas 2005; Wilkoff et al. 2001; Cuerda and Minguillón 2005), although fully functional developments already existed in the second half of the 1990s, it is, primarily, after 2002[2] when CMS begin to become established within the technological panorama.

It was precisely at that time that an important change in the use of the Internet environment by its users, and especially companies, took place. Throughout the 1990s, corporations had identified the possibility of using the Internet phenomenon for their own benefit.

In this sense, on the one hand, the Net was beginning to be seen as a source of business identifying new marketing channels and giving rise to what we now call e-commerce and to everything linked to this business strategy. On the other hand, the Net was identified as the perfect technological resource for improving and making the internal operation of organisational structures and processes involved in these types of organisations more efficient. Finally, the Net was ultimately identified as a unique opportunity that until that time had not been considered for reinventing and channelling teaching–learning processes, with e-learning strategies and all their subsequent development being established this way.

In this new context, in order to tackle these new challenges successfully, static and unarticulated web pages soon became insufficient, and the use of other types of more dynamic web pages capable of allowing continuous changes – more scalable web pages, in a manner of speaking – would increasingly be required to meet the needs of the environment.

However, the challenge was not only a technological one, but it also had to respond to economic restrictions. It was necessary to find a tool that would enable all this to be done, but which would also enable it to be done cheaply; in other words, that would allow someone with minimal IT knowledge to be able to use it and develop the required solutions quickly and in a straightforward way. CMS, by taking advantage of the advances developed in the field of information and documentation management, came about in response to this dual technological and economic need.[3]

But how do these systems help achieve these aims? In the context of an organisation, we usually find an infinite number of documents (or digital resources) that contain different types of data. So, for example, we can identify documents with textual data, numerical data, images and/or sounds or even documents that simultaneously

---

[2] Although, strictly speaking, by 1995 some companies, such as Vignette, had already launched this type of product on the market.

[3] These origins are so closely connected to the web, as we shall see, that some authors (including Wilkoff et al. 2001) refer to these types of systems as Web Management Systems rather than Content Management Systems.

include all these different types of data. In addition, these documents, with their variety of data, may come in very different formats. Thus, there are documents that have been created on a word processor, spreadsheets, web pages, e-mails or multimedia files, to name just a few examples. If we look for a suitable type of management for these digital resources that come in a huge range of formats, we will surely have to go with the segmentation of that type of management and the use of different management systems, with the problems of reduced efficiency and limited thoroughness that these types of strategies involve.

Strictly speaking, as some authors point out (Browning and Lowndes 2001), CMS are technological tools that have been created to meet the priority aim of increasing and automating the processes that effectively and efficiently sustain Internet communication. In this sense, CMS are articulated sets of IT applications – although from the user's point of view, there is a feeling that they are a single program – which, as far as possible, usually integrate documents with different formats and directly create new documents in XML format. These resulting documents or digital resources are generically known as "content".[4]

The CMS keep the content separate from its appearance or final presentation, which leads to significant benefits for operations, and they provide the tools needed for the efficient management of these contents that may aid the communicative dimension (in a broad sense) of the web of which they are part of. The tools they provide and which allow the complete lifecycle of a web page to be covered are characterised by the fact that they enable this management to be implemented very easily and quickly which means that we do not have to be constantly entrusting a webmaster or specialist with these tasks, thus saving time and money and achieving the flexibility that this entails. More practical detail about this subject can be found in Chap. 8.

1.2.2   Social Software

As already outlined, the term CMS has ended up being used as a label to describe an extensive and disparate group of technological products that are invading the market. The group is so heterogeneous that in some instances it is difficult to find the reasons that have led to a product being given this label.

In this group, social software can be identified as a special type of content management product. Strictly speaking, unlike other CMS, a part of social software is not directly related to the main objective of aiding and supporting the creation, management and use of the contents of web pages. However, this type of solution has a very important relevance in the field of knowledge management and e-learning.

---

[4] As McKay (2004) says, content is a unit of data with certain associated information. In this sense, strictly speaking, these types of resources would contain the semantic part of contents with a minimum degree of presentation.

Intuitively, social software is a set of applications designed to aid (synchronous and diachronous) communication, the personalised creation of contents and the exchange of information between users (individuals and groups) in such a way that this communication and exchange, in turn, generate the spontaneous creation of social networks or communities. As will be presented in detail in Sect. 1.4.2, all those applications can help in the adequate implementation of the critical operations involved in e-learning contexts.

Leaving some tools aside (such as the e-mail, mailing lists, instant messaging or news groups), which could also be identified, albeit indirectly, as software of this type, the most popular social software are weblogs, RSS systems, wikis and social bookmarking.

Let us first deal with weblogs. The weblog is a tool that allows for the construction and online publication of personal web pages, without the need for technical knowledge. They present a list of news items (texts or articles by one or more authors) arranged inversely with regard to their publication date and offer the possibility of being commented on by other people. Examples of this type of tool are Blogger (http://www.blogger.com/start), Manila (http://manila.userland.com/), Movable Type (http://www.movabletype), pMachine (http://www.pmachine.com/) and TypePad (http://www.typepad.com/).

In a strict sense, weblogs produced by a single user (just to post news) cannot be considered a genuine social software tool. Only in the cases where this news is then commented on by others can we regard it as being imbued with a real social dimension. In these cases, the weblog acts as a catalyst for a virtual community formed by the author of the weblog and the people commenting on their news, where the list of the people taking part in the discussions and the opinions, thoughts and stances that each one adopts are published.

Yet the social dimension of this tool does not end here in the creation of a community following the possibility of commenting on the news. In a further stage, when reference is made to other weblogs and their addresses are included in these comments or in the news item itself, a multiplying element appears. In these cases, what is generated is no longer a virtual community, but a virtual community of virtual communities; a transversal network of communities formed by the social articulation of the communities generated autonomously by each of the weblogs. As will be observed later, this social dimension and this multiplying effect open up a new world of possibilities in the use of weblogs in the field of knowledge management and e-learning.

Looking briefly at Really Simple Syndication (RSS) systems from first a technical point of view, this type of system is a tool that permits web retransmission or syndication. They allow users to receive an alert (or summary), automatically and normally in their e-mail, of updates or news – in some cases, they can even receive the update or news item itself – from a page in which they are interested without the need to enter and look at this page continuously.

Although this kind of system can be applied to the syndication of any type of information in XML format, the most common use of this class of resource is in the context of weblogs. Applied to these tools, they allow the user to automatically receive all the new additions (news or comments) to the weblogs in which they are interested without having to visit them. In this sense, it strengthens the social dimension of weblogs even further, diachronously connecting the RSS user to all those people who form part of the communities derived from each weblog. Some examples of tools that allow for this type of collective subscription include Bloglines (http://www.bloglines.com), BlogBridge (http://www.blogbridge.com) and Feedburner (http://www.feedburner.com).

Let us now tackle the subject of wikis. Wikis are a type of tool that permits the collaborative, quick, easy and online creation and publication (and the management of that publication) of content by a group of users. This type of tool allows a history of changes to be retained that includes both the changes made and their authorship, and which also permits any previous version of this content to be retrieved. In many cases, this type of solution usually includes a special section called a sandbox where novice users can practise before using the system publicly. The most famous example of a product created using a tool of this type is Wikipedia.

As can be seen in its definition, the social component of the wiki lies in the possibility of being able to create content collectively and in the possibility of this content being amended, corrected and evaluated by the other members of the community of users. Thus, by using this type of tool, the content created is submitted to an "ecological" context in which only the content that stands up to the criticism and evaluation of the community survives.

Concluding this brief overview, the last of the social software tools will be analysed, i.e., social bookmarking. Traditionally, when someone found a web page that was of interest or use to them, what they usually did was register it or mark it (with a bookmark), using the tools offered by their browser. This register of bookmarks is set in the user's browser. This strategy offered interesting benefits: it allowed them to return to that page without having to waste time in another search on the browser. However, the fact that the register of bookmarks is kept in the user's browser means that this type of information is relegated to their exclusive use without others being able to access and take advantage of it.

To solve this limitation, as an alternative, social bookmarking systems permit these bookmarks to be stored outside the Internet user's browser and made accessible to a set or community of other users. This community of users may be public or limited in number and of restricted access. As well as storing these bookmarks, they are also usually classified or categorised (based on what is known as a folksonomy).

This strategy of accessible storage and categorisation is what turns social bookmarking systems into genuine social software. When a user marks a web page and classes it simultaneously, these labels are made accessible to the rest of the members of the community. By making them accessible, they permit significant benefits to be obtained.

On the one hand, this system allows subsequent information search strategies used by the members of the community to be improved. When one of the members of the community is searching for web pages related to that label, the system will offer them as search result the pages that have been classed with the label previously by other members of the community. On the other hand, by being based on an intellectual indexation procedure (produced by humans), this information search and retrieval system offers better results than automated retrieval systems based on algorithms (such as that of search engines). In addition, one should not forget that the results of this type of search are offered in the form of a ranking – based on the criteria of the number of users who have marked a page – and that this ranking is also determined by intellectual decisions (made by humans) and not by algorithmic calculations, with the advantages of suitability with regard to the expected information that this involves. Finally, by sharing the labels, the members of the community also share and group knowledge and personal opinions on the contents of the web that they have previously selected.[5] Two examples of this type of system are Del. icio.us (http://del.icio.us) and Furl (http://www.furl.net).

1.3 Knowledge Management and E-Learning

Following the review of the technological panorama for content management, it is possible to look at the subject of knowledge management and e-learning.

One could state that knowledge management can be understood as a discipline; the main aim of which is to design systems that enable knowledge to become a value for an organisation. This means that, by implementing these systems, knowledge should clearly contribute to the achievement of the aims sought by the organisation. E-learning, by contrast, can be viewed as a discipline; the aim of which is to design a series of strategies geared towards achieving the creation, transfer and consolidation of a person's knowledge by means of online resources.

The design of these types of systems and strategies that sustain both disciplines, however, cannot be planned and implemented adequately without previously taking into account a series of restrictions imposed by the object to which they should be applied. In this sense, it is essential to first look at the different types of knowledge that can be found in a teaching–learning environment and in the context of an organisation. This examination will enable us to understand the properties of the institution examined and will also help us profile their transfer and management. Once this examination has been fully completed, the critical operations that would need to be implemented for the knowledge to fully achieve this central role within the organisational environment and for its correct transfer within an e-learning context will be analysed.[6]

---

[5] It is also important to point out that social bookmarking systems present some limitations. For example, on the one hand, the fact of not using a controlled documentary language when assigning categories to the web pages causes the typical problems of documentary noise and silence when these systems are used as information search and retrieval strategies. On the other hand, there is also the danger of these systems being used fraudulently (and unethically) to promote specific web pages with ulterior motives beyond informational criteria.

[6] The starting point for this section can be found in a number of ideas proposed by Pérez-Montoro (2005). Specifically, this paper aims to be a reformulation and generalisation of those ideas extending them to the e-learning scenario.

1.3.1 Types of Knowledge

Analysing both the context of an organisation and an e-learning context, we find that both appear to be involved in different types of knowledge. However, in both contexts, in organisations and in online teaching–learning environments, it is also possible to verify whether these same types of knowledge are repeated. In other words, the same common types of knowledge appear in both contexts. These different common types of knowledge have their own characteristics and, therefore, require personalised, or a la carte, management and transmission which takes into account this unique nature (Table 1.1).

Referring to the specialist literature, it is not difficult to see that there are different and disparate knowledge classification proposals involved in these types of contexts that we are analysing. This chapter does not endeavour to support any of these proposals, but to introduce an alternative classification (summarised in Fig. 1.1) based on a dual and intuitive distinction. This classification will subsequently enable us to characterise with greater precision the operations involved in the processes in which knowledge is managed and transferred. The first distinction will refer to the format of the knowledge, the second, in turn, will focus on its intrinsic (or propositional) properties.

We shall first start with the distinction based on format. Usually, knowledge in these types of contexts (organisational and online teaching–learning) can be found in two different formats. On the one hand, one has *knowledge as human capital*. This is knowledge residing, as a mental state, in the heads of the members of the organisation or of the person undergoing an e-learning process. It comprises the sum of all the knowledge (tacit and explicit) that these individuals have in their heads. On the other hand, one can identify *knowledge as information*. This comprises the knowledge represented – materialised, in a manner of speaking – in the form of documents (in any of their formats).

Let us now consider the second distinction, which focuses on the intrinsic or propositional properties of knowledge. Using these properties, it is possible to discriminate between *explicit knowledge* and *tacit knowledge*.

Explicit knowledge is characterised for being directly codifiable in a representation system such as natural language. Thus, it is easily transferable or communicable and is therefore directly accessible to other individuals. To show that a person, A, has this type of knowledge, it is usual to use the expression, "A knows that P" (where P is usually a heading). Consequently, knowing that a water molecule comprises two hydrogen atoms and one oxygen atom or knowing that when the red light on a photocopier goes on, the ink needs changing are two examples of this type of knowledge.

Table 1.1 Type of knowledge in an organisation

According to its format	According to its intrinsic properties
Knowledge as human capital	Explicit knowledge
Knowledge as information	Explicitable tacit knowledge
	Non-explicitable tacit knowledge

Tacit knowledge, by contrast, corresponds to knowledge based on personal experience and in many cases is identified with the skills of the person. Its main characteristic is that it is difficult to transfer or communicate – verbalise, in a manner of speaking – and, therefore, it is not directly accessible to other individuals. To show that a person, A, has this type of knowledge, it is usual to use the expression, "A knows how to P" (where P is usually a verb). Consequently, knowing how to swim, knowing how to ride a bicycle, knowing how to drive a car, knowing how to speak a language, knowing how to speak in public or knowing how to motivate and manage a group of people are a number of examples of this type of knowledge. In turn, it is possible to discriminate two types of tacit knowledge: tacit knowledge, which, although with difficulty, can be made explicit (verbalised), and non-explicitable tacit knowledge. Knowing how to multiply would be an example of the first type; and knowing how to speak a language, an example of the second type.

If we adequately use Cartesian multiplication,[7] the two underlying sets of categories of this dual distinction (knowledge as human capital and knowledge as information, on the one hand; and explicit, explicitable tacit and non-explicitable tacit knowledge, on the other hand), the result obtained is a classification of all the knowledge that potentially exists in the contexts that we are analysing. The four categories that define it would be as follows: explicit knowledge as human capital, explicitable tacit knowledge as human capital, non-explicitable tacit knowledge as human capital and knowledge as information. This classification will enable us, in

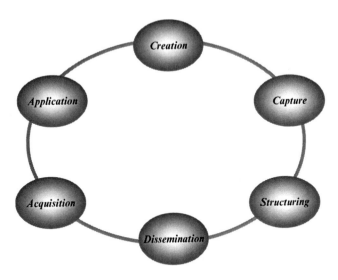

Fig. 1.1   Critical operations in knowledge management

---

[7]In this case, it does not make sense to multiply the knowledge category as information of the first distinction by the categories of the second because, as we have already indicated above, this type of knowledge is, by definition, knowledge (explicit or explicitable tacit) that has been explained and represented in a document form.

the next section, to characterise more adequately the critical operations of the knowledge management programs and e-learning strategies.

1.3.2 Critical Operations in Knowledge Management and E-Learning

Now that it is clear what the different types of knowledge (and their specific characteristics) are in organisational and e-learning environments, the critical operations that define both the knowledge management discipline and the e-learning strategies will be identified.

1.3.2.1 Critical Operations in Knowledge Management

We begin with the subject of knowledge management. As stated previously, knowledge management seeks for knowledge to become a value for an organisation and for knowledge to contribute clearly to the achievement of the objectives sought by the organisation. In general terms, this is achieved when it is ensured that all of the knowledge that is in the organisation can be used by anyone who needs it to act appropriately at all times in that context.

However, behind this aim is a series of critical operations on whose proper development depends to a large extent on the success or failure of a knowledge management program. This series would be formed by the following operations: the creation of knowledge, its capture, its structuring and processing, its dissemination, its acquisition and the application of the knowledge. It is important to point out that for these programs to work, these operations must be articulated between themselves forming a circular chain structure where each of them is applied to the result obtained from the application of the previous one. The representation of the chain in which these operations are articulated can be found in Fig. 1.1.

Let us start by tackling the first of the operations, i.e., the creation of knowledge. This operation can be defined as the process whereby new knowledge is generated in the head of a member of the organisation. The result is usually knowledge in the form of human capital, although it may be tacit or explicit. This new knowledge is usually generated on the basis of the everyday practice of the individual in the organisation. Among all of this knowledge created, one can highlight that it is due to the role it plays in the context of an organisation, i.e., best practices. Best practices are solutions to problems (knowledge, in short) that an individual has found and which, by being imitated by the rest of the community, saves effort and helps the organisation.[8]

---

[8]Allied to this concept is also that of worst practices: incorrect solutions (pseudo-knowledge) that should not be imitated and in which more effort should not be invested in the context of the organisation. These should be considered to be as or more important than best practices.

And, now the second of the operations, i.e., the capture of knowledge. Capture may be understood as the series of operations aimed at the identification and extraction of the knowledge residing in a person's head (knowledge as human capital) to place it within the grasp of the rest of the community that needs it. In the case of explicit knowledge, this capture is made by means of its coding or representation in the form of documents. The result of this capture is the transformation of knowledge as human capital into knowledge as information. In the case of an explicitable tacit knowledge, it is first verbalised and then submitted, as in the case of the explicit, to its coding or representation in the form of documents. However, in the case of non-explicitable tacit knowledge, capture is transmitted through socialisation strategies between the individual who possesses it and the rest of the community. In this last case, the knowledge continues in its format of knowledge as human capital.

Structuring and processing is the next critical manoeuvre and focuses on (explicit or explicitable tacit) knowledge represented in a document form. These documents are submitted to a treatment that includes a series of operations. On the one hand, the document is submitted to a dual revision. In this revision, specialists (a publication committee) decide whether the knowledge represented is relevant (whether it really can help achieve the objectives sought by the organisation) and does not harbour any risk (if it includes any type of sensitive information that may harm the organisation in some way). If the document passes the dual revision, it may be considered to have been approved. On the other hand, once the document has been approved, it is submitted to a formal and semantic examination where a documentary analysis is made. Finally, following this examination, the document is incorporated into the documentary system (it is published in the system), which has been designed to ensure that documents such as this, depending on the interests of the organisation, are accessible and shared by all the members that may need them.

The following operation is described, i.e., dissemination (or sharing). Dissemination can be understood as the series of operations aimed at the knowledge involved in the organisation reaching the members of the community that need it through its transfer and dissemination. In the case of explicit knowledge and explicitable tacit knowledge, this dissemination is usually made through the transfer and dissemination of the documents in which it is represented. In the case of the non-explicitable tacit knowledge, however, this dissemination is again made through socialisation strategies between the individual that possesses it and the rest of the community interested in it.

The next critical operation is that of acquisition. This operation can be understood as the perception by the members of the community of the knowledge that circulates through it as the result of dissemination. This cognoscitive perception is always made on the basis of the background (set of beliefs and knowledge that govern the conduct of an individual) of the person receiving this knowledge (the receiver). In the case of the explicit and explicitable tacit knowledge represented in a document form, this operation is carried out on the basis of the interaction between the receiver and the document where the knowledge is represented. The result of this interaction is the transformation of knowledge as information into knowledge as human capital. However, in the case of the non-explicitable tacit knowledge, the acquisition is again achieved through socialisation strategies between the individual who possesses it and the potential receiver. In this case, the knowledge remains knowledge as human capital.

The last of the operations in this chain is that of application. In this operation, the person who has acquired the knowledge, applies it and reuses it in their daily practice in the organisation. In many cases, the receiver reuses this knowledge in new contexts different from the one that originated it, creating a reinterpretation of it that offers as a result, the creation of new knowledge. With this new knowledge created, the stock of knowledge in the organisation is increased and the circle is closed, restarting the whole management process by activating the first link in the chain of operations.

The result of applying the circular chain of critical operations articulated in knowledge management is highly profitable and beneficial. Whenever a piece of knowledge completes all of the processes involved in this chain of management, there is an increase in the quantity of useful knowledge that circulates throughout the organisation and access to it is improved. This directly and positively benefits the internal operation of the organisation, improving the strategies designed and meeting the objectives. Simultaneously, and recursively, thanks to the circular nature of the process, this knowledge again supplies the same chain and, in turn, generates new knowledge. A practical approach for creating a minimal CMS can be found in Chap. 7.

1.3.2.2 Critical Operations in E-Learning

In order to be able to tackle the critical operations of e-learning adequately, we first have to briefly introduce a small distinction with regard to the learning models. This distinction will allow us to set the context of e-learning correctly.

Traditionally, since the Age of Enlightenment, learning has been carried out in strictly formal contexts. In these contexts, each of the protagonists and elements that comprised it presented clearly set and well-defined roles. The teacher was the academic authority, the origin of knowledge, the person who in these contexts possessed and transmitted the knowledge. The student was the passive subject in these contexts, the person who received the knowledge from the teacher and consolidated this in their own background as memory. The teaching materials or contents were, by contrast, an important part of the personal strategies through which the teacher organised the transmission of the knowledge to the student. These materials were created by the teacher in a closed way that could not be manipulated by the student. The ultimate aim sought in these formal education contexts was for the student to acquire a series of specific knowledge items by direct transfer from the teacher and through memory strategies.

In recent decades, however, and especially with the change of millennium, this formal and static way of understanding educational contexts is opening up to give way to a new, much less formal and more social way of understanding and developing the teaching–learning processes.

In this new type of learning, the roles are not so defined but are blurred and become indistinct. In this new context, the teacher is no longer the only source of knowledge, or the only one responsible for the process. Neither does the student have that passive profile that they did in the previous model. In this new scenario, the students take a much more active role in their learning processes and the materials used for these processes are not created nor do they come exclusively from the teacher's planning. In addition, new actors are introduced into this process: the different communities in which the student and the teacher may be integrated and the contents and comments that the members of these communities may offer them at any time now complete and enrich the whole teaching–learning process in which the students are the protagonists. In this sense, compared with the previous model, the responsibility for the process is reduced with regard to the teacher and it is the context or the social network (the social network of learning), through the various communities, that takes on an important role that it previously did not have.

With this distinction between traditional learning and social learning in hand, it is now possible to adequately set the context for e-learning. Through the resources and strategies that it allows to be implemented, e-learning becomes a clear ally for the development and consolidation of the whole of this new social scenario for teaching and learning. It becomes, in short, a strategy in which the teacher, the student, the contents and the communities share the protagonism in the educational process, and its critical operations also incorporate this new social dimension.

As already mentioned, unlike knowledge management, e-learning does not directly seek to turn knowledge into value in the context of an organisation but tries to design and implement a series of strategies aimed at achieving the creation, transfer and consolidation of knowledge in individuals by means of online resources.

Yet although this difference may seem to point in the opposite direction, the critical operations that comprise it do not differ substantially from those that articulate knowledge management. In this sense, it can be stated that the series of critical operations on which the success or failure of an e-learning program depends to a large extent are again the creation of knowledge, its capture, its structuring and processing, its dissemination, its acquisition and the application of the knowledge. Let us see how each one of these operations should be understood in this context.

Let us tackle the first of the operations: the creation of knowledge. In e-learning contexts, this operation can be understood in the same terms that are used to define it in the field of knowledge management, as generation of new knowledge (in the form of human capital) in a person's head. The main difference is that in e-learning contexts, this operation is used by the teacher or person responsible for the teaching process as a learning strategy. In this sense, the teacher previously possesses the knowledge but designs strategies so that the student is able to generate or discover it and so incorporate it into their stock of knowledge. This apart, it is also important to stress that the social network of learning in which the student is immersed, through the exchange of contents and ideas, contributes to their creation of new knowledge.

Let us now look at the second of the operations: the capture of knowledge. Once again, this second operation may be understood in the same way. The difference in the e-learning context lies in the fact that the result of this operation is also used to evaluate and check, by the person responsible for the process, what the knowledge is that the student possesses and to what degree or level they have acquired it.

The structuring and processing is also focused in this context on (explicit or explicitable tacit) knowledge represented in a document form. It is used primarily so that the documents involved in the teaching–learning process may be managed aptly by the technological tools implemented for their management.

In these contexts, the dissemination (or sharing) is made by means of the transfer and conveying of the documents involved in the learning process (explicit knowledge and explicitable tacit knowledge) and through online socialisation strategies that may be established between the teacher and the students and between the students and the social network of learning in which the student is involved (non-explicitable tacit knowledge).

The operation of acquisition consists again of the perception by the student of the knowledge that circulates as the result of the dissemination and made on the basis of the student's background. Similar to what occurred in the organisational contexts, the explicit and explicitable tacit knowledge represented in a document form is acquired from the interaction between the student and the document where the knowledge is represented. The non-explicitable tacit knowledge acquisition is again achieved through online socialisation strategies between the individual that possesses it (teacher, student or member of the social network of learning) and the potential receiver (student).

In the last of the operations which is that of the application, the student who has acquired the knowledge applies it. This application is corrected or validated by the social network of learning and is used by the person responsible for the teaching–learning process as an indicator of the degree of acquisition of this knowledge by the student.

1.4   Content Management Systems in Knowledge Management and E-Learning

So far, first, content management has been defined and the main operating capacities offered by CMS and social software have been set out. Second, the critical operations that govern both knowledge management and e-learning processes have been analysed. What remains is to examine to what extent these systems can help in the adequate implementation of these critical operations.

To achieve that aim, the following sections will be looked at: first, analysing how CMS can help with the appropriate development of these critical operations. Second, without losing sight of the fact that strictly speaking some of the solutions are already integrated into a significant part of CMS, the fact how social software solutions can contribute to the correct implementation of these operations are analysed. Complementary work on the relationship between content management and e-learning can be found in Chap. 2.

1.4.1 Content Management Systems and Critical Operations

In order to analyse the contribution of CMS, we are going to monitor lineally the chain of operations that comprise both knowledge management and e-learning. This monitoring will enable us to assess the adaptation of technological solutions to these critical operations.

We will start by looking at the first operation: the creation of knowledge. CMS, with their functionalities, can play a very important role in developing this operation correctly.

Thus, if with the help of the system, we design a database that stores documents containing represented knowledge, the students (in the case of e-learning) and the members of the organisation (in the case of knowledge management) can access and retrieve these documents from the repository and, using their content, generate new knowledge.

The search and retrieval of these documents that allow knowledge to be generated can be done more adequately and efficiently if we include other functions of the CMS. So, for example, we can enrich this whole search and retrieval process by including resources such as a thesaurus, taxonomy or even an ontology to aid users' use of the repository. However, in addition to this, by taking advantage of the fact that the repository also includes users' details and preferences, user profiles can also be designed which, systematically and ergonomically, offer the user the documents that may help them generate knowledge. This user and profile management means that, through a content syndication system, the user can obtain new documents which contain knowledge and which have been created automatically on the basis of documents that represent knowledge stored in the repository. All of this is possible with complete security control and the option, by means of user profile control, to prevent the user from having access to other documents that may not be related to their aims (organisational or teaching and learning).

The role of the CMS in the creation of knowledge can be completed through the possibility of developing collaborative environments using the technological solutions that these offer. As some authors point out (von Krogh et al. 2000, for example), one of the bottlenecks in the creation of knowledge is created by the fact that people reach a point where individually and autonomously no more knowledge can be created. Having reached this point, a good strategy for overcoming this situation is to work in groups to create knowledge. Through the use of CMS tools which allow virtual meeting spaces (forums) to be created, it is possible to ensure that the people who form part of these groups can communicate (synchronously and diachronously). This communication usually produces an intense exchange of ideas which, naturally, may lead to the generation of knowledge among the protagonists of these communicative acts (members of the organisation, teacher–student and student–student).

Let us now move on to the second operation, i.e., the capture of knowledge. As in the case of creation, again, CMS can be seen to be an ideal global solution for its correct development.

In the case of the capturing of explicit and explicitable tacit knowledge, CMS play a central role. They enable a person with this type of knowledge to capture and represent it in a document. Likewise, they can make any necessary changes or revisions to it as it evolves. They can carry out this capture, representation and revision quickly, easily and, most importantly, online. To do so, they can use the text editor, focusing, almost exclusively, on the quality of the knowledge and not worrying about the final appearance and display of the document where this knowledge is represented. This solution means that the capturing process does not become complicated, more expensive and slowed down due to the need to entrust these tasks to a second person (other than the person who possesses the knowledge) who has capturing skills and solid notions regarding web page creation and design.

The capture of this type of knowledge also benefits from another of the functionalities of CMS. The workflow solutions that these incorporate can also be used to allow the documents that represent knowledge to be created by different people. Different people who have the same knowledge can work in collaboration to represent it using this functionality, decentralising the capture process and offering the benefits that this involves. All these processes, at all times, have a high security control and are covered by legal control through an audit inspection based on historic reports.

In the case of non-explicitable tacit knowledge, capture is based on other utilities provided by the CMS. As we have already seen in the case of creation, we can also help the capture of this type of knowledge by developing collaborative environments. By creating virtual meeting spaces, we allow socialisation strategies to occur, through communication, between the individual who possesses this special type of knowledge and the rest of the community (organisational or educational) that are needed for its direct capture.

Let us now focus our attention on the structuring and processing operation. As we have already stated, this critical operation focuses on (explicit or explicitable tacit) knowledge represented in a document form. In the case of knowledge management, by using the workflow solution provided by CMS, we can simplify and rationalise to a great extent the operations involved in the dual revision (risk and relevance) to which the members of the publishing committee submit the documents that represent knowledge and which are likely to form part of the repository. Once the document has completed the dual revision and can be considered approved, it is possible in the same process to enrich the assessed documents with control standards (metadata) that result from its formal and semantic analysis, thus ensuring a much more effective subsequential documentary use.

Finally, CMS also provide a system that enables us to design a database containing the documents that result from the process that has just been described.

This database enables documents of this type to be registered or removed according to the interests of the organisation or accessed and shared by all of its members who need them. This database also stores data relating to the documents (versions created, authors, publication, change and expiry dates, etc.), permitting version control.

Let us now look at the next operation, i.e., the dissemination of knowledge. As in the case of capture, we need to present the potential contribution of a CMS to the dissemination operation by specifying at all times the specific type of knowledge involved in the operation.

As we have already shown, in the case of explicit and explicitable tacit knowledge, dissemination usually occurs through the transfer and diffusion of the documents in which it is represented. In this sense, CMS are a highly effective tool for implementing this operation. By providing a database management system that allows for the design of a database (as described above) which stores the documents in which knowledge is represented, a CMS aids the dissemination or compartmentalisation of knowledge through the use (search and retrieval) of all the knowledge-holding documents in the repository.

As in the knowledge creation operation, the dissemination that occurs through the search and retrieval of these documents can be done in a much more adequate and efficient way. So, for example, the process can be enriched through the use of documentary resources, such as thesauruses, taxonomies or ontologies. In addition, by taking advantage of the user profile management utility, the system can be programmed to systematically and ergonomically offer the user documents that may be of use to them and, through content syndication, enable them to obtain new documents that contain knowledge created automatically on the basis of documents previously held in the repository.

In the case of non-explicitable (and, to a degree, explicitable) tacit knowledge, the processes of socialisation between the individual that possesses it and the rest of the community (organisational or educational) represent the most suitable strategy for dissemination. With CMS, virtual collaborative environments can be designed that allow knowledge to be disseminated on the basis of communicative exchanges and the particular interests of the users of these spaces.

The next critical operation is that of the acquisition of knowledge. As in the previous cases, CMS, with their functions, can play a central role in the adequate development of this operation. However, as also occurred above, the contribution varies according to the type of knowledge involved.

In the case of explicit and explicitable tacit knowledge represented in a document form, the acquisition is indirect. This is usually made by means of the interaction between a member of the community and the document where the knowledge is represented and which they have obtained after a process of search and retrieval in the repository created on the basis of the functions of the CMS.

In order to improve this acquisition mediated by the receiver–document interaction, various strategies may be implemented. So, for example, on the one hand, the noise and the silence in the retrieval of the documents that contain knowledge can be reduced by taking advantage of the user profile management utility and content syndication. This reduction leads to the series of documents with which the individual has to interact being much more adequate and useful. On the other hand, the interaction can also be improved by managing and personalising the display of these documents using content publication tools.

As occurred in the previous operations, in the case of non-explicitable (and, to a degree, explicitable) tacit knowledge, acquisition is, again, achieved through socialisation strategies between the individual that possesses it and the potential recipient. Through the use of CMS, virtual collaborative environments can be designed so that this socialisation (virtual in this case) occurs to enable acquisition.

It is important to highlight that the acquisition, mediated or not by documents, is aided greatly by one of the capacities that characterise the latest CMS products: functionality on mobile platforms (PDA or mobile telephones, for example). This functionality allows the acquisition of knowledge, be it through documents or socialisation, to be developed regardless of the physical location of the individuals involved.

This analysis is ended together with this section, by tackling the last of the operations in this chain, i.e., the application of knowledge. In this operation, the role of the CMS is a little more indirect than in the previous cases.

They do not take part directly in the application and the reuse of the knowledge acquired. They do intervene, however, and very directly, in the diffusion of the results of this application, especially in knowledge management contexts when the receiver uses this knowledge in contexts other than those in which it originated and, on the basis of a reinterpretation of it, new knowledge is produced.

In these cases, the CMS offers the possibility of integrating this new knowledge in the database where the documents which contain represented knowledge are stored, again activating the whole chain of critical operations which can be supported on this technological resource. Furthermore, through the possibility of developing collaborative environments, these systems allow the knowledge created from the application to new contexts to be diffused to the rest of the community with the aim that all of this knowledge being used by anyone who needs it must act appropriately with it at all times. This type of resource is particularly effective when it is applied to the practice communities, i.e., to the communities or groups of people who share interests and experiences on a series of common topics.

It is important to end by noting one of the most interesting virtues of the CMS in helping the implementation and the correct operation of knowledge management and e-learning processes: its capacity to integrate external applications into the system. Using this capacity of the CMS based on Applications Programming Interface (API)-type resources, the whole knowledge management system can be enriched, integrating in an articulated and ergonomic way, other IT resources that are commonly used in this type of program and using all of these resources online thanks to Internet standards.

Thus, other resources can be included in the CMS such as the data warehouse, data mining or text mining programs that can help in the creation, capture, structuring, dissemination and acquisition of knowledge on the basis of the management of documents that contain represented knowledge. However, we can also enrich the system and complete these resources with the inclusion of a digital subject index that classes all of the documents involved, taking advantage of the taxonomy derived from a knowledge map and permitting easy internal browsing.

It is also possible, in the case of knowledge management, to integrate a decision-making support system that helps members to improve their contributions to the organisational objectives on the basis of better suited, more streamlined and less supervised decision-making. Finally, it is by no means superfluous to directly integrate some type of search engine or metasearch engine. The search engine allows members to conveniently browse the organisation's web (intranet) and offers the chance to search for new external information on the Internet without intermediaries. In contrast, by combining all of the information retrieval power of various search engines, a metasearch engine aids and, to a great extent, reinforces an exhaustive search for new and interesting knowledge of quality for the organisation in the same Internet context.

1.4.2 Social Software and Critical Operations

Finally, it is necessary to examine to what extent social software tools (blogs, RSS systems, wikis and social bookmarking) can help in the adequate implementation of the critical operations of knowledge management and e-learning.

We start by stressing, as we outlined above, that the main virtue of these types of IT solutions is that they allow the user to use them to create and enter different social networks in which they can communicate (synchronously and diachronously) and exchange content and knowledge. In the context of knowledge management, all these networks built using social software will be called the social knowledge network. In the case of e-learning, the set of these networks will be called the social learning network.

The common feature that defines these types of tools is that, in allowing these social knowledge and learning networks to be created, they ensure that the person opens up and pours out their most internal mental content (explicit and tacit) onto the network or community and that, simultaneously, they can receive and benefit from the influence and the internal mental content of each member of the network.

Looking more closely, it can be seen that these social knowledge and learning networks that surround a person are, in turn, usually built using the concentric articulation of three different types of networks or communities (Dalsgaard 2006). At the core is the network formed by the group of individuals who work in collaboration to achieve a common aim. In the case of the social knowledge network, the working team in which the member of an organisation is involved could be an example of this type of network. In the case of the social learning network, groups of students who work collaboratively on a joint activity would be an example. In the second sphere, we would find the networks comprising people who share a common organisational context. This is a network of people who are not working on the same project, but who have access, to a certain extent, to the productions of the other people who form part of that community. The members of the same department (in the context of the social knowledge network) or the students from the same academic year (in the case of the social learning network) could be examples of this second type of network. Finally, the more general sphere would contain the networks of people who, although they are not part of the same organisation, share a common field of interest. The social networks that are created around a subject and which include members of different organisations (in the context of the social knowledge network) or pupils and students from different centres who are interested in the same subject (in the case of the social learning network) could be examples of this last type of network.

The combined and personalised use of social software tools allows individuals to behave and move easily inside all these types of networks and, by doing so, find in them the resources (or content) and people who can help them solve their knowledge problems. This is all possible and articulated in a way as to allow them to enjoy significant benefits, with the help of the social software, when implementing the critical operations that govern the knowledge management and e-learning contexts.

In terms of the knowledge creation operation, these types of social software tools can play a very important role in helping to overcome the barrier determined by the fact that people reach a point at which they individually and autonomously can no longer create more new knowledge.

Thus, on the one hand, the members of these social (knowledge and learning) networks can meet other individuals who, by interacting with them and sharing their knowledge, enable them to overcome the barriers to individual knowledge creation. On the other hand, these social networks offer them access to content created by other members that can help them unblock the process of creation. Likewise, it allows for the creation of personalised content and its distribution to others for them to use in their creation processes. Finally, they can also benefit from the searches that other members have made using social bookmarking to efficiently find content outside the network or community (throughout the World Wide Web) that can help them in the gestation of new knowledge.

We will now look at the second operation, i.e., the capture of knowledge. Social software plays a central role in the case of the capture of explicit and explicitable tacit knowledge. It allows individuals with this type of knowledge to capture and represent it in contents. Likewise, they can make any necessary changes or revisions to it as it evolves. They can carry out this capture, representation and revision quickly, easily and, most importantly, online. To do so, they can use the blog or wiki's text editor, without the need for solid notions of web page creation and design. The capture of this type of knowledge also benefits from another wiki functionality and its collaborative dimension: different people who have the same knowledge can work in collaboration to represent it using this functionality, so decentralising capture and offering the advantages that this involves.

In the case of non-explicitable tacit knowledge, capture is based on the development of collaborative environments or social networks by means of social software tools. By creating these networks, we allow socialisation strategies to occur, through communication, between the individual who possesses this special type of knowledge and the rest of the community (organisational or educational) that are needed for its direct capture.

We are now going to focus our attention on the structuring and processing operation carried out on (explicit or explicitable tacit) knowledge represented in a document form. Once again, using the social software we can create networks where, collaboratively, the members of the publishing committee submit the documents that represent knowledge and are likely to form part of the repository to a dual revision (risk and relevance).

We will now look at the next operation, i.e., the dissemination of knowledge. As we mentioned, in the case of explicit and explicitable tacit knowledge, dissemination is usually carried out by means of the transfer and diffusion of the documents in which it is represented. Thus, social software allows every member of the (knowledge or learning) network to offer their documents where they have represented their knowledge to the rest. As in the knowledge creation operation, the dissemination developed through the search and retrieval of these documents can be improved and made more efficient if the members of the network take advantage of the social bookmarks that have previously been entered.

In the case of non-explicitable (and, to a degree, explicitable) tacit knowledge, the processes of socialisation between the individual that possesses it and the rest of the community (organisational or educational) represent the most suitable strategy for dissemination. With social software, virtual collaborative environments can be designed that allow knowledge to be disseminated on the basis of communicative exchanges and the particular interests of the users of these spaces.

The next critical operation is that of the acquisition of knowledge. As stated, in the case of explicit and explicitable tacit knowledge represented in a document form, acquisition is indirect. This is usually achieved through the interaction between the member of the community and the document where the knowledge is represented and that which they have obtained from the (knowledge or learning) networks generated by the social software. In order to improve this acquisition, the bookmarks that have been used by the members of these networks or communities can also be used.

As occurred in the previous operations, in the case of non-explicitable (and, to a degree, explicitable) tacit knowledge, acquisition is, again, achieved through socialisation strategies between the individual that possesses it and the potential receiver. Through the use of social software, virtual collaborative environments can be designed so that this socialisation (virtual in this case) occurs to enable acquisition.

We will end this analysis, and this section, by tackling the last of the operations in this chain, i.e., the application of knowledge. As occurred with the CMS, the role of social software in this operation is a little more indirect than in the previous cases. They do not intervene directly in the application and reuse of the knowledge acquired. They do intervene, however, and very directly, in the diffusion of the results of this application. In these cases, the social software tools offer the possibility of diffusing these results to the rest of the community over the networks, again activating the whole chain of critical operations which can be supported by this social technological resource.

References

Browning, P.,& Lowndes, M.(2001). JISC techwatch report: Content management systems. *Techwatch Report TSW 01-02, The Joint Information Systems Committee*. September 2001.
Cuerda, X., & Minguillón, J. (2005). Introducción a los Sistemas de Gestión de Contenidos. CMS) de código abierto. *Mosaic*, núm. 36. ISSN: 1696-3296. Retrieved March 1, 2005, from http://www.uoc.edu/mosaic/articulos/cms1204.html
Dalsgaard, C. (2006). Social software: E-learning beyond learning management systems. *European Journal of Open and Distance Learning*. Retrieved November 10, 2007, from http://www.eurodl.org/materials/contrib/2006/Christian_Dalsgaard.htm
Shegda, K., Chin, K., Gilbert, M., Logan, D., & Lou, T. (2006). *Magic quadrant for enterprise content management*, Gartner RAS Core Research Note G00143653.
Tramullas, J. (2005). Open source tools for content management. *Hipertext*. Retrieved March 2010, from http://www.hipertext.net. ISSN 1695-5498
Wilkoff, N., Walker, J., Root, N., & Dalton, J. (2001). What's next for content management? *The techRankings techInsight*. Retrieved March 1, 2005, from http://www.forrester.com/ER/Research/TechInsight/Excerpt/0,4109,13920,00.html

Bibliography

Addey, D., Ellis, J., Suh, P. & Thiemecke, D. (2002). *Content management systems*. Birmingham: Glasshaus.
Adelsberger, H., Kinshukm, P., Pawlowski, J. M., & Sampson, D. (Eds.) (2008). *Handbook on information technologies for education and training*. London: Springer.
Asilomar Institute For Information Architecture. (2003). The problems with CMS. *The Information Architecture Institute*. Retrieved March 1, 2005, from http://aifia.org/pg/the_problems_with_cms.php
Baumgartner, P. (2005). The zen art of teaching. En *elearningeuropa.info*. Brussels: European Commission. Retrieved November 10, 2007, from http://www.elearningeuropa.info/extras/pdf/zenartofteaching.pdf
Bluebill Adv. (2003). The classification and evaluation of content management systems. *The Gilbane Report, 11*(2). Retrieved January 22, 2005, from http://www.gilbane.com/gilbane_report.pl/86/The_Classification__Evaluation_of_Content_Management_Systems.html
Boiko, B. (2001). *Content management bible*. New Jersey: Wiley.
Boisot, M. H. (1998). *Knowledge assets*. Oxford: Oxford University Press.
Brown, J., Iiyoshi, T., & Kumar, M. S. (Eds.) (2008). *Opening up education: The collective advancement of education through open technology, open content, and open knowledge*. Boston: The MIT Press.
Davenport, T., & Prusak, L. (1998). *Working knowledge*. Boston: Harvard Business School Press.
Doyle, B. (2003). Open source content management redux. *The Gilbane Report, 11*(3). Retrieved March 1, 2005, from http://www.gilbane.com/gilbane_report.pl/87/Open_Source_Content_Management_Redux.html
Dretske, F. I. (1981). *Knowledge and the flow of information*. Cambridge: The MIT Press/Bradford Books.
ERP Software. (2003). *Content management tutorial*. Retrieved March 1, 2005, from http://erptoday.com/CMS/Content-Management-Tutorial.aspx
Fahey, L., & Prusak, L. (1998). The eleven deadlist sins of knowledge management. *California Management Review, 40*(3), 265–276.
Fraser, S. (2002). *Real world ASP.NET: Building a content management system*. Berkley: Apress.

Gilbane, F. (2000). What is content management? *The Gilbane Report, 8*(8). Retrieved March 1, 2005, from http://www.gilbane.com/gilbane_report.pl/6/What_is_Content_Management

Gingell, D. (2003). *A 15 minutes guide to enterprise content management*. Pleasanton: Documentum Inc.

Gorey, R. M., & Dobat, D. R. (1996). Managing in the knowledge era. *The Systems Thinker, 7*(8), 1–5.

Gottlieb, S. (2005). From enterprise content management to effective content management. *Cutter IT Journal, 18*(5), 13–18.

Gupta, V. K., Govindarajan, S., & Johnson, T. (2001). Overview of content management: Approaches and estrategies. *Electronic Markets, 11*(4), 281–287.

Han, Y. (2004). Digital content management: The search for a content management system. *Library Hi Tech, 22*(4), 355–365.

Hasan, H., & Pfaff, C. (2006). The Wiki: An environment to revolutionise employees' interaction with corporate knowledge. *ACM International Conference Proceeding Series, 206*, 377–380.

Hüttenegger, G. (2006). *Open source knowledge management*. Berlin: Springer.

Jennings, T. (2002). *Defining the document and content management ecosystem*. London: Butler Direct Limited.

Keyes, J. (2007). *Knowledge management, business intelligence, and content management: The IT practitioner's guide*. London: Auerbach Publications.

McKay, A. (2004). *The definitive guide to plone*. Berkley: Apress.

McKeever, S. (2003). Understanding web content management systems: Evolution, lifecycle and market. *Industrial Management and Data Systems, 103*(9), 686–692.

Instituto Universitario Euroforum Escorial. *Medición del capital intelectual: Modelo Intelect*. (1998). Madrid: Instituto Universitario Euroforum Escorial.

Nakano, R. (2002). *Web content management. A collaborative approach*. New Jersey: Prentice Hall.

Nonaka, I., & Takeuchi, H. (1995). *The knowledge creating company*. Oxford: Oxford University Press.

Pérez-Montoro, M. (2003). El documento como dato, conocimiento e información. *Tradumática*, núm. 2, 2003. Retrieved December 12, 2003, from http://www.fti.uab.es/tradumática/revista ISSN 1578-7559

Pérez-Montoro, M. (2005). Sistemas de gestión de contenidos en la gestión del conocimiento. *BiD: textos universitaris de Biblioteconomia i Documentació*, junio, núm. 14, 2005. Retrieved July 18, 2005, from http://www2.ub.es/bid/consulta_articulos.php?fichero=14monto2.htm ISSN 1575-5886

Pérez-Montoro, M. (2007). *The phenomenon of information*. Maryland: Scarecrow Press.

Pérez-Montoro, M. (2008). *Gestión del Conocimiento en las organizaciones*. Gijón: Trea.

Robertson, J. (2002a). How to evaluate a content management system. *Step two designs*. Retrieved March 1, 2005, from http://www.steptwo.com.au/papers/kmc_evaluate/index.html

Robertson, J. (2002b). What are the goals of a content management system? *Step two designs*. Retrieved March 1, 2005, from http://www.steptwo.com.au/papers/kmc_goals/index.html

Robertson, J. (2003a). Is it document management or content management? *Step two designs*. Retrieved March 1, 2005, from http://www.steptwo.com.au/papers/cmb_dmorcm/index.html

Robertson, J. (2003b). Metrics for knowledge management and content management. *Step two designs*. Retrieved March 1, 2005, from http://www.steptwo.com.au/papers/kmc_metrics/index.html

Robertson, J. (2003c). So, what is a content management system? Step two designs. Retrieved March 1, 2005, from http://www.steptwo.com.au/papers/kmc_what/index.html

Robertson, J. (2003d). Why a small website needs a content management? *Step two designs*. Retrieved March 1, 2005, from http://www.steptwo.com.au/papers/cmb_needcms/index.html

Robertson, J. (2004). Open-source content management systems. *Step two designs*. Retrieved March 1, 2005, from http://www.steptwo.com.au/papers/kmc_opensource/index.html

Rockley, A. (2003). *Managing enterprise content. A unified content strategy*. Worcester: New Riders.

Smith, M., & Salvendy, G (Eds.) (2007). *Human interface and the management of information. Methods, techniques and tools in information design*. London: Springer.

Veen, J. (2004). Why content management fails? *Adaptive Path*. Retrieved March 1, 2005, from http://www.adaptivepath.com/publications/essays/archives/000315.php

von Krogh, G., Ichijo, K., & Nonaka, I. (2000). *Enabling knowledge creation*. Oxford: Oxford University Press.

Chapter 2
From Content Management to E-Learning Content Repositories

Julià Minguillón, Miguel-Angel Sicilia, and Brian Lamb

Abstract The concept of content in an educational context is very different from the one in other fields such as publishing or electronic newspapers, for example. From textbooks to exercises, from software simulations to data sets containing educational data, it is necessary to rethink the way these educational resources or "learning objects" are managed. One of the major concerns for teachers using e-learning environments is the availability of the appropriate structures and tools for organizing such learning resources and making them accessible to learners. This is especially true for e-learning virtual environments where learners have access to both digital libraries and also to any other Web resource, through Google or other conventional search engines. Nevertheless, these systems are usually not directly integrated in the learning process and content and metadata management requires the use of different tools. Furthermore, new pedagogical approaches consider the learner as an active element in the learning process, promoting the acquisition and development of competences through activities which involve the use and creation of learning resources. This chapter explores the relationship of traditional content management systems and the broader scope of virtual learning environments, including aspects of metadata standards, content personalization, the use of semantic web techniques and ontologies, the use and annotation of learning resources and the possibilities offered by the use of Web 2.0 technologies. At the end of this chapter, the possible learning scenarios that will be derived from all the changing forces, combining methodological, technological and organizational issues will be described.

J. Minguillón (✉)
Computer Science, Multimedia and Telecommunications Department,
Universitat Oberta de Catalunya, Barcelona, Spain
e-mail: jminguillona@uoc.edu

N. Ferran and J. Minguillón (eds.), *Content Management for E-Learning*,
DOI 10.1007/978-1-4419-6959-0_2, © Springer Science+Business Media, LLC 2011

2.1 Introduction

Nowadays, e-learning is one of the most promising and growing applications that are essential to an information society. The growth of the Internet is approaching online education to people in corporations, institutes of higher education, the government, and other sectors (Rosenberg 2002), and both the growing need of continuous education and the inclusion of new multimedia technologies become crucial factors for the expansion of lifelong learning. Besides pure virtual colleges and universities, more and more traditional educational institutions are adopting the use of Information and Communication Technologies (ICT) to provide learners with a richer environment for their learning process. Furthermore, new Web 2.0 technologies such as wikis and blogs have generated new possibilities for creating and sharing educational content. This fact, combined with the concept of open educational resources, enables a new environment for learners that view the whole Web as a learning space with many possibilities, with no time or space barriers. Quoting Wiley (2007), "content is infrastructure," the learning process must be created on top of such infrastructure, and there is a real need for managing all those contents available on the Web.

Content management has been traditionally related to content producers such as publishers, portals, news agencies, newspapers, and so on. Web-based content management systems (CMS) support all the phases of content management, from creation to delivery (Boiko 2001). In fact, many educational institutions such as universities are nowadays also the publishers of their own contents, mainly generated by their teachers. These contents are mainly textbooks, but also research papers in academic journals or formal project deliverables such as technical reports (i.e., gray literature). Nevertheless, there are many other contents that are not managed and maintained by the educational institution but by the teachers themselves, such as exercises, resources used in the classroom, or teaching notes. In consequence, the concept of content in educational institutions has not been a simple one by only definition; it depends on the context and the learning goals that must be achieved. Therefore, using CMS in educational institutions needs to face new requirements caused by two main factors: first, content granularity and typologies are very diverse, and second, content should be created and shared with reusability in mind. Reusability has been hypothesized to create economies of scale and to be a major factor in the universal accessibility of high-quality educational resources, which are in general expensive to produce (Downes 2001).

With the creation of the new European Higher Education Area (EHEA), also known as the "Bologna Process" (Ade et al. 1999), it has become necessary to shift from heavily content-based courses to others where the concept of activity is the key. Contents or learning resources in general will become secondary pieces in the learning process, while the activities and the competencies developed by such activities will become the focus of any educational action. This approach has been widely accepted as the most appropriate for providing learners with a learner-centered pedagogical model, instead of a content-driven one. Learners need to acquire and develop competencies which will be part of their future professional profile. In order to do so, learners follow a sequence of learning activities which have been designed as the basic pieces of the learning process instead of that of contents. Ideally, the learning process is supported by intelligent tutoring systems which help users (learners but also teachers and course managers) to achieve their goals. The learning process becomes a complex path including the handling of educational resources, formative and evaluation activities, interaction with other students and the teacher, so the concept of content management needs to be redefined. From the secondary place of contents in activity-based learning, the need for breaking down contents in smaller, more reusable pieces follows.

In another direction, the appearance of the Web 2.0 paradigm makes the traditional producer–consumer model obsolete, as all the participants in the learning process can easily create and share resources. These new technologies have also changed the definition of content: from books or large pieces of content to microcontents, which can be created and reused in different contexts. The range of content typologies becomes wider: textual, multimedia elements, but also simulations and even datasets can be considered learning resources, as well as blog posts or wikipedia entries. Furthermore, teachers are not the only content producers: students can also participate actively in the process of creating and sharing content which is part of the learning process. This shift, from a producer–consumer model (one-to-many) to a create–remix–share model (many-to-many), also changes all the aspects related to content management, such as granularity, metadata, and which need to be reconsidered in order to be created and managed collaboratively.

This chapter describes how these methodological changes (that are central to the new EHEA paradigm) together with the technological ones (virtual learning environments plus the new Web 2.0 paradigm and the slow adoption of the Semantic Web approach) have modified the requirements of CMS in educational institutions. Section 2.2 describes the learning process in virtual learning environments as something that is much more than just providing learners with digitized content. Section 2.3 describes the concept of learning object and learning object repositories (LORs) and their relationship to CMS and also discusses their differences with Web 2.0 applications with respect to managing content. The semantic approach to describing learning objects in repositories is discussed in Sect. 2.4. Finally, Sect. 2.5 outlines and discusses the open questions related to the use of LORs in virtual learning environments and its intersection with new trends such as social learning and connectivism.

2.2   The Learning Process in Virtual Learning Environments

Distance education has radically changed with the intensive use of ICT. The use of the internet for not only content delivery but also for improving communication and interaction between students and teachers has created a completely new scenario. Distance education is no longer conceived as just delivering content but as a whole learning process supported by a virtual learning environment. Learning in virtual environments is more than just accessing PDF or PPT files with content; the whole learning process must be transformed, not just translated, as stated by Thomas et al. (1998).

In this sense, e-learning scenarios can be characterized by three different dimensions: users, platforms (or services), and contents (Holmes and Gardner 2006). A single learner using his or her personal computer for taking a course available in CD-ROM is a possible e-learning scenario, although this is far from the current understanding of what e-learning is nowadays. In fact, we adopt the fourth e-learning generation as described by Taylor (1999), where there is an asynchronous process that allows students and teachers to interact in an educational process specifically designed in accordance with these principles. The place where these interactions occur is the virtual learning environment, which supports users (learners, teachers, managers, etc.), resources, and services. Through the appropriate services, virtual learning environments can be used to provide learners with better support for the new needs created by the Bologna process: personalization issues, a true learner-centered model, an active and more participative learning process, competence-based instead of content-driven activities, etc. In this virtual space, learning is a combination of interaction and content consumption, through the supervision of the teacher, who becomes more a facilitator of the learning process instead of a content producer and provider.

Within this framework, content management clearly becomes one of the most important services that the virtual learning environment must deal with. In fact, most universities already implement what is called the digital library, which tries to reproduce the usual services available in a traditional brick-and-mortar library, i.e., borrowing books and documents, accessing external databases, etc. Nevertheless, the concept of content is much wider, as it needs to include all the resources used by teachers and learners in the virtual classroom: exercises, multimedia resources, simulations, software, etc. Furthermore, it is also necessary to encourage learners to use the resources in the digital library, promoting an active learning process, and not just being a place where to find learning resources. Therefore, it is necessary to rethink the concept of digital library, which is content centered and based on the producer–consumer model, in order to improve the integration of content management as part of the learning process. As we will describe in Sect. 2.3, LORs (as a specific case of institutional repositories) become a key element for supporting a user-centered learning process, combining the services offered by digital libraries with the flexibility of directly providing contents through a simple interface (Conway 2008). In Chap. 4 of this book, the relationship between instructional design (the core of the learning process) and content management is discussed.

2.2.1 New Methodological Approaches

As previously mentioned, the new EHEA paradigm promotes a shift from a content-based learning process to a competence-based one. Instead of creating content-centered courses with the aim of transmitting knowledge about such content, the lowest competency level in the Bloom's (1956) taxonomy, learning is seen as an active process supported by a set of activities which guide the learner toward the acquisition and development of a set of competences. Each one of these activities involves the use of one or more learning resources which might be different according to the learner's profile and the specific context. In fact, these learning resources can depend on the learner's preferences, with or without a default learning resource related to such activity. It is exactly the "content is infrastructure" sentence as stated by Wiley (2007). Furthermore, these resources are not just chunks of content given that a high degree of interactivity is expected. Readings but also videos, simulations, and exercises are, among others, typical learning resources used in virtual learning environments. In fact, learning objects (which will be addressed in the following section) were initially supposed to be consumed by the learner in only 15 or 20 min, in short sessions, although these figures are nowadays being questioned, as learners request even smaller chunks of content that can be easily downloaded and digested. Learners (and teachers) also request to be part of the workflow of the institutional repository, as they can create their own digital assets and share them easily (Thomas and Rothery 2005). This new scenario causes a fragmentation of the original content (i.e., textbooks, collections of exercises) in a large collection of very small contents which are absolutely related to each other, with some of these relationships directly generated by users.

Therefore, as stated in Sumner and Marlino (2004), it is necessary to bridge the gap between educational scenarios and digital libraries by means of providing users (learners and teachers) with the appropriate tools for creating and sharing knowledge and capturing all the richness of the learning process in virtual learning environments. In order to achieve an ideal learning scenario that gives complete support to its users (Dreher et al. 2004), we propose to introduce the use of LORs as one of the elements of the learning process as true CMS adapted to the specific needs of teaching and learning in virtual learning environments.

2.3 Learning Objects and Learning Object Repositories

The concept of a learning object has been deeply discussed many times in the literature since its appearance. Many authors have provided their own definition, which has not helped to clearly convey the concept, causing confusion and constant reformulations (McGreal 2004). Nevertheless, most of the existing definitions have three main characteristics in common: learning objects are available in digital format; they are described using metadata according to proposed standards formats, and they are oriented to maximize reusability by breaking the resources into pieces that can be reused independently. Reusability can be addressed as an integral part of the instructional design process (Wiley 2000) and it can be approached without a consideration of standards and specifications, i.e., reusing regular content with no specific metadata (Wiley et al. 2004). However, it is by using advanced metadata schemas that educators can expose the contents and their basic description more explicitly, thus sharing also educational indications and even the prescribed sequencing. The concept of learning object and its implications with respect to content management are deeply discussed in Chap. 3 of this book.

Several specifications address the structure of digital learning resources. For example, ADL SCORM[1] provides a way to structure contents in packages that can be transported across platforms. The structure of SCORM 1.2 is very simple, but other specifications as its successor SCORM 2004 or IMS Learning Design (LD)[2] offer much more flexible languages for expressing concrete instructional sequencings that are the outcome of instructional design methods (Reigeluth 1999). Concretely, IMS LD focuses on describing learning activities, including multiple learner and tutor roles, sequencing of activities and services, including the resources or "learning objects" that must be used by each role kind in each concrete activity. Furthermore, metadata standards such as IEEE Learning Object Metadata (LOM)[3] allow for defining some basic properties that are interesting from an educational perspective like that of interactivity, and more importantly, they provide a way to define types of resources, e.g., differencing exercises from expositive material and the like. Other specifications are very specific to some of these resources, e.g., IMS QTI[4] is targeted to the representation of tests. These issues are covered in Chap. 9 of this book.

In spite of the diversity of resource types and characteristics of their structure that are covered in current metadata schemas, they are not commonly used nowadays as search criteria in repositories. In consequence, content management in current repositories is still not exploiting these special kinds of characteristics, but many of them stay at the level of "media files" with basic, general-purpose metadata. For example, uploading an IMS LD unit of learning is considered by existing repositories as a single, opaque ZIP-compressed file, and the structure and descriptions of the activities are not inspected and not used for search of versioning, just to name two typical CMS functionalities.

Learning objects are stored in LORs, which can be considered a specific kind of CMS for educational resources. Although, as stated before, traditional CMS tools can be used to store, describe, and share learning objects (such as Drupal or OpenCMS, among many other open source software tools), these tools are usually oriented toward Web content. According to Heery and Anderson (2005), repositories are differentiated from other digital collections because the content is deposited in the repository together with its metadata; and such content is accessible through a basic set of services (i.e., put, get, search, etc.). Depending on the specific needs of the community using the repository, this will provide additional tailored services, but all repositories should at least provide two basic ones: content

---

[1] http://www.adlnet.gov/scorm.

[2] http://www.imsglobal.org/learningdesign.

[3] http://ltsc.ieee.org/wg12/files/IEEE_1484_12_03_d8_submitted.pdf.

[4] http://www.imsglobal.org/question.

preservation and content reusing (Akeroyd 2005). As stated in Ferran et al. (2007), it is important to fully integrate the LOR in the learning process in order to promote its usage by learners during the whole learning process. Furthermore, there are several requirements that should be fulfilled in order to ensure a successful repository (McNaught 2006). Chapter 10 of this book covers this subject with more detail.

2.3.1 Learning Object Repositories and Content Management Systems

It would be useful to start by considering how a LOR and a CMS differ. The main features of CMS products are content creation, maintenance and versioning, publishing workflows usually within a predefined work structure with concrete roles and responsibilities, and content dissemination through portal and search facilities. It is also common that a CMS provides a way to add some basic metadata to contents as an aid to search, and that they provide a way for users to provide feedback about the contents, e.g., in the form of ratings or grades. If we think in the development of a digital learning resource from scratch, the aforementioned functionalities of a CMS is still required for its development, at least when the contents are not created in isolation by a single educator, but they are produced by a team in a systematic way. This could lead us to the conclusion that the equation CMS = LOR is correct. However, a more accurate judgment is that a CMS can be used as a platform for the development of learning resources, whenever the functionalities of a CMS are required. In fact, systems such as *Connexions*[5] do actually provide group editing facilities, versioning, and other functionalities that are typical of a CMS. But there are many LORs that do not support such functionalities for the production of contents, but simply act as mere repositories of the contents produced elsewhere. Merlot[6] is a popular example of such a system. Moreover, repositories such as DSpace[7] are useful to keep frozen versions of learning materials of any kind, thus providing the services of a permanent archive that will resist the course of time.

Then, it is worth wondering what are the key distinguishing characteristics of a LOR that make them especially valuable for learners or educators when contrasted with a portal or with a conventional Web search engine. Examining a current LOR considered as best practice (Nash 2005), the following list of elements can be considered as a summary of the aspects that can be found and are specific, even though each LOR provides only part of them or only to a certain extent.

---

[5]http://cnx.org.

[6]http://www.merlot.org.

[7]http://www.dspace.org.

1. Specific metadata descriptions, addressing information relevant for educational purposes, such as those in the IEEE LOM schema. A typical example is the "educational level" of the target learning, which can be expressed as an age range or an indication of an educational level such as "K12" or "Higher Education."
2. Special formats that specify instructional sequence or interaction schemes, like those supported by different proposed standards like SCORM or IMS LD. This includes formats for the interchange of interactive materials that are specific for educational settings as the tests that can be specified with the IMS QTI schema.
3. Categorizations used as browsing mechanisms for the learning resources that are significant of the structure of formal education.
4. Search mechanisms based on the specifics of educational metadata and formats.
5. Quality control or quality assessment mechanisms that consider educational aspects. This includes a wide range of possibilities, from user ratings to formal peer reviews conducted by experts in the pedagogy of specific subject areas.
6. An orientation to breaking down the resources in parts that are independent and self-standing, so that they can be reused in an easier way.

In addition to the aforementioned specificities, the actual practice of producing and sharing learning resources is in many cases very different from the production of contents in portals. This is mainly because a large number of learning resources are contributed by individual educators willing to share the products of their instructional preparation for their courses (which may be online, face-to-face, or hybrid). Furthermore, the resources are part of an instructional design process (Gagné et al. 1992), so that a LOR would ideally support such processes (but nowadays none of them provide such explicit support), including educational assessment and the recording of instructional design decisions (Sicilia 2007). Further to this, the emergence of the "open educational resource" paradigm can be considered as the principal driver of the widespread adoption of a LOR as an independent system, as will be discussed later, and this is also a distinguishing characteristic.

Therefore, any LOR featuring all the above characteristics will ideally be:

- More reliable and freer of noise than any portal or web-based CMS, as it has quality control based on educational properties
- Providing more effective search and browsing mechanisms
- Enabling a higher level of effectiveness in the reuse of learning resources produced by others
- Providing resources better prepared for sequencing and delivery within a learning management system (provided that both the LMS and the resource implement the same standards and specifications)

But there is still a long way to go before we have such an "ideal" LOR, as discussed in Dreher et al. (2004). Nonetheless, the constant development and upgrading of tools and learning technology standards and specifications have progressively increased the adoption of the paradigm behind the above characteristics. That paradigm can be called the "learning object" paradigm, which has been previously discussed.

The aforementioned aspects that are a characteristic of LORs also help in separating them from systems that allow the uploading of user-generated contents. Popular examples of such kind of repositories are Flickr[8] or YouTube.[9] These systems emphasize the community and informal sharing aspect of resources, but they are not concerned specifically with education. This is not to say that educators cannot find excellent resources for learning in these sites and actually quite the opposite is true, and they are a source of ideas on the important topic of building communities around repositories (Monge et al. 2008). But there is not any kind of education-oriented quality control or categorization. Then, a typical practice for exploiting these sites with user-generated content is that of describing selected resources such as entries in a LOR, so that the LOR acts as a filter for the mass of contents. This can be easily done, for example, using Merlot. Anyone can create an entry in Merlot referring (with a URI) to a YouTube video and then complete metadata about its potential educational usage, and eventually that resource will be reviewed and assessed by experts with regards to its educational properties. Nevertheless, as universities are places where knowledge is generated before and during the learning process, LORs are tailored to store content, not just links pointing to it, pursuing preservation and minimizing the problem of broken links. Furthermore, teachers (and, in some cases, learners) can also act as curators with respect to content quality issues.

2.3.2   Repositories and Virtual Learning Communities

As already mentioned, a key element for having a successful repository is the community of users built around it. Indeed, the success of many Web 2.0 applications such as YouTube lies in that they were able to attract a critical mass of users that either provide contents or add value to the existing contents in the site by commenting, rating, and bookmarking. Merlot can be mentioned as an example of a LOR that has succeeded in attracting an active user community, and today Merlot offers the possibility to navigate the resources through the profiles of registered users. Merlot has several mechanisms to award recognition to active users that provide high-quality contributions. Moreover, users are able to select some resources and link them in their "*Personal collections*" (Akeroyd 2005), as repositories cover all the range from individual to national scale (Peters 2002).

Personal collections represent a form of "user profile" or "user model," because we can reasonably assume that the resources included in the collection of an individual determine indirectly his/her preferences or interests. This opens possibilities for personalization in repositories and digital libraries (Ferran et al. 2005). In this case, a rudimentary but effective way of personalization can be based on computing individuals with similar interests. Trivially, two users A and B that have many resources in common in their personal collections can be assumed to have similar interests. Then,

---

[8]http://www.flickr.com.

[9]http://www.youtube.com.

whenever one of them adds a new resource to his/her personal collection, the system could take the risk of "recommending" that item to the other for potential inclusion in his/her personal collection. This similarity-based approach combined with quantitative correlation measures based on numerical ratings is actually the basis of existing approaches to collaborative or social filtering (Konstan et al. 1997), which is also implemented in many e-commerce sites as the popular Amazon bookstore. Personalized actions such as the basic recommendation mechanism provided above can be found in many systems, and synergize with the development of active and engaged user communities (Littlejohn and Margaryan 2006). In fact, it is the information extracted from the real usage that the community makes of the service (or the repository) as the main source for building a recommendation system (Herlocker et al. 2004).

2.4 Semantic Repositories

As discussed above, LORs provide an alternative to search engines such as Google for finding educational resources, and metadata is a key distinguishing aspect. The typical implementation of metadata in learning resource repositories provides compatibility with a widely used metadata schema as Dublin Core[10] or IEEE LOM (or use metadata elements that are similar to them). Metadata-based search represents a significant step in seeking more accurate svearch functionalities. But current metadata schemas such as IEEE LOM are limited in several aspects. They still rely on natural language descriptions (even though they are given some structure), and in general, the metadata produced is not good enough to be machine understandable. Machine understandability is an ideal in metadata that promises to enable learning object composition, precise selection of learning objects for given learning resources, instructional design aware search, and other advanced functionalities. These capabilities require the use of formal metadata statements and their link with domain ontologies (Sicilia et al. 2005).

To clarify these concepts, the description of a YouTube video clip about genetics will be considered. A fragment of IEEE LOM metadata might be similar to the following:

```
<?xml version="1.0" encoding="UTF-8" ?>
<lom xmlns="http://ltsc.ieee.org/xsd/LOM"
xmlns:xsi="http://www.w3.org/2001/XMLSchemainstance"
xsi:schemaLocation="http://ltsc.ieee.org/xsd/LOMhttp://ltsc.ieee.org/xsd/lomv1.0/
lom.xsd">
<general>
  <identifier>
    <catalog>URI</catalog>
    <entry>http://www.youtube.com/watch?v=WsofH466lqk</entry>
  </identifier>
```

---

[10]http://dublincore.org.

```
<title> <string language="en">DNA Transcription</string> </title>
<language> en </language>
</general>
<classification>
  <purpose>
    <source>LOMv1.0</source>
    <value>educational objective</value>
  </purpose>
  <description>
    <string language="en">Introduces the process of DNA transcription.</string>
  </description>
</classification>
</lom>
```

This fragment describes some basic properties of the video, namely its location, title, language, and its educational objective. This kind of metadata is useful for a structured search; however, semantics go one step further by using ontologies. Ontologies are formal, shared conceptualizations (Gruber 1993) that are nowadays being shared through the Web by means of common languages such as OWL, which are part of the foundations for a Semantic Web (Berners-Lee et al. 2001). For example, if we use the Gene Ontology[11] (GO) in an IEEE LOM metadata record, we can have something similar to the following:

```
<classification>
  <purpose>
    <source>LOMv1.0</source>
    <value>educational objective</value>
  </purpose>
  <taxonPath>
    <source>
      <string>GO</string>
    </source>
    <taxon>
      <id>0006351</id>
      <entry><string language="en">transcription, DNA-dependent</string></entry>
    </taxon>
  </taxonPath>
</classification>
```

In this classification, the GO has been used as an external classification system and pointed to a concrete node in that system, with ID 0006351. This represents a "biological process" in GO and is defined as "The synthesis of RNA on a template of DNA," and we can from this, identify specific classes of that process (for example, "mRNA transcription with identifier GO:009299"), parts of that process (for

---

[11] http://www.geneontology.org.

example "transcription initiation," GO:0006352), or related regulation processes, so that we could use these related elements to search for related learning objects. The difference is subtle, but with this, we have unambiguously identified a knowledge objective and we are able to reuse the investment of the community of researchers that created and maintain this GO. This is thanks to the fact that the GO is formally defined in term of classes and relationships as "part of" or "is a." The ontology thus becomes a mediator for relating some resources to others. This is only a simple approach to "semantic annotation," but there are several different approaches reported in the literature (Gaševic et al. 2007).

But connecting standardized metadata elements with existing ontologies is only half of the story. The metadata statements themselves need to be expressed in formal terms and the learning process requirements need to be given an advanced expression and finally, instructional design or pedagogical information has to be also made available in terms of ontology languages. These are aspects still subject to intense exploratory research. Semantic repositories are still in their infancy, even though there are several implementations already available.[12] There are several issues about the use of semantic technology in repositories that make them harder to implement and maintain. These issues include how to provide semantic annotation tools that are usable and produce useful formal statements; how to use ontologies for navigation and in general, how to represent learning needs and pedagogical requirements. Furthermore, semantic repositories have added overhead in the management of metadata, since they in turn rely on the evolution of ontologies.

The complete integration of repositories into the learning process will not be possible until the whole virtual learning environment is driven by ontologies, establishing the appropriate relationships between resources, services, and users. The LOR, seen as a sophisticated service part of the virtual learning environment, needs to provide learners with better support for searching and browsing activities but also for storing, tagging, rating, and even evaluating learning resources. That will enable learners to seamlessly integrate the LOR into their learning process and use it continuously as part of it.

2.5   Discussion

Nevertheless, the most important issue for a LOR integrated in a virtual learning environment is being able to build a true social learning network around it, promoting the creation, sharing, and reuse of learning resources among the members of the learning community, mainly both learners and teachers. This can be only done if the LOR, regardless of its technology, provides its users with a virtual learning

---

[12]http://sourceforge.net/projects/ont-space.

environment and a true learning experience. Obviously, a semantic layer which establishes the appropriate relationships between resources and the learning process will be a first step toward maintaining such a social network. But the learning process in virtual learning environments is far from being completely and concisely described. Although the new EHEA paradigm focuses mainly on formal learning, bridging higher education and lifelong learning, some of the ideas behind it can be adopted to any educational level. The shift from a content-based curriculum to a competence-based one is one of the main methodological issues, calling for new technologies such as LORs, as aforementioned.

New learning theories such as connectivism (Siemens 2005) establishes that learning is produced during the process of establishing new relationships between contents and concepts, rather than in the already acquired knowledge. LORs are important elements in the network built by the learner during his or her learning process, as they store not only the learning resources but also all the details of the learning experience itself with respect to the learner, with the help of the appropriate ontological support. In fact, nowadays we live in an age of content abundance, as resources are easy to find, create, remix, and share; the main problems for learners now are quality assessment and the lack of feedback, which are informational competences that must also be acquired and developed as part of the learning process. This subject is deeply discussed in Chap. 5 of this book.

We have discussed that the shift promoted by the new EHEA paradigm also causes a shift from traditional CMS, aimed at storing and preserving digital content with unidirectional interaction (the producer–consumer model), to LORs, which provide users with a dynamic vision of content (e.g., infrastructure), promoting a higher degree of interactivity, framing interactions, and learning experiences. In this sense, content is not something static, it evolves multidirectionally from an initial source, as it is "used" by learners. Therefore, the concept of preservation is at stake and needs to be possibly redefined. On the other hand, LORs must offer content as infrastructure, but the learning process is performed everywhere else. The LOR is an important element of the virtual learning environment but it is not the only one and, of course, learners may search for resources outside the institutional "barriers." This is one of the key elements in connectivism: learning happens anytime and anywhere; it is the learner (and not the institution) who decides and takes control over his or her learning process, going where his or her particular learning goals might be satisfied and at the same time combining multiple sources. This new landscape shapes new roles, as teachers and institutions must become guides, enablers, capacity builders, facilitators, more than just content creators and providers. Any learning management system based on a simple content management solution is, simply, condemned to death.

Therefore, LORs seem to be one of the basic elements of any virtual learning environment, but they must be built based upon these principles: they need to serve a community of users which share a common interest; they must allow users to store any kind of content, in any format, as well as to establish the appropriate relationships with other content already in the repository; users should be also allowed to add their own tags, ratings, or comments about the content; browsing and searching should be semantically supported; personalized services should be provided according to each user profile; and, finally, system usage should be analyzed to discover any potential problem or improvement. All of these characteristics will be only possible when repositories will become a collection of semantic services being part of a semantic learning management system which operates at a higher level.

References

Ade, J., Allegre, C., Arsenis, G., Bladh, A., Catenhusen, W.-M., Dowling, P. et al. (1999). The Bologna Declaration of 19 June 1999. Available at http://www.bologna-bergen2005.no/Docs/00-Main_doc/990719BOLOGNA_DECLARATION.PDF

Akeroyd, J. (2005). Information management and e-learning. Some perspectives. Aslib *Proceedings: New Information Perspectives, 57*(2), 157–167.

Berners-Lee, T., Hendler, J., & Lassila, O. (2001). The semantic Web. *Scientific American, 284*(5), 28–37.

Bloom, B. S. (1956). *Taxonomy of educational objectives, the classification of educational goals – Handbook I: Cognitive domain.* New York: McKay.

Boiko, B. (2001). *Content management bible.* New York: Wiley.

Conway, P. (2008). Modeling the digital content landscape in universities. *Library Hi Tech, 26*(3), 342–354.

Downes, S. (2001). Learning objects: Resources for distance education worldwide. *International Review of Research in Open and Distance Learning, 2,* 1.

Dreher, H., Krottmaier H., & Maurer, H. (2004). What we expect from digital libraries. *Journal of Universal Computer Science, 10*(9), 1110–1122.

Ferran, N., Casadesús, J., Krakowska, M., & Minguillón, J. (2007). Enriching e-learning metadata through digital library usage analysis. *The Electronic Library, 25*(2), 148–165.

Gagné, R., Briggs, L., & Wager, W. (1992). *Principles of instructional design* (4th ed.). Boston: Wadsworth Publishing.

Gaševic, D., Jovanovic, J., & Devedžic, V. (2007). Ontology-based annotation of learning object content. *Interactive Learning Environments, 15*(1), 1–26.

Gruber, T. R. (1993). A translation approach to portable ontologies. *Knowledge Acquisition, 5*(2), 199–220.

Heery, R., & Anderson, S. (2005). *Digital repositories review.* Bath: UKOLN and Arts and Humanities Data Service. Retrieved November 15, 2007, from http://www.jisc.ac.uk/uploaded_documents/digital-repositories-review-2005.pdf

Herlocker, J. L., Konstan, J. A., Terveen, L. G., & Riedl, J. T. (2004). Evaluating collaborative filtering recommender systems. *ACM Transactions on Information Systems, 22*(1), 5–53.

Holmes, B., & Gardner, J. (2006). *E-learning: Concepts and practice.* Thousand Oaks: Pine Forge Press.

Konstan, J., Miller, B., Maltz, D., Herlocker, J., Gordon, L., & Riedl, J. (1997). GroupLens: Applying collaborative filtering to Usenet News. *Communications of the ACM, 40*(3), 77–87.

Littlejohn, A., & Margaryan, A. (2006). Cultural issues in the sharing and reuse of resources for learning. *Research and Practice in Technology-Enhanced Learning, 1*(3), 269–284.

McGreal, R. (2004). Learning Objects: A practical definition. *International Journal of Instructional Technology and Distance Learning, 1*(9), pp. 21–32.

McNaught, C. (2006). *Are learning repositories likely to become mainstream in education?* Proceedings of the 2nd International Conference on Web Information Systems and Technologies, Setubal, Portugal, April 11–13, 2006 (pp. IS9–IS17). Keynote address.

Monge, S., Ovelar, R., & Azpeitia, I. (2008). Repository 2.0: Social dynamics to support community building in learning object repositories. *Interdisciplinary Journal of E-Learning and Learning Objects* (formerly the *Interdisciplinary Journal of Knowledge and Learning Objects*), 4.

Nash, S. S. (2005). Learning objects, learning object repositories, and learning theory: Preliminary best practices for online courses. *Interdisciplinary Journal of Knowledge and Learning Objects, 1*. Retrieved May 15, 2006, from http://ijklo.org/Volume1/v1p217228Nash.pdf

Peters, T. A. (2002). Digital repositories: Individual, discipline-based, institutional, consortial or national? *Journal of Academic Librarianship, 28*(6), 414–417.

Reigeluth, C. M. (Ed.) (1999). *Instructional-design theories and models, volume II: A new paradigm of instructional theory.* Mahwah, NJ: Lawrence Erlbaum Assoc.

Rosenberg, M. J. (2002). *E-Learning: Strategies for delivering knowledge in the digital age.* New York: McGraw-Hill.

Sicilia, M. A. (2007). Beyond content: Sharing the design of open educational resources In: Open educational resources [on-line monograph]. *Revista de Universidad y Sociedad del Conocimiento (RUSC). 4*(1). UOC. http://www.uoc.edu/rusc/4/1/dt/esp/sicilia.pdf.

Sicilia, M. A., García-Barriocanal, E., Sánchez-Alonso, S., & Soto, J. (2005). A semantic lifecycle approach to learning object repositories. *Proceedings of the Advanced Industrial Conference on Telecommunications*, pp. 466–471.

Siemens, G. (2005). Connectivism: A learning theory for the digital age. *International Journal of Instructional Technology and Distance Learning, 2*(1), 3–10.

Sumner, T., & Marlino, M. (2004). Digital libraries and educational practice: A case for new models. *Proceedings of the 4th Joint Conference on Digital Libraries*, pp. 170–178.

Taylor, J. C. (1999). Distance education: The fifth generation. *Proceedings of the 19th ICDE World Conference on Open Learning and Distance Education*, Vienna, Austria.

Thomas, P., Carswell, L., & Price, B. (1998). A holistic approach to supporting distance learning using the internet: Transformation, not translation. *British Journal of Educational Technology, 29*(2), 149–161.

Thomas, A., & Rothery, A. (2005). Online repositories for learning materials: The user perspective. *Ariadne, 45*, available at www.ariadne.ac.uk/issue45/thomas-rothery/.

Wiley, D. (2000). *Connecting learning objects to instructional design theory: A definition, a metaphor, and a taxonomy.* In D. A. Wiley (Ed.), *The instructional use of learning objects: Online version,* http://reusability.org/read/chapters/wiley.doc.

Wiley, D. (2007). Content is infrastructure. *Terra incognita* [online]. Available at http://blog.worldcampus.psu.edu/index.php/2007/10/03/content-is-infrastructure/.

Bibliography

2009 Horizon Report. (2009). Various authors. Retrieved February 19, 2009, from http://wp.nmc.org.horizon2009

Alsagoff, Z. A. (2008). University learning = OCW + OER = Free! *ZaidLearn.* Retrieved February 19, 2009, from http://zaidlearn.blogspot.com/2008/06/university-learning-ocw-oer-free.html

Downes, S. (2005). The fate of eduSource. *OLDaily.* Retrieved February 19, 2009, from http://www.downes.ca/cgi-bin/page.cgi?post=15

Downes, S. (2008). The future of online learning: Ten years on. *Half an Hour.* Retrieved February 19, 2009, from http://halfanhour.blogspot.com/2008/11/future-of-online-learning-ten-years-on_16.html

Ferran, N., Mor, E., & Minguillón, J. (2005). Towards personalization in digital libraries through ontologies. *Library Management, 26*(4/5), 206–217.

Hirst, T. (2008). OER custom search engine. *OUseful Info.* Retrieved February 19, 2009, from http://ouseful.open.ac.uk/blogarchive/014895.html

Leslie, S. (2008). Dynamic Wiki-driven OER search engine. *EdTechPost.* Retrieved February 19, 2009, from http://www.edtechpost.ca/wordpress/2008/06/20/google-coop-on-the-fly/

Wiley, D. et al. (2004). Overcoming the limitations of learning objects. *Journal of Educational Multimedia and Hypermedia, 13*(4), 507–521.

Chapter 3
Learning Objects, Content Management, and E-Learning

David Wiley

Abstract For better or worse, e-learning is still primarily a matter of delivering course materials via the world-wide web. With the increasing ubiquity of high-bandwidth connections to the home, even multimedia materials like videos and simulations are commonly delivered in-browser. This melding of education with the web brings a new variety of problems to educators who are already required to have a wide-ranging set of interdisciplinary skills.

3.1 Where Education and the Web Meet

For better or worse, e-learning is still primarily a matter of delivering course materials via the World Wide Web. With the increasing ubiquity of high-bandwidth connections to the home, even multimedia materials like videos and simulations are commonly delivered in-browser. This melding of education with the web brings a new variety of problems to educators who are already required to have a wide-ranging set of interdisciplinary skills. Andersson et al. (2005) nicely summarize the problems involved in running Web sites:

It is easy to build and maintain a Web site if:

- One person is publisher, author, and programmer
- The site comprises only a few pages
- Nobody cares whether these few pages are formatted consistently
- Nobody cares about retrieving old versions or figuring out how a version got to be the way that it is

Fortunately, for companies and programmers that hope to make a nice living from providing content management "solutions," the preceding conditions seldom

D. Wiley (✉)
Instructional Psychology and Technology, Brigham Young University, Provo 84602, UT, USA
e-mail: david.wiley@gmail.com

N. Ferran and J. Minguillón (eds.), *Content Management for E-Learning*,
DOI 10.1007/978-1-4419-6959-0_3, © Springer Science+Business Media, LLC 2011

obtain at better-financed Web sites. What is more typical are the following conditions:

- Labor is divided among publishers, information designers, graphic designers, authors, and programmers
- The site contains thousands of pages
- Pages must be consistent within sections and sections must have a unifying theme
- Version control is critical

We have all seen online courses that fit the first description: a few pages, formatted inconsistently, only some of which have been updated recently. We have also seen examples of the second kind of e-learning: thousands of consistently formatted pages that seem to have been created by faceless masses for faceless masses.

But we can productively extend Andersson and colleagues' example of methods of developing Web sites to an example of e-learning (which involves both doing education and developing Web sites) by considering the three possible configurations of people who might be involved in an e-learning project:

- The single educator who gains some technical expertise
- The single engineer who gains some educational expertise
- The specialized, division-of-labor, multiperson team including content experts, instructional designers, graphic designers, and programmers

We can also associate the configurations of people with the type of projects they work on. The single educator with some technical expertise puts his/her university course online in blackboard. The engineer with some educational expertise develops e-learning standards and reference software implementations. The multiperson team develops 15 courses at a time for delivery in a standards-conforming enterprise e-learning system.

Much of the e-learning "innovations" of the past decade have come from the second kind of person – the engineer with some educational expertise. Everything from IMS specifications, to IEEE LTSC standards, to ADL SCORM is primarily attributable to this kind of person. I've frequently wondered why educators tolerate this state of things; perhaps the answer is the obvious observation that it is much easier for an engineer to be lulled into a belief that they understand education than it is for an educator to be lulled into the belief that they understand engineering. See Chap. 9 for a more detailed discussion on this subject.

3.2   Enter Learning Objects

The topic of many of the e-learning specifications, standards, and reference software implementations of the last decade has been "learning objects" and the variety of problems related to appropriate content management practices for learning objects, including cataloging, managing, and moving learning objects between systems.

What exactly are learning objects? This question has been asked and answered too many times to warrant original writing. Wiley (2008, p. 347) summarized:

> The learning objects notion is confusing in part because there are dozens of definitions of the term learning object (LO), as well as several phrases referring to the same notion of reusable digital educational resources. The most frequently cited definition of learning objects, and the most all-inclusive, is that put forth by the Institute of Electrical and Electronics Engineers' Learning Technology Standards Committee (IEEE 2005):
>
> "Learning Objects are defined here as any entity, digital or non-digital, which can be used, re-used or referenced during technology supported learning... Examples of Learning Objects include:
>
> • Multimedia content
> • Instructional content
> • Learning objectives
> • Instructional software and software tools
> • Persons, organizations, or events referenced during technology supported learning"

The reaction against this extremely broad definition has been very strong. Wiley (2000, p. 23) struggled to constrain the definition somewhat with "any digital resource that can be reused to support learning," but even this is still very broad. More colorfully, people have reacted by writing pieces such as *My Left Big Toe Is a Learning Object* (Levine 2004) and *Urinal as a Learning Object* (Leinonen 2005).

To add to the confusion, there are a number of other terms synonymous with learning object, including Merrill's *knowledge object* (Merrill 1998), Gibbons' *instructional object* (Gibbons et al. 2000), the Advanced Distributed Learning Initiative's *sharable content objects* (ADL 2004), Hannafin's *resources* (Hannafin et al. 2000), and Downes different use of the term *resources* (Downes 2004).

The stated end-goal of much of the learning objects work is the automated selection of learning objects from a content management system for just-in-time assembly and delivery to a learner. Hodgins (2000) compares this future software system to a childhood tale:

> For those who recall the story of Goldilocks and the Three Bears, this is the "Baby Bear" analogy – we get it "just right": not too big, not too small, not too hot, not too cold, etc. In the case of learning objects, we get them in "just the right"

• Size/amount
• Time
• Way (learning style)
• Context, relevance
• Medium of delivery (paper, DVD, on-line, synchronous, on screen, etc.)
• Location (desk, car, house, palm, field, etc.)

While there are obvious benefits for the learner in such a system, the instructional design and content management issues involved in designing and building the system are incredibly complex. In fact, I believe these issues to be so complicated as to be intractable, at least as the problem is currently framed. In the discussion that follows, I will make this argument while touching upon several educational and content management issues.

3.3   Problems with Baby Bear

Academic work on learning objects has centered on questions like "what is the optimal size for a learning object?" Standards work on learning objects has focused on questions like "what is the optimal method of cataloging learning objects to support later findability and retrieval?" Technical work on learning objects has focused on questions like "what is the optimal database structure in which to store learning objects to support later findability and retrieval?" These questions are generally asked in the context of the Baby Bear context of automated selection and assembly, providing each learner with a completely personalized learning experience. However, careful thought will show that the Baby Bear goals are simply unachievable for all the most simplistic cases.

In order to carry out this thought process with sufficient precision, a number of definitions are required. The core issue to understand is the role of context in influencing and creating meaning. With advance apologies to the reader for presenting a list of terms, the following terms and definitions are used throughout the remainder of the chapter:

1. *Learning object*: a digital resource that can be reused to mediate learning.
2. *A learning object's internal context*: the media elements juxtaposed within a learning object. This juxtaposition may be spatial, as in the case where a caption appears beneath a photo, and the juxtapositions may be temporal, as in the case where a voiceover describes a scene in a video. The notion of context as spatial or temporal juxtaposition is a key to the experiment.
3. *Small learning object*: a single media element uncombined with any other, like a single jpg photograph.
4. *Large learning object*: many media elements combined to make a bigger, aggregate learning object, like a webpage including several text elements, images, and an animation.
5. *A learning object's external context*: the elements (including other learning objects) against which a learning object is juxtaposed either spatially or temporally in order to mediate learning.
6. *Instructional use of a learning object*: the process of placing of a learning object within an external context, whether done by a software system or a person.
7. *Instructional fit*: the degree to which the instructional use of a learning object, as opposed to other variables, mediates learning. For example, a module on the Pythagorean theorem would not "fit" well in a second grade spelling lesson.

I pause here to give a few more examples of the idea of context as juxtaposition. Take the word "no" for example. Notice the very different meanings the word takes on in the following two short dialogues:

Dialogue 1

Police officer: Good evening ma'am. I'm sorry to have to inform you that your husband has been in a car accident.

Woman: *No!* Surely you have the wrong house!

Dialogue 2

> Teenager: Mom, seriously. Everybody is going. I don't know what you're so
>   uptight about.
> Woman: *No!*
> And if you ask me again it will be a week until you drive that car again.

The word "no" is used in each of the dialogues, punctuated exactly the same way (with an exclamation point), and delivered by the same character (the Woman). However, it is clear to even the casual reader that the "no!" in dialogue one means "please tell me it isn't so" or "I don't believe you;" while the "no!" in dialogue two means "absolutely not." How is it that we are able to understand different meanings of the two identical words, punctuated identically, and spoken by the same person? by the *context* in which her remarks are made. The words that come before and come after the word "no" actually influence the meaning of the word. Vygotsky (1962) called this phenomenon the "influx of sense":

> The senses of different words flow into one another – literally "influence" one another – so that the earlier ones are contained in, and modify, the later ones.

Vygotsky's use of the word "earlier" tells us that he is really speaking about temporal juxtaposition. As we will explore below, the importance of context in determining meaning is a key problem for content management practices as they apply to e-learning, and particularly learning objects. When learning objects are stored in a database, without an external context other than the database itself, it can be difficult to decide exactly what a learning object is supposed to mean and where it might or might not fit.

A few more definitions:

8. *Learning object user*: a software system or human that makes instructional use of a learning object.
9. *Metadata*: descriptive information about some of the properties of a learning object.
10. *Learning object discovery*: the process by which a user locates learning objects which are a candidate for a specific instructional use.
11. *Objective metadata*: properties of a learning object to which meaningfully falsifiable values can be assigned, such as the learning object's author, file size, or mime type.
12. *Subjective metadata*: properties of a learning object to which meaningfully falsifiable values cannot be assigned, such as the learning object's meaning or usefulness.
13. *Instructional architecture*: a known configuration of external contexts. For example, instructional templates which learning objects may be "plugged into" in order to mediate the learning process.

For the purposes of this exploration, we assume that two sizes of learning objects exist: "small" and "large." In practice, the designators "small" and "large" represent ends of a continuum on which all learning objects may be measured. While more sizes of learning objects exist than simply "small" and "large," these two types do exist, and the differences between them as discussed below remain when additional types of objects are admitted to exist along the continuum between them. The argument below could be extended to these other types of learning objects with some effort, but this effort is unnecessary to make the point that it is not practically possible to automate the assembly of learning objects in order to support the learning process.

Building on the definitions provided above, then, we can both make and defend a number of assertions, and draw out their implications for content management practices.

3.4 Assertions and Implications

Assertion 1. A learning object has no meaningful external context independent of its instructional use. External context is defined as the juxtaposition of a learning object against other elements, including other learning objects. When a learning object is stored in a digital library, it can be juxtaposed against thousands of other objects in search results, or juxtaposed against no other objects when the learning object itself is viewed. Spatial juxtaposition against thousands of other items in a list of search results contributes only random noise to our interpretation of the learning object's meaning. And when we do drop into the object view from the search results, the temporal juxtaposition of the learning object itself against the list of search results adds very little to our understanding. The most meaningful external contexts for interpreting the meaning of a learning object are those spatial and temporal juxtapositions purposively made to support the learning process.

One of the implications of Assertion 1 is that content management practices regarding learning objects should include a process for capturing, preserving, and later presenting one or more of the external contexts of instructional use for each learning object in the collection. Complementary work on this subject can be found in Chap. 4.

Assertion 2. The number of external contexts in which a learning object will fit instructionally is a function of the internal context of the learning object. Consider an art history web page as an example of a large learning object. This web page might contain an image of the Mona Lisa, an image of Leonardo da Vinci, captions for both images, and some text describing Leonardo da Vinci's life and what we know about the creation of the famous portrait. The images, captions, and texts have been selected and juxtaposed in a way that strongly suggests that we interpret their meaning in a specific way – a way that teaches us about the history of art. This large learning object is easily usable in an art history curriculum because the component learning objects have been selected and instructionally used specifically to facilitate learning in the domain of art history.

Assertion 3. A large learning object has a greater internal context than a small learning object. Two or more small objects are contained in a large object. Because the internal context of the large object consists of the internal contexts of its component parts and the juxtaposition of the components against each other, we can safely assert that a large learning object has a greater internal context.

Assertions 4. Large learning objects fit into fewer external contexts than small learning objects. This follows from Assertions 2 and 3. The art history web page described above fits clearly in many art history contexts, but would fit poorly in bioinformatics or music theory contexts. This is because the juxtapositions of images, captions, and text work together to create a meaning that suggests this page belongs in an art history context.

Contrast the page's specificity of suggested meaning with one of the page's component small learning objects, like the image of the Mona Lisa. This individual image fits in the art history context, but the specificity of the art history domain is in the image's external context, and is solely a function of its instructional use. Independent of that use, the learning object will fit units on popular culture, attitude, or in the treatment of digital images.

One of the content management implications of Assertion 4 is that learning objects should be stored in the smallest pieces possible, in order to maximize their potential for reuse. This has been a maxim of the learning objects movement for sometime. However, as we will see below, this implication turns out to be faulty on further inspection.

Assertion 5. Metadata facilitates the discovery, and therefore the instructional use of, learning objects. Because many learning objects are nontextual, they cannot be discovered via full-text searching. Metadata provide a way for these learning objects to be located. Additionally, information about the learning object that would not necessarily appear within the resource can be represented. For example, the total amount of time the average learner would spend on a resource can be captured and presented. A learning object cannot be used unless the user knows about it.

One of the content management implications of Assertion 5 is that learning objects should be indexed with metadata. Best practices would indicate that one of the existing metadata standards like Dublin Core + ED, SCORM, or IEEE LOM should be used to capture this information.

However, notice the interaction between the implications of Assertions 4 and 5. On the one hand, it would seem that we should cut existing resources down into the smallest learning objects possible in order to maximize their potential for reuse. On the other hand, it would seem that we should create metadata for each of our objects. If we pursue both of these recommendations, we end up with hundreds of thousands or even millions of small learning objects for which we must create metadata records containing dozens of values. The cost of indexing all these small learning objects will quickly outgrow the cost of creating all the objects. These two implications are therefore at odds with one another when the practicalities of cost are considered.

Wiley (2004) discusses a similar problem called "the reusability paradox":

> Because humans make meaning by connecting new information to that which they already know, the meaningfulness of educational content is a function of its context. As the module's context is further elaborated and made more explicit, a learner working with the module has an easier time understanding how this information relates to what they already know. *The more context a learning object has, the more (and more easily) a learner can learn from it.*

To an instructional designer, learning object "reuse" means placing a learning object in a context other than that for which it was designed. The fit of learning objects into these new contexts depends on the extent to which the learning object's internals contain explicit statements of context. For example, statements within a learning object like "as you will recall from the last module…" make it very difficult to reuse the learning object in a context other than that for which it was designed. *To make learning objects maximally reusable, learning objects should contain as little context as possible.*

It turns out that reusability and pedagogical effectiveness are completely orthogonal to each other. *Therefore, pedagogical effectiveness and potential for reuse are completely at odds with one another.*

Assertion 6. Metadata about the internal context of large learning objects is more valuable to users of a learning object than metadata about the large learning object's previous external contexts. A large object has an internal context sufficient to restrict its use to a closed set of learning (or external) contexts (via Assertion 4). Before a learning object can be used instructionally the possible externals contexts of use must be identified, and a decision must be made regarding the instructional fit of a learning object into the target external context. Fit can only be assessed by examining the internal context of the learning object and comparing it to the target external context, making metadata regarding the internal context of the learning object necessary to its use (assuming that users will not examine every learning object individually and will rely on metadata to support learning object discovery).

Assertion 7. Metadata about the previous external contexts of small learning objects is more valuable to users of a learning object than metadata about the small learning object's internal context. Small learning objects are by definition single elements. While small learning objects exhibit some juxtaposition of internal elements (e.g., the foreground and background of a photograph), this internal context is much less significant than that of a large learning object, meaning that the possible external contexts of use of a small learning object are significantly greater in number than those of a large learning object. Since the internal context of a small learning object does not eliminate it from use in many external contexts (as the large learning object's internal context does), metadata regarding the internal context of a small learning object provides less information to users making decisions regarding the small learning object. However, examples of the manner in which other users have used the small object may provide valuable data that support small learning object use decisions by learning object users.

Assertion 8. The potential for instructional use of different types of learning objects will be maximized by different types of metadata. This follows from Assertions 6 and 7.

One of the content management implications of Assertion 8 is that the difficulty of combining Assertions 4 and 5 is exacerbated by the need to capture different kinds of metadata about different kinds of learning objects. Because of the additional decision processes involved in categorizing learning objects in order to decide which type of metadata they should have, the implications of Assertions 4 and 5 are even more expensive to implement conjointly than we previously thought.

Assertion 9. The value of objective metadata in facilitating learning object discovery is stable across learning object types, be they small or large, and should be captured for all learning objects. Assertion 8 states that different types of metadata must be used to maximize the potential for discovery and use of different types of learning objects. Assertions 6 and 7 demonstrated that the specific metadata needed to facilitate discovery (and therefore instructional use) relate to the internal and external contexts of the learning object. Because the interpretation of context is a subjective matter, the differences in necessary metadata are differences in subjective metadata, meaning that the value of objective metadata is the same for all learning object types.

Some additional content management implications of Assertions 6, 7, and 8 are that subjective metadata for small learning objects should focus on capturing the previous external contexts of use of the small learning objects. Conversely, subjective metadata for large learning objects should focus on capturing the internal context of the large learning object.

Assertion 10. Automation of the instructional use of large learning objects may be possible in simple cases. The internal context of a large learning object significantly limits the external contexts into which it will fit instructionally (Assertion 4). This limitation of possible external contexts of use can be combined with a highly constrained instructional architecture (a known configuration of external contexts) to facilitate the automated selection and placement of large learning objects into well-known external contexts in which they will fit.

For example, say a learning objects developer creates three large learning objects that are equivalent in terms of their instructional outcomes, but differ in their presentation in order to cater to differing students' preferences (say, didactic instruction, a digital storytelling approach, and a simulation-based approach). An automated system is certainly capable of reading learner preference information out of a learner profile and choosing the best fitting of these three objects. Note, however, that the automated system has not made any instructional choices in terms of how to combine smaller objects to generate an instructional message – the system has simply chosen a large object (inside which all these instructional message-generating decisions have already been made) according to an aesthetic or preference criterion.

Another case where large learning objects can play into the Baby Bear strategy is when they are automatically ignored – not selected. For example, if large learning objects are linked to learning outcomes, and a student demonstrates mastery of some outcomes, an intelligent system can leave out the associated large learning objects.

Another case in which we approach the Baby Bear case is a large learning object automatically assembled from smaller components, where the large learning object is mostly preassembled by hand, with a small number of templated slots into which an intelligent system can automatically insert one of several smaller media elements, depending on learner profile information. For example, a system might select a soldier in a blue uniform for presentation to a member of one branch of the armed services, and a soldier in a green uniform for presentation to a member of another branch of the armed services.

A content management implication of Assertion 10 is that if learning objects are to be used in an instructional approach that relies on information outside the learning object (like learner preferences) as part of its selection criteria, these decisions must be made in advance. Creating an additional field in metadata to capture this kind of information costs relatively little if it can be done as part of the initial indexing process. The relative costs are very high, however, if a project comes to the realization later and has to go back and re-index every object.

Assertion 11. The instructional use of small learning objects cannot be safely automated. The internal context of a small learning object constrains the number of external contexts into which it could fit much less than the internal context of a large learning object does (Assertion 4). This necessitates the use of additional decision support data to select one of several potentially fitting learning objects. That is, it forces instructional fit decisions to rely on data other than those expressed in metadata. Deprived of the data necessary to support this kind of decision, an automated system is incapable of reliably using small learning objects.

Wiley et al. (2004) describe the risk inherent in assembling small learning objects with what they call the "Sixth Sense Effect":

> Even if an automated system could successfully select and sequence learning objects correctly the vast majority of the time, a mistake at any point could cause a "Sixth Sense Effect" due to the influx of sense, in which previously understood material is reinterpreted in light of new information. The "Sixth Sense Effect" is the common school experience of understanding a lecture up to a certain point and then "realizing" that you haven't understood it at all. "I was with you right up to the last sentence; but now I think I must not have understood anything you said."

> It is entirely possible that a single, misplaced object could, via this Sixth Sense Effect, undo significant portions of previous learning as students struggle to reinterpret what they have previously understood in terms of new material presented inappropriately. For example, imagine concept instruction teaching the identification and classification of Baroque period music. After several examples and non-examples are displayed, a twentieth century example is inappropriately selected and presented as an example of Baroque. One can imagine students thinking back to the previous examples and non-examples, struggling to understand how Stravinsky fit the mental model they had worked so hard to develop. While humans may make occasional selection errors of this kind, we believe that machines are much more likely to err in this manner – especially in more complex instructional domains where meaning-making plays a more significant role.

Assertion 12. Different types of learning objects are best suited to instructional use by different types of learning object users. Following from Assertions 10 and 11, it is clear that smaller, more reusable learning objects should only be combined for instructional use by people and not by automated systems. It is also clear that large learning objects can, in some cases, be made amenable to real-time selection and delivery by automated systems.

The primary content management implication of the final assertion is that an important decision must be made before implementing a learning objects strategy. If personalized, automated assembly of learning objects is the goal of your project, you must decide on a learning object architecture comprised of larger learning objects and the surrounding metadata early on. Everything must conform to the architecture for the automated system to make use of it. Relationships between learner preferences and profiles and learning objects must be mapped out in advance. Connections between learning objects, assessments, and learning outcomes must be specified ahead of time. Merrill's knowledge objects approach is one example of an approach that relies on highly specified content that can be reused by an intelligent system (Merill 2000).

3.5 Discussion and Openness

One of the primary reasons people are interested in "learning objects" is their purported reusability. Reusability, if achieved, facilitates the creation of generative systems, adaptive systems, and scalable systems; in fact, it facilitates the creation of generative, adaptive, scalable systems. Gibbons and his associates claim that these three properties are nothing less than the goals of computerized instruction (Gibbons et al. 2000). For this reason the automated approach to learning object assembly, which is necessary to achieve these three goals, has been reverenced as the one true goal of the learning objects movement, if such a thing can be said to exist. However, there is another view of the desirability of reusable educational content.

When educational media is created as a learning object, that is, when it is created in a digital format, the economics of media use change. In the physical world, educational media is created, horded, and occasionally used (South and Monson 2000). The ratio of production cost to number of uses is prohibitively high. However, in the digital world, where any number of people can access and use a single learning object simultaneously, the ratio changes. With the repeated reuse facilitated by the growing ubiquity of the ICT, cost recovery can become a reality. More importantly, however, once the ratio of production cost to number of uses nears zero, access to learning objects can be made available for free. Better yet, open source development models can be adopted to drive the cost of learning object creation toward zero (the ratio of development work to volunteer developers), making learning objects freely available from their genesis. Finally, advertising will continue to support free access to some online content and services. Each of these scenarios can provide teachers and learners with access to high quality educational materials they could never afford or produce individually. The "open education movement" as represented by projects like MIT OpenCourseWare and the recent Cape Town Open Education Declaration are pushing this agenda of free and open access to educational opportunity.

Having attended public schools in a very rural area as a child, I speak about this viewpoint with a certain passion. Access to interactive maps for geography study, Java applets for physics study, and graphing scientific calculators for use in math would have been wonderful. Today, each of these and many more "learning objects" are freely available on the Internet.

While the goal of automated instructional systems based on learning objects is worthwhile, there are two important reasons that the by-hand, human assembly of learning objects should not be passed over.

First, human assembly of learning objects works best with small objects. Fortuitously, the majority of the data available on the public Internet are "small objects" – images, text files, etc. If promoting reuse is the goal of the learning objects movement, how can it ignore dozens of terabytes of existing learning objects? And yet it is being ignored, mostly because it will not fit into automated systems like those designed by Merrill. If services existed to facilitate the instructional use of these "small objects," the educational impact could be significant. A number of systems exist to support the by-hand assembly of objects, including the Instructional Architect (Recker et al. 2005).

Second, common sense would suggest that we can only automate that which we know how to do by hand. Could the automation of coal mining or automobile assembly ever have occurred without the lessons learned by years of humans performing these same tasks by hand? I do not believe so. Likewise, before humans can build automated systems to assemble learning objects, they must first learn the lessons to be gained combining those objects by hand. These experiments must be supported, documented, evaluated, and published in order to build a body of content management, pedagogical, and technological expertise sufficient to support the automated assembly of small learning objects by intelligent systems.

Bibliography

Andersson, E., Greenspun, P., & Grumet, A. (2005). *Software engineering for Internet applications*. Retrieved February 11, 2008, from http://philip.greenspun.com/seia/content-management

Gibbons, A. S., Nelson, J., & Richards, R. (2000). The nature and origin of instructional objects. In D. A. Wiley (Ed.), *The instructional use of learning objects: Online version*. Retrieved February 11, 2008, from http://reusability.org/read/chapters/gibbons.doc

Hodgins, H. W. (2000). The future of learning objects. In D. A. Wiley (Ed.), *The instructional use of learning objects: Online version*. Retrieved February 11, 2008, from http://reusability.org/read/chapters/hodgins.doc

Merrill, M. D. (2000). Knowledge objects and mental models. In D. A. Wiley (Ed.), *The instructional use of learning objects: Online version*. Retrieved February 11, 2008, from http://reusability.org/read/chapters/merrill.doc

Recker et al. (2005). Teaching, designing, and sharing: A context for learning objects. *Interdisciplinary Journal of E-Learning and Learning Objects, 1*, 197–216. Retrieved February 11, 2008, from http://ijklo.org/Volume1/v1p197–216Recker.pdf

South, J. B., & Monson, D. W. (2000). A university-wide system for creating, capturing, and delivering learning objects. In D. A. Wiley (Ed.), *The instructional use of learning objects: Online version*. Retrieved February 11, 2008, from http://reusability.org/read/chapters/south.doc

Vygotsky, L. S. (1962). *Thought and language*. Cambridge: MIT Press.

Wiley, D. (2004). *The reusability paradox*. Retrieved February 11, 2008, from http://cnx.org/content/m11898/latest/

Wiley, D. et al. (2004). Overcoming the limitations of learning objects. *Journal of Educational Multimedia and Hypermedia, 13*(4), 507–521.

Chapter 4
On the Relationship Between Pedagogical Design and Content Management in eLearning

Sandy Britain

Abstract This chapter explores the relationship between pedagogical design and content management in the creation and use of online learning resources. A strong relationship between the two concepts is presented and in particular that the strategies and considerations around content management in eLearning systems impose a number of constraints on the variety of pedagogical designs and methods that are available to teachers using these technologies. For instance, it exposes the problems that arose when changing from one Virtual Learning Environment (or Learning Management System) to another one. It also outlines the issue of re-usability which is a crucial factor of many aspects of e-learning content management and pedagogy.

The first thing I feel I ought to do in this chapter is to explain the title. First, it contains at least two words that are the subject of ongoing debate within education theory and research, namely Pedagogy and Content. So, for the sake of clarity, I should provide some working definitions for the purposes of this chapter. In plain English then, "content" refers to the stuff that you teach (or learn); the tangible stuff communicating ideas, concepts and information, such as the results of research for example. You can listen to it, perhaps watch it, usually you can read it. You can talk about it, present it or write it. Content, you might say, is the "it" of education. When we talk about the content of a book, an article or a course, we are referring to what is in there in terms of information and ideas which might influence our own knowledge, understanding or views. While many commentators (myself included) have argued that education in general (and e-learning in particular) can get too over-focussed on the content, I rather think that a course that was truly devoid of content would be somehow unsatisfactory.

S. Britain (✉)
Director, Terrascan Ltd., New Zealand
e-mail: sandybritain@gmail.com

N. Ferran and J. Minguillón (eds.), *Content Management for E-Learning*,
DOI 10.1007/978-1-4419-6959-0_4, © Springer Science+Business Media, LLC 2011

So if content is the "it," then pedagogy can be thought of as how you teach "it." By this I mean the particular combination of didactic instruction, discussion, collaborative knowledge construction activities, practical exercises, personal reflection, research activities and so on that the teacher may decide to employ in their teaching to provide the optimal learning experience for their students.

Assuming this is acceptable as a working definition, it may still be a little unclear what a "pedagogical design" is. This is the second thing contained in the title I should perhaps explain. It is intended to convey the idea that it is possible to express the combination or sequence of pedagogical activities or methods such as those listed above as a "design" or design pattern (after Alexander 1977), independently of the content that will be taught. For precedents in the use of the term in this way see for example Kolås and Staupe (2004) or Lakkala (2007). I could have equally used the terms pedagogical approach or model here as I have in the past (e.g. Britain and Liber 2004) or the term learning design as it was used in Beetham and Sharpe (2007). I think the idea of design is important in the context of this chapter, yet the term learning design has received some criticism for applying design to the wrong thing (i.e. a teacher can only apply design to their teaching, not to learning, which is a consequence of what goes on in the students heads). The point is arguable, but I can certainly see the logic of the argument, so pedagogical design it is.

The third and final thing I need to explain about the title is that it contains an implicit assumption that there is, in fact, a relationship between pedagogical design and content management within e-learning. This contention lies at the heart of the themes and content of this chapter. I believe that there is a strong relationship and in particular that strategies and considerations around content management in eLearning systems impose a number of constraints on the variety of pedagogical designs and methods that are available to teachers using these technologies. I also suggest that an explicit awareness and open discussion of these issues will help design and employ more flexible architectures for the future.

4.1 Organisational Context, Content Management and Pedagogy

In a traditional face-to-face teaching context whether it is school, college or university, it isn't so much content management that constrains the pedagogical design of teaching sessions but the organisational context and physical environment the teacher is operating in. For example, a first year undergraduate course might consist primarily of lectures with 100 students or more filling a lecture theatre containing seats arranged in an amphitheatre and bolted facing the front. This situation places severe constraints on the variety of teaching strategies the lecturer can employ; small-group discussion, for instance, is hardly an option. A school-teacher in a classroom might have 30 students and have a wider variety of options in the organisation of their space and the opportunities to engage the students in different kinds of activities but there are still restrictions imposed by the timetable and other organisational devices (Gilbert 2005).

One of the often-stated benefits of eLearning is to free the teacher and students from the oganisational constraints of face-to-face teaching and afford greater pedagogical variety (Laurillard 2002; Britain and Liber 2004). Some of this is obtained simply by enabling students to access course content and information outside of allotted teaching time. But what is more exciting is the capability for teachers to use a creative blend of a variety of digital media (HTML, video, podcasts and animations) with activities and assessments to create an engaging learning experience using the online environment. In this way, e-learning blurs the distinctions between learning content and learning activities. Content can be embedded within an activity – such as a hyperlink to an external resource within an online discussion. Alternatively, activities can be embedded within content. Thus, a web page containing content about a topic can also contain a hyperlink to an online discussion. Furthermore, activities for some students can be used as content by others. For example, the transcript of an online discussion (an activity for some) can simply be read as a source of information (content) by others (Conole 2007).

For teachers, the blurring of the boundaries between content and learning activities undoubtedly provides new opportunities in pedagogical design, but it also can have unexpected consequences.

In a face-to-face environment where there is less mutual dependence on the learning resources providing the content (textbooks, papers, handouts etc.), the learning activities and the environment of delivery, the teacher has a very high level of flexibility in their pedagogical approach. So much is this state of affairs taken for granted that for many teachers pedagogical design is a tacit process and not something they can articulate verbally or at least have never thought to do so (Sharpe and Oliver 2007). In contrast when faced with the task of designing an online course or lesson, a teacher has to explicitly think about the instructions and activities they provide to the students. It is not enough merely to upload a document to a course space in a VLE, it also needs a direction to the students to read it, and some indication of why it should be read, questions for the students to consider as a result of reading it and perhaps a further activity they should undertake as a result.

The teacher needs to consider at the outset how they are going to provide the context for the resource. If they are working within a VLE such as Blackboard or Moodle, should they provide this context in a posting to a "course bulletin board"? Should it be written into a description of the activities for that week or topic on the main course page? Or should the context be provided on a separate web page along with the link to the resource itself? Perhaps they are operating in a blended teaching situation and decide that the context can be given verbally in class and it is simply enough to use the VLE as a content repository, but then again, they might ponder whether that is after all the most helpful strategy when students come to actually read and digest the material outside of the classroom environment?

These decisions do not solely affect pedagogical design, they are also content management decisions, and this is just one example of many similar questions at a micro-design level. Inevitably, design questions at this level require us to make some macro-level decisions, if we have not done so already. These include: Is the course going to be managed entirely online or using a blended approach? Is the course going to be predominantly teacher-led or will the teacher play more of a facilitative role? How are assignments and assessment going to be handled? Answers to these questions also affect both pedagogical and content management issues in online environments.

In the examples above, I have begun to make the assumption that the teacher or course designer is developing their course including the resources and activities within a VLE. Although by no means all online teaching and learning is conducted this way, this isn't an unreasonable assumption as this is by far the most widely used technology to support e-learning today. So let's explore some of the specific characteristics of using a VLE.

4.2 Virtual Learning Environments and the One Ring Model of Online Education

These days just about everybody involved in formal education is familiar with the idea of a Virtual Learning Environment (VLE) or Learning Management System (LMS).[1] There are many different flavours available, and you can either buy them or use the free open-source ones – it is up to you.

The core idea behind a VLE is to provide a single integrated system for authoring web-content, designing and constructing courses, actively conducting teaching and learning activities online and storing both content and course structures. The idea of a one-stop shop to cater for all your eLearning needs has proved to be very attractive to institutions for a number of reasons and most higher education institutions today have at least one such system, whose staff are encouraged to use by teaching and learning support units. One of the obvious advantages from a teacher's perspective is that it provides an easy way to link online digital resources to topics that they are teaching in the context of a designated private course space, which can be accessed by both teacher and students. Typically, a teacher will set up and configure a course space into which they might put reading materials (or links to materials), instructions for why they should be read, discussion activities, quizzes, instructions for assignments and so-on.

This kind of custom hand-built approach to course design and creation within a VLE can work perfectly adequately particularly in cases where the teacher is the sole administrator of the course. But there are various content management pitfalls with this approach, particularly as courses grow larger and/or more than one teacher begins to administrate the course.

As I have already indicated, course information, instructions for activities, hyperlinks and other references to materials can easily become duplicated and

---

[1]The terms can be used entirely interchangeably in my opinion. Although I have seen some definitions that attempt to draw a distinction I think it is just a difference in terminology for essentially the same thing. E-learning platform or system is possibly the most general and neutral term. I will mostly just use VLE in this chapter for brevity and convenience.

sprinkled about across several pages. This can quickly become a real headache when a teacher wants to change an activity or some of the instructions or perhaps a reference to some external materials, and as a result they have to search their entire course and make changes in multiple places to ensure consistency. Courses structured as deeply nested trees (topics within units within modules etc.) can be especially problematic in this respect.

These are the same category of problems faced by designers of hand-built websites and the reason that content management systems have become popular for authoring and managing larger websites. As a response to this issue several of the larger VLE/LMS systems have adopted a similar strategy and either incorporated some CMS functionality into their application or supplement the LMS application with an additional LCMS (Learning Content Management System). This is all well and good but for many educators who find just using a VLE baffling enough, the addition of more enterprise-grade software into the mix is not necessarily helpful.

Another serious problem with the VLE/LMS model is what happens when your institution decides they want to move from one VLE to a different one? How will all the courses be transferred? In many cases where they have been hand-built entirely within the VLE environment there is simply no choice but to recreate everything in the new environment. For a large institution, the costs involved can be astronomical. Recently, a UK university estimated that moving all their courses from one VLE to another would be a 3 year project costing in the region of three million Euros. Of course, if you are in the business of selling VLEs, the answer is simple – encourage everyone to use the same system and the problem is instantly solved. It is not just VLE vendors who are prone to applying this sort of logic, I have heard the same argument from open-source VLE afficionados too. But, to use a well-worn mantra, "one size does not fit all", and no one software environment is capable of the variety necessary to adequately support all teaching and learning contexts. In terms of pedagogy alone, any software environment imposes a certain workflow or "way of doing things" that inevitably channels the user towards particular ways of working and I don't believe that uniformity on that level is either desirable or practical across the full spectrum of a national education system.

The final issue we consider here is that of re-use of content. This is a crucial factor affecting many aspects of both e-learning content management and pedagogy and it is a recurring theme throughout this chapter. For now, I just highlight a couple of points. Let's say you are an educational publisher and you want to create some online learning content which can be embedded within multiple e-learning environments. You don't want to create a different version for each system; that would clearly be unsustainable. Or let's say you are a teacher who has created some content and you want to share it with your colleagues who use different VLEs, or even present it on the web outside of an VLE. To handle these situations, a standard exchange format is required to support content portability

These are all legitimate concerns with the "one ring to hold them all" model of a VLE. One solution to the limitations of the VLE approach is to separate content authoring from design and delivery.

4.3   Learning Objects and the Promise of Re-usability

Re-usability is a seductive notion, not just within eLearning but across most areas of design, development and manufacture for the obvious efficiencies in time and costs that can be gained by not having to custom-build from scratch all the time. Software developers have developed object-oriented methodologies to encapsulate functions and data into objects in the hope of facilitating code re-use. Systems architects have developed Service-Oriented Architectures to promote software component re-use. And within the domain of e-learning, the concept of Learning Objects is intended to promote re-use of digital learning content. The idea behind learning objects is that discrete chunks of digital learning content, activities and perhaps assessment can be encapsulated in a stand-alone package and can then be embedded in multiple course instances either within the same VLE within an institution, or if one of the standard packaging formats such as ADL SCORM or IMS Common Cartridge is used, then the package can be embedded within different VLEs (assuming of course that the VLE can interpret or "un-package" and run the content).

The rationale behind the approach undeniably makes sense. For example, almost every undergraduate social sciences degree course will run a Research Methods module in the first year. This is a module that tends to be pretty much the same whichever social science discipline you are studying and whichever institution you are studying at. Thus, it seems highly advantageous for an institution to be able to collaboratively create, buy or otherwise obtain one version of this module for online use and then re-use it in multiple contexts rather than creating innumerable slightly different versions of the same thing, as happens now.

The concept of learning objects is of course also highly appealing to educational publishers and other commercial content providers who want to be able to market their content to as wide an audience as possible while, keeping the costs of production to a minimum. The emerging IMS Common Cartridge specification for packaging learning objects contains a number of features to explicitly appeal to commercial providers, such as a DRM mechanism and it is no accident that a number of the major educational publishers have been closely involved with the creation of the specification.

Another feature of packaged learning objects is that they can be supplied with extensive metadata using a standard metadata format (e.g. IEEE LOM) and accessed through a digital learning objects repository. There are now many commercial and open-source learning content repositories available to support this model.

But while the learning objects model of course design has significant advantages over the cottage-industry model of hand-building courses in a VLE in terms of economies of scale, distribution and content management, what effect does it have on pedagogical design?

Critics of the learning objects paradigm have argued that the learning objects model tends to lead to a sterile, de-motivating and disconnected learning experience, characterised by passive page-turning content or a content-"n"-quiz model at best. Some go even further, Wilson (2005) proclaims of learning objects "They don't work!." Wilson goes on to support this quite radical statement with arguments both from pedagogical and re-usability perspectives. I return to explore some of his arguments later in the chapter.

Certainly, it is immediately apparent to anyone who has tried to construct a course in a VLE, say Moodle for example, from SCORM-packaged learning objects that the flow of narrative, content and activities within the VLE becomes awkward and interrupted. The student is required to launch an external window to view the SCORM content, so the SCORM content and activities are now separated from the VLE content and activities. Any activities that the teacher wants to create to provide an educational context for the content can no longer be intertwined with the narrative flow of the content. For example, you can no longer link to a discussion forum from within the package, you have to work your design around it. It is true that this is less of problem if you are dealing with multiple small content packages rather than a few large complex ones. Nevertheless, it still creates an uncomfortable limitation for the course designer and a loss of flow in the learning experience for the students.

A further problem is that SCORM packages and Common Cartridges are not easy to create without specialist tools (e.g. RELOAD). Even then, it requires a level of technical knowledge which presents a significant barrier to many teachers. This means that the production of learning objects is skewed towards commercial providers. One of the crucially important factors for successful design with learning objects (and as it turns out for the re-usability of objects) is the capability for teachers to adapt, customise or re-purpose packages. As noted by Wilson (2005), most commercial packages are designed to be used "as-is" under the terms of the licensing agreement and in any case the teacher has no tools to break the packages apart to customise or repurpose them for their own context.

In the next section, I look at examples of recent software developments intended to address some of these issues by enabling teachers to generate their own packaged digital learning resources in a way that also provides support for pedagogical design.

4.4 Tools to Support Authoring of Learning Content and Pedagogical Design

Before looking at any specific software tools let's briefly consider what is involved in creating a pedagogical design. Good practice guides for pedagogical design whether it is for a single lesson, a module or an entire course (let's call it a unit of learning for want of a better general term) typically centre around the following four components:

1. Defining the learning outcomes for the unit.
2. Creating an assessment which will demonstrate the achievement of the learning outcomes.

3. Selecting the content that will be taught including any resources that will be used.
4. Designing activities that will engage the students with the content to best promote effective learning for those particular students in that particular learning context.

While many variations on this theme exist (Laurillard 2002; Sharpe and Oliver 2007), most educators will recognise this general model. It is an approach that is intended to ensure that there is a rational internal consistency within the unit of learning between the desired learning outcomes and what is assessed, that the content provided is relevant to both the outcomes and the assessment and finally that the activities included are appropriate to both the students and the content and, in addition, fit the instructor's teaching philosophy. Clearly, it is this final step that is the most difficult to reconcile with that of creating generalised, reusable learning objects.[2] Consequently, it is the component that is typically omitted. Unfortunately, many learning theorists and educators see it as the crucial component of this scheme in order to create active, meaningful learning experiences. This is perhaps part of the reason many commercial learning objects produced to date ultimately fail to engage learners.

One recent area of attention within learning technology is the development of tools that support both the process of content authoring and pedagogical design. One such project that I was involved with as project manager for two years was the eXe project and it provides some useful insights.

Exe (http://www.exelearning.org) is an open-source educational content authoring tool that was developed in New Zealand to address some of the problems mentioned above. It is an offline, educational XHTML editor, which is designed to be easy to use for teachers who want to create online learning resources and package them for use, either in the context of a VLE, or independently as a stand-alone website. An important innovation within eXe is that it uses a library of pedagogical design templates (known as iDevices) combined with tips on their usage to allow the teacher to easily blend content in a variety of rich media forms with activities as a natural part of their authoring and design process. The sorts of activities available in eXe are things like a reading activity, where the author simply specifies what should be read, why it should be read and some reflection questions as prompted by the iDevice template. The software then configures this information into an XHTML representation according to the chosen style. When the learning resource has been developed, the author can choose from a menu of styles for the display of the content (or create their own) and can use menu options to add metadata and export the content as a SCORM object, an IMS Content Package, an IMS Common Cartridge or as a Zip file for upload to a web-server. The software has been translated into 29 languages and seen uptake in Europe as well as in Australia, South America and New Zealand.

---

[2] For an overview of the "reusability paradox" a term coined by David Wiley which is related to this issue see Wiley (2004) and Wiley (2010).

At a purely practical level, the offline authoring capabilities provided by eXe appeal to many teachers who find authoring in an online environment unnatural or impractical due to bandwidth constraints (still, sadly, a common problem in New Zealand). However, what educators who have used the software typically find most useful is the template-driven model of design embedded within the software. As one learning technologist at a UK university noted, academics like to write books. If you give them a word processor for authoring learning content, then it looks like you are inviting them to write a book. If you give them a tool like eXe, then it sends the clear message that you are inviting them to structure their content around learning activities.

While eXe represents a substantial improvement in supporting pedagogical design for teachers through the use of iDevice templates, it still has many limitations. For example, because eXe is an authoring tool only, there is no way to specify and launch "interactive" activities involving other learning tools such as a discussion forum or a chat session. Currently, the only way to achieve that level of integration is to use an integrated environment for both authoring and delivery (or run-time behaviour). A well-known example of such a tool is the LAMS environment (http://www.lamsinternational.com).

LAMS employs an activity sequencing approach as its design metaphor and allows the building of pedagogical templates as sequences of learning activities. Because LAMS also integrates a run-time environment with the authoring tools, it is capable of creating and instantiating interactive online activities as well as providing the instructions to perform them. One of the interesting features of the LAMS approach to pedagogical design is the idea that you can save created sequences of activities as a template, independent of the content associated with it, effectively creating a design pattern that could be re-used in multiple contexts. This provides an alternative model of re-use to the classic learning objects model previously described.

Two ongoing developments in the standards and specifications world which are relevant to the current discussion are IMS Learning Design and IMS Learning Tools Interoperability. IMS-LTI is a specification designed to support the instantiation of the run-time tools of a VLE from within a learning object (packaged as a Common Cartridge). IMS-LD is intended to support the abstract specification of a learning design (or pedagogical design) and again is being actively developed for incorporation into the Common Cartridge model. While both these specifications are still relatively immature, they offer promise for substantial improvements in the flexibility and sophistication of packaged learning objects.

4.5 Learning Objects and the Curse of Re-usability

So far in this chapter, I have highlighted a number of areas in which content management issues have an impact on the pedagogical design of online learning. Many of those issues are connected in some way with the goal of achieving a level of re-usability of learning resources. In many instances in the fields of software development and enterprise architecture, the goal of re-usability has turned out to be somewhat quixotic, and so too in the field of eLearning. Wiley (2004; 2010) refers to the "paradox of re-usability". Simply put, the more educational context that is associated with a learning resource, the more useful and yet the less re-usable it is. Conversely, resources with less educational context are less pedagogically effective and yet more re-usable. Wiley goes on to point out that while smaller learning objects containing less educational context are more likely to be re-used, the costs of applying metadata to many thousands of small learning objects are likely to outweigh the efficiency gains from investing in re-use (Wiley 2010).

Costs are not the only source of concern relating to learning object metadata. Metadata quality is an on-going problem, especially for teacher-created objects. Search algorithms applied to digital repositories rely on metadata to find relevant materials (packaged materials or non-text objects are not searchable using full-text search methods). Poor quality metadata can make learning objects essentially invisible to search tools. The creation of high-quality metadata is a specialist activity (Barton et al. 2003), yet it is usually left to the author to provide metadata for objects they create. Since many teachers neither appreciate the importance of metadata in the creation of objects intended for re-use nor know how to create quality metadata, learning object repositories can become clogged with lost, unused learning objects.

A further problem for re-use within the learning objects paradigm is that in most instances re-use requires some level of editing, re-contextualisation or re-purposing of existing resources for them to be useful as was indicated above. But the fact that many learning objects cannot be easily adapted either because of licensing restrictions or because they have been created or packaged using tools requiring a high level of technical expertise limits both their pedagogical value and their re-usability.

The concerns raised here lead us to ask whether e-learning has taken a wrong turn somewhere in pursuing the goal of reusability through learning objects, SCORM and IMS packaging standards, LOM metadata and Learning Object repositories.

SCORM was developed by ADL, an organisation with a focus on the education and training needs of clients such as the US Department of Defense and the aviation industry. The educational vision behind SCORM and related architectures is that students will be able to work through sequenced learning content automatically supplied by a learning management engine from a database of learning objects. The sequence may be adapted depending on a profile of the learners current training needs. This world-view does not however necessarily coincide with the educational goals of schools and universities. Similarly, IMS Common Cartridge will find natural support among commercial content developers but the question remains as to whether it will really serve the needs of teachers seeking to develop resources and activities for their students. Unless tools are made freely available which make it easy and intuitive for teachers to both author new materials in Common Cartridge format as well as break-up, edit and re-purpose existing Cartridges, it is unlikely.

The case is put succinctly by Wilson (2005):
"Lecturers like reusing materials

- Provided the materials are good
- Provided the materials appear to be free of charge
- Provided they can change the materials to fit their context
- Provided they are in a usable format

So, if we really wanted to make learning objects useful for lecturers...

- They would be "open source"
- They would be liberally licensed
- They would be *easy to edit* and repurpose without special tools
- You could easily *make and publish your own* objects"

So what options are there for an alternative model to the learning object paradigm that would match Wilson's criteria? In the next section I explore the growing interest in Open Education Resources (OERs) and the increasing variety of technologies to support their creation and distribution

4.6   Open Education Resources and the WikiEducator Model

Following a remarkable decision by MIT to open up its course materials online to the general public through its Open CourseWare Initiative in 2002, other higher education institutions have followed suit, for example, the UK Open University with its OpenLearn initiative and Otago Polytechnic in New Zealand. Support for the Open Education movement is rapidly growing as more institutions make their content freely available with licensing policies to encourage re-use.

While OER initiatives such as these signify a major step forward in making digital learning resources freely available, how easy is it to edit and repurpose these materials or to embed them within your own learning materials? The answer is, well – it depends! Many OERs consist simply of un-structured HTML pages, so you can simply link to them, or manually copy and paste material from them (depending on the nature of the licensing agreement) but there is no easy way to load their contents into a structured authoring environment such as eXe, LAMS or a VLE for re-contextualisation or editing. One of the early complaints about OERS was that they could consist of an unpredictable mix of Word documents, Powerpoints, web-pages and other formats with little or no metadata attached. While it seems slightly unreasonable to complain about getting content for free, the amount of work required to re-contextualise it to make it useful did dampen the enthusiasm of some early adopters. More recently, resources have been substantially cleaned up (OpenLearn, for example, are packaging many of their materials as Common Cartridges) but still without the rigorous application of metadata to many OERs, it can be hard to know whether you are accessing relevant material or not. As with the web in general, the problem is not finding content – there is an overwhelming quantity of content; it is more a question of finding high-quality, relevant content.

A key aspect of the value proposition for OERs is that the costs of re-use (in terms of the time and effort involved in re-purposing a resource) must not exceed the benefits of doing so when compared to simply using existing resources or creating them from scratch. This means that both open licensing policies and open formats for content are essential to the success of OERs.

One approach to both the development and content management of online educational resources is provided by recent advances in Wiki software technologies. Consider the example of Wikipedia based on the MediaWiki engine. Here is a collaborative model of online content development, which rather than leading to the creation of many different content objects on the same topics, leads naturally as a result of the collaborative model to a convergence of effort on creating a single resource multiple contributors offering their expertise. Arguably this model also builds in a quality-assurance model by the nature of its open editing design. The resulting resource can be continually improved so is less likely to become stale or go out of date, gathering cobwebs in a learning object repository. And the resource is open to full-text searching, so is accessible to ordinary search engines on the web without the need for specialist search tools. One initiative that has adapted the Wikipedia approach to the creation of online education resources is WikiEducator (http://www.wikieducator.org). Started at the Commonwealth of Learning, WikiEducator is an open learning content development environment based on the Mediawiki platform. Furthermore, because WikiText is structured then in the same way that Wikipedia uses templates for content development, a Wiki for developing learning resources could employ pedagogical templates for structuring resources around learning activities as well as content along the same lines as eXe. As a demonstration of this Wikieducator has incorporated the facility to use eXe templates for structuring activities. An additional advantage of the structured format of wikitext is that it can readily be imported into a variety of other learning technologies such as offline editors such as eXe or integrated environments like VLEs or LAMS if so desired.

An issue that we have not even touched on is the need to be able to deliver learning resources in different formats depending both on the teaching and learning context and to cater for differences in student needs. An example is where print output is required as well as online materials. The Collection extension to the MediaWiki platform provides a means to render the contents of a Collection in a variety of print formats. It is possible to imagine that iDevices could specify different behaviours for output from the collection for different types of media. Thus, for rich media objects such as audio and video, a collection could be formatted for export as a CD of resources instead of a text document. An exciting implication of this scheme is supporting accessibility requirements. For example, a Collection could be exported formatted for Braille readers.

The collaborative OER development model presents a radical alternative to the classic model of learning object development and storage as described in this chapter and it has the advantage of stripping away much of the administrative complexity associated with that approach such as LOM metadata, content packaging standards, learning object repositories and so on. As a consequence, many of the content management constraints on pedagogical design are removed, while maintaining (or even increasing) the potential for re-usability through the use of open formats and licensing models.

Of course this model of learning object development and management does not work very well for the kind of automated adaptive sequencing model which SCORM 2004 was developed to support. Nor does it include the sort of DRM protection and access control that educational publishers would find in IMS Common Cartridge or Digital Repositories. But for the development of open, flexible, re-usable learning resources by both educators and students, this approach holds great promise.

4.7 Conclusions: A Question of Variety and Interoperability

Through the course of this chapter I have explored the relationship between pedagogical design and content management in the creation and use of online learning resources using three broad models of content development and management commonly employed in eLearning today. First, I described the characteristics of the cottage-industry model of the hand-crafted VLE course in which the course development tools are integrated with the content management system and the delivery environment. Second, I reviewed some of the benefits and issues associated with separating content development, storage and delivery in the creation of re-usable learning objects. Third, I turned my attention to the development of OERs using the example of WikiEducator. The models that I have presented here are of course generalisations (some might say caricatures), solely intended to highlight some key differences between these approaches and does not represent the myriad combinations of these approaches actually in use. The real world of eLearning is much more messy than I have presented it here. Courses developed in VLEs can be made available as OERs, OERs can be packaged as IMS Common Cartridges, LAMs sequences can be embedded in some VLEs. A wide range of possibilities exist within the scope of current technologies and the relentless pace of innovation in web technologies ensures that it is impossible to make hard and fast distinctions that are valid for very long. In particular, current developments in the area of web-services and mash-ups means that it is becoming more common to be able to invoke external services such as run-time environments for interactive content or other learning tools from within VLEs or other applications being used to support online learning. In this chapter, we have discussed the way the mediaWiki platform (a general purpose content editing engine) has been co-opted for the specialist purpose of authoring educational content. There are other applications that could also be adapted for this purpose. The Google Apps suite, for example, includes GoogleDocs a general purpose online word processor that can support real-time collaborative editing. Given Google's increasing interest in providing services to education, it would be easy to imagine that GoogleDocs could be adapted to include pedagogical templates for authoring learning content.

A fair question to ask is what is the best model of content development and content management for the future in eLearning? It is a fair question, but it is possibly not the right question. First, we have to understand, and to a certain extent accept, the variety or complexity that exists within education today. There are educators who like to work solely within the confines of a VLE and there are those who wish to work only in Blogs or Wikis. There are educational content providers who wish to widely distribute their content while protecting their licensing rules and there are organisations who want to make their content freely available to anyone with a web-browser. There are contexts in which the automated generation of personalised training sequences is required for self-directed learning and there are contexts in which content is only used as material to support conversations between teachers and students. This variety in the eLearning landscape can only be adequately supported by a variety of approaches to both content management and pedagogical design. With that in mind, it is important that technology developers, systems integrators, standards developers and institution managers pay attention not just to re-usability but also to interoperability. Teachers want to be able to find, access and re-use content, but they also want to be able to break it apart, edit it, embed it within their own context according to their own pedagogical design and deliver it through the technology medium of their choice. Helping to achieve that goal is a worthwhile challenge for all involved.

References

Alexander, C. et al. (1977). *A pattern language: towns, buildings, construction*. New York: Oxford University Press.

Barton, J., Currier, S., & Hey, J.M.N. (2003) Building Quality Assurance into Metadata Creation: an Analysis based on the Learning Objects and e-Prints Communities of Practice. In Sutton, S. and Greenberg, J. and Tennis, J., Eds. Proceedings 2003 Dublin Core Conference: Supporting Communities of Discourse and Practice – Metadata Research and Applications, Seattle, Washington (USA). http://eprints.erpanet.org/83/

Beetham, H., & Sharpe, R. (2007). *Rethinking pedagogy for the digital age – designing and delivering e-learning*. Abingdon: Routledge.

Britain, S., & Liber, O. (2004). 'A framework for the pedagogical evaluation of eLearning environments'. Retrieved March 10, 2009 from http://www.cetis.ac.uk/members/pedagogy/files/4thMeet_framework/VLEfullReport.

Conole, G. (2007). 'Describing learning activities. Tools and resources to guide practice'. In H. Beetham & R. Sharpe (Eds.), *Rethinking pedagogy for the digital age – designing and delivering e-learning*. Abingdon: Routledge.

Gilbert, J. (2005) *Catching the knowledge wave: the knowledge society and the future of education*. Wellington, NZ: New Zealand Council for Educational Research.

Kolås, L., & Staupe, A. (2004). 'Implementing delivery methods by using pedagogical design patterns'. In L. Cantoni & C. McLoughlin (Eds.), *Proceedings of world conference on educational multimedia, hypermedia and telecommunications* (pp. 5304–5309). Chesapeake, VA: AACE. Retrieved March 10, 2009 from http://www.editlib.org/p/11834.

Lakkala, M. (2007). 'The pedagogical design of technology-enhanced learning'. Retrieved March 10, 2009 from http://www.pedagogy.ir/index.php?view=article&catid=125%3Ateaching-learning-approaches&id=305%3Athe-pedagogical-design-of-technology-enhanced-collaborative-learning&option=com_content&Itemid=162.

Laurillard, D. (2002) *Rethinking university teaching – a conversational framework for the effective use of learning technologies*. London: RoutledgeFalmer.

Sharpe, R., & Oliver, M. (2007). Designing courses for e-learning'. In H. Beetham, & R. Sharpe (Eds.), *Rethinking pedagogy for the digital age – designing and delivering e-learning*. Abingdon: Routledge.

Wiley, D. (2004). 'The reusability paradox'. Retrieved March 10 from http://cnx.org/content/m11898/latest/.

Wiley, D. (2010). 'Learning objects, content management and e-learning'.

Wilson, S. (2005). 'Learning resources – a (personal) educational view from UK HE'. Retrieved March 10, 2009 from www.knownet.com/writing/elearning2.0/entries/scott_wilson_on… resources/scottwilson-eduresources.pdf/…/scottwilson-eduresources.pdf.

Chapter 5
Information-Related Competencies for Teachers and Students in an E-Learning Environment

Núria Ferran and Sirje Virkus

Abstract This chapter explains the concept of "information competence." After defining the concept in the broader context of digital competences, we explain how important is to develop such competence in the context of workplace skills required in a knowledge society, and specially, in an e-learning environment. Being competent in the use of information is a requirement for life-long learning. In that sense, the information competence development has been a controversial aspect since their implications on the learning and teaching process makes difficult to see it as an isolated concept. We try to explain the skills, attitudes and all other aspects linked to the information seeking and use process, and how their acquisition is quite different if we talk about teachers or about students. We try to explain the implications of information competence on the benefit and exploitation of a content management system and finally, we offer some recommendations of the aspects of information competence that must be taken in account in order to design systems that helps teachers and students to be more competent in their use.

5.1 Introduction

Our society, referred to in so many diverse ways as the information society, the knowledge society, the network society or the informational mode of development (Castells 1996), is undergoing a process of rapid change. Information generation, processing and transmission have become the fundamental sources of productivity and power in this society (Castells 1996). There have been several calls for the "need for rethinking the whole learning enterprise" and the need for lifelong and life-wide

N. Ferran (✉)
Department of Information and Communication Sciences, Universitat Oberta de Catalunya, Barcelona, Catalonia, Spain
e-mail: nferranf@uoc.edu

N. Ferran and J. Minguillón (eds.), *Content Management for E-Learning*,
DOI 10.1007/978-1-4419-6959-0_5, © Springer Science+Business Media, LLC 2011

learning of each citizen if "we are to succeed in this changing knowledge-based society" (ACOL 2001, p 18; OECD 2006). In fact, the new European Higher Education Area promotes the design of a learner-centred learning process that focuses on the acquisition and development of competencies rather than content in order to "create" professionals with appropriate skills to manage information in the new society.

This chapter explores the importance of "information-related competencies" (IRC) in our society and its relationship with content management. The chapter is structured into four parts. The first part explores the concept of IRC. The second explains the importance of IRC in education, in the workplace and in everyday life. The third part focuses on the role of IRC in the academic environment in the context of e-learning and life-wide learning; the fourth discusses the IRC of students and staff. Finally, some recommendations on the aspects of IRC will be offered and that should be considered in designing systems and tasks in order to help teachers and students to be more competent in finding and using information for learning purposes.

5.2   The Concept of Information-Related Competencies

In this era of the global economy, countries around the world are recognizing that information and knowledge are central to societal development. The ability to find, evaluate, use and communicate information effectively and efficiently is essential to live in the information society. In library and information science (LIS) literature, these competencies are called "information literacy" (IL). It is believed that IL is absolutely critical literacy for living and working in the twenty-first century (Bruce 2002) and a prerequisite for participative citizenship, social inclusion, the creation of new knowledge, personal and professional productivity and learning for life (Bundy 2003; Correia 2002).

However, there is no single generally accepted definition of IL. Many individuals and institutions have offered their definitions of IL. For example:

> Information Literacy encompasses knowledge of one's information concerns and needs, and the ability to identify, locate, evaluate, organize and effectively create, use and communicate information to address issues or problems at hand; it is a prerequisite for participating effectively in the Information Society, and is part of the basic human right of life-long learning(UNESCO2003)

> Information literacy is the adoption of appropriate information behaviour to obtain, through whatever channel or medium, information well fitted to information needs, together with a critical awareness of the importance of wise and ethical use of information in society (Johnston and Webber 2003, p.336)

> Information literacy is knowing when and why you need information, where to find it, and how to evaluate, use and communicate it in an ethical manner (CILIP 2005)

> Information literacy means the set of skills, attitudes and knowledge necessary to know when information is needed to help solve a problem or make a decision, how to articulate that information need in searchable terms and language, then search efficiently for the information, retrieve it, interpret and understand it, organize it, evaluate its credibility and

authenticity, assess its relevance, communicate it to others if necessary, then utilize it to accomplish bottom-line purposes (Horton 2008, p.53)

However, among the many definitions, perhaps the most widely accepted and cited is that provided by the American Library Association (ALA) Presidential Committee on IL:

> To be information literate, a person must be able to recognise when information is needed and have the ability to locate, evaluate and use effectively the needed information (ALA 1998)

Some authors perceive IL as an "umbrella" concept incorporating many other literacies (Shapiro and Hughes 1996; Breivik 2000; Bawden 2001; Boekhorst 2003) and numerous alternative terms (e.g. "infoliteracy," "informacy," "information empowerment," "information competence," "information competency," "information competencies," "IL skills," "IL and skills," "skills of IL," "IL competence," "IL competencies," "information competence skills," "information handling skills," "information problem solving," "information problem-solving skills," "information fluency," "information mediacy" and "information mastery") have been offered to refer to these competencies as well. There are many overlapping concepts (e.g. study skills, learning skills, learning to learn skills, academic skills, digital literacy, media literacy and e-literacy) and several other concepts closely related to them. IL is viewed as a set of competences (Boekhorst 2003), a way of learning (Kuhlthau 1993; Lupton 2004), a way of knowing (Lloyd 2003) and a habit or a way of life (Hinchliffe 2001; cited in Virkus 2003, 2006).

However, how people perceive and define IL depends on how they perceive and define other related terms: for example, information, literacy, competence, competency, skill, learning and knowing. There are numerous definitions and interpretations about all these terms/concepts and a lack of commonly understandable terminology. But, many authors do not adequately define the exact nature of the concept to which they are referring to in their publications and leave a lot of freedom for interpretations (Virkus 2003).

Nevertheless, according to Anttiroiko et al. (2001), the development of the information society seems to be intrinsically related to competence issues. In several countries in Europe, the terms used for IL also clearly refer to competencies. For example, in Denmark the term informationskompetence, in Finland informaatiokompetenssi (also informaatiolukutaito), in Germany informationskompetenz, in Norway informasjonskompetanse and in Sweden informationskompetens have been used for IL (Virkus 2003).

The concept of competence also has different meanings, and it is not always clear whether competence refers to identifiable skills, or is it related to patterns of behaviour. The New Oxford Dictionary of English defines: "competence (also competency) as the ability to do something successfully or efficiently; the scope of a person's or group's knowledge or ability; a skill or ability." Savolainen (2002) points out that there are several other concepts closely related to them and belonging to the same family of concepts: "ability," "capacity," "expertise" and "know-how" and it can be difficult to find out whether these form a conceptual hierarchy or whether they reside at the same level of generality (Virkus 2003).

Anttiroiko et al. (2001, p. 31) refer to competing research approaches to the phenomena of competence. Rationalistic theories approach competence as a set of relatively stable attributes possessed by actors or the set of requirements characteristic of specific work. On the contrary, the interpretative approaches emphasize the importance of the ways in which actors experience the settings of action and construct meanings concerning action. They conclude that competence has two dimensions – knowledge and skills. Knowledge may be seen as our understanding of how our everyday world is constituted and how it works. Skills involve the ability to pragmatically apply, consciously or even unconsciously, our knowledge in practical settings. In this setting, "skills" can be conceived as the technical aspects of competence, emphasizing the aspect of "how to do" (Virkus 2003).

Several scholars, mainly outside the LIS discipline, however, approach competence as a quite complicated phenomenon and also distinguish between competence and competency (Keen 1992; Cheetham and Chivers 2000; Kirschner et al. 1997; Koper 2000).

Keen (1992), for example, notes that competencies refer to the ability to operate in ill-defined and ever-changing environments, to deal with non-routine and abstract work processes, to handle decisions and responsibilities, to work in groups, to understand dynamic systems and to operate within expanding geographical and time horizons. In other words, competencies are a combination of complex cognitive skills (that encompass problem solving, qualitative reasoning and higher-order skills such as self-regulation and learning-to-learn), highly integrated knowledge structures (e.g. mental models), interpersonal skills and social abilities and attitudes and values. In addition, competencies assume the ability to flexibly coordinate these different aspects of competent behaviour (Kirschner 1999; cited in Virkus 2003).

In a learning environment, according to the researchers of the Dutch Open University, competencies can be construed as the abilities that enable learners to recognize and define new problems in their domain of study and future work as well as to solve these problems. A competency is the ability, within a certain (professional or academic) domain, to make use of already learnt as well as new knowledge and skills across traditional subject areas to adequately solve real-life, poorly defined problems. These competencies are made up of component knowledge, skills and attitudes (Kirschner et al. 1997). Koper (2000) puts it this way:

I consider a competency to be the ability to act consciously and responsibly in a specific context. By 'consciously' I mean a man's ability to freely choose how to act, and to do so with a certain passion and attitude. The choice is dependent on an assessment of the situation and on specific underlying motives such as interests, values or the need to solve a problem. With 'responsibly' I am referring to people's ability to justify their choices and actions, and explain them to others, without putting it down to circumstances beyond their control or automatic behaviour, but rather to their own, carefully considered values and choices. In using these terms, I wish to clarify that I view a competency as the combination of cognitive, conative and affective aspects that collectively determine behaviour in a given situation

Which competencies are involved always depends on the domain and the contexts within that domain. And he concludes that there is, as yet, no conceptual framework that is widely accepted in this area (Koper 2000).

The authors of this chapter prefer to use the term "information-related competencies" instead of IL. The reasons for using this term is the conviction that the concept of IL is very elusive, its essence is hard to grasp and the meaning is not always clear in the higher education (HE) environment. It is believed that the concept of competencies is more familiar and better understood among academic staff, students and senior managers in HE settings (Virkus 2006).

In addition, the concept "information-related competencies" allows to differentiate several blocks of competencies related to information finding, handling and use; for example, identifying, locating, gathering, selecting, storing, recording, retrieving and processing information from a variety of sources and media; developing successful information seeking and retrieval strategies; mastering complex and multiple information systems; organizing, analysing, interpreting, evaluating, synthesizing and using information and presenting and communicating information clearly, logically, concisely and accurately. Thus, it might be easier to perceive how to integrate or embed different competencies or blocks of competencies into the learning process at a different educational level and thereby facilitating the development of these competencies. However, the term IL might be a useful research construct and also as a strategic concept or goal – a political, economic and educational one (Virkus 2003). Information-related competencies in this chapter are defined as the skills, knowledge, attitudes, experience, attributes and behaviour that an individual needs to find, evaluate and use information effectively (Virkus 2006).

5.3 Information-Related Competences in Several Contexts

In spite of the confusion around the concept/phrase "IL is receiving increasing attention worldwide" Webber (2007, p. ii), especially among library and information professionals, Goff (2007, p. 125), notes:

> In the past decade, Information Literacy, sometimes called Information Competence or Information Fluency, has become a well-established educational goal through the United States and Canada. Associations and institutions have defined it, written tutorials to teach it, developed standards, rubrics and tests to assess it and librarians have devoted entire careers to helping their users achieve these competencies

The concept of IL has also permeated strategic thinking in Australia (Muir and Oppenheim 2001) and has been highlighted in several influential reports produced by the HE sector and by the government. Virkus (2003) also notes that there has been considerable interest in IRC in Europe; this can be illustrated by the number of projects, conferences, workshops, working groups, adaptation of IL competency standards, teaching initiatives in many institutions, development of Web sites, journals and Web-based tutorials and in the area of research.

Increasing interest in IRC is caused partly because of information overload, especially related to the growth of digital information, and partly because of the increasing focus on learning in a lifelong learning context.

The exponential growth of information is not a new phenomenon, but the pace has increased rapidly in the last decades. For example, Wurman (1989) notes that, "A weekday edition of the New York Times contains more information than the average person was likely to come across in a lifetime in seventeenth-century England". In 2002, the world produced about 5 exabytes of new data stored in print, film, magnetic and optical storage media which is roughly 800 MB of information for every man, woman and child on the planet. It is equivalent in size to the information contained in half a million new libraries, the size of the Library of Congress print collections. About 90% of information currently produced is created in a digital format (Lyman and Varian 2003).

The large growth of information both in print and electronic form can lead to information overload. Information overload generally refers to the state of having or receiving too much information to make effective use of it. The psychologist David Lewis, who proposed the term "information fatigue syndrome" (IFS), also described the symptoms resulting from information overload, which include the paralysis of analytical capacity, constant searching for more information, increased anxiety and sleeplessness, as well as increasing self-doubt in decision-making. He believed that IFC might soon be recognized as a medical condition (Lewis 1996). With the advent of the Web 2.0 and the thousands of social network sites and blog communities, issues related to information overload have become even more critical. Basex, a business research firm, claims in the report Information Overload: We Have Met the Enemy and He is Us and that a "problem of the year" for 2008 is information overload (Spira and Goldes, 2007).

Information overload has been acknowledged as a serious problem in areas such as psychology and management (Klausegger et al 2007) and in a variety of contexts: in education, in work settings as well as in daily living.

Breivik (1998) believed that no one in HE could escape from information overload, either on campus or at home, and information overload will only increase in the future. The huge volume of information available requires enhanced competencies from students in finding, processing, evaluating, using and sharing information. New learning approaches and greater emphasis on resource-based and problem-based learning also demands a higher degree of IRC (Virkus 2004). IRC is needed during the students' formal study, but is also needed as a preparation for a lifelong learning in a future working life and for functioning as active citizens in society. It is believed that an integration of IRC into learning would also have a positive impact on students' mastering of context, fulfilling research tasks and problem solving, becoming more self-directed and assuming greater control over their own learning (Todd 1995), enabling individuals to engage in a variety of learning situations and opportunities in optimal ways (George and Luke 1995).

IRCs are also essential competencies in workplaces and in gaining a competitive advantage. Information is seen as a strategic resource for organizations; for their existence, achieving their goals, developing new products and services and making decisions. Economic and business success depends more and more on the access to relevant information and the competencies of finding, evaluating and using information. Lloyd (2003) notes that information literate people in a workplace context have the ability to make informed decisions based on the ability to integrate and synthesize operational and cognitive information that is gained through the engagement and interaction with information environments, information systems, resources, information services, colleagues and other individuals. However, according to O'Sullivan (2002), "employees and particularly knowledge workers faced with information overload have difficulty finding what they need quickly and efficiently, and are struggling with issues of quality and credibility with the information they do find."

Several studies have shown the significant extent to which overload is becoming a serious problem in the work settings (Reuters 1996; Waddington 1997; Basex 2007).

Everyday tasks also present information overload. We also need IRC in our daily lives to make many consumer decisions: such as which house, car or computer to purchase – these are also critical and require efficient and effective information finding, evaluation and use. IRCs are also necessary for participating fully in a democratic society as an informed citizen by understanding issues and voting. IRCs allow disadvantaged people and groups such as the disabled, unemployed and elderly people and also several minority groups to locate, use and exchange relevant information according to their needs. Relevant information helps to make decisions, conclusions and communicate efficiently.

However, Candy (1998) found that IRCs needed in the workplace are different from those needed in formal study and that it is the responsibility of both the individual and the organization to maintain and update these competencies. In the professional and community contexts, social sources are the most habitual forms and information is mostly acquired informally while in educational settings textual sources are the more essential ones (Lloyd 2005).

According to some authors, it could be possible to acquire and then transfer some competencies from one sphere to another (Misko's 1998, Anderson et al. 1996, cited in Lloyd 2003). But, the transferability of competencies from one sphere to another is the least studied aspect in terms of the competences developed in the search for and use of information (Lloyd 2006). One qualitative research that was performed with e-learning students of the Open University of Catalonia showed that the transfer of competences from an e-learning environment to the workplace or daily life was mostly dependant on the attitude, that is to say if students who showed a motivated informational behaviour (i.e. participates in the non-evaluated classrooms debates, attend seminars which are not evaluated), they appear to be more IRC expert in the other contexts. The cognitive approach also showed to be related with IRC expertise in that if learners were more focused on the learning process rather than with the academic results, they were more likely to achieve a higher level of IRC in the academic context and then in the workplace and in their daily lives. So, e-learning environments could be the nest for acquisition of ICR and some of these competences can later on be transferred to the workplace or daily life context, if it is required, as e-learning students are people that mostly have, besides their academic duties, professional family and/or community responsibilities (Ferran 2010). That could be a way to overcome the situation described by Virkus of the lack of initiatives related with the development of IRC in the workplace, community and lifelong learning (2003).

5.4   IRC in the Academic Context

Both the Delors Report (1996) and the Bologna Declaration (European Ministers of Education 1999) established that the core of HE institutions should be to develop lifelong learners.

Originally, the concept of lifelong learning was to address the continuous education that adult students were taking and were valuing learning for its own sake and the pursuit of personal fulfilment through it. Some authors use the term life-wide instead of lifelong as "traditional distinctions between formal and informal learning, or between different institutional contexts, become less significant since learning might occur in the workplace, the home, the car, the internet café, as well as the college. We learn not only for the purposes of gaining formal qualifications but also to obtain and keep employment, develop expertise in a leisure activity, deal with changes in relationships, or manage personal finances" (Harrison et al. 2002).

Otherwise, e-learning nowadays provides the possibility to learn at anytime and from anywhere as it provides access to a wealth of resources and new forms of communication and virtual communities (Conole 2004). There is a shift from a linear knowledge space (the classroom, the library) towards a random knowledge space (the Internet, computer-based learning) (Christensen et al. 2008). Then, e-learning is the key for making education and lifelong learning more effective, efficient and pervasive (OLCOS 2007).

However, e-learning can take very different forms but it is the practices that decide what kind of e-learning is employed and whether this makes a real difference in education and lifelong learning that play a vital role. In this sense, the Open e-Learning Content Observatory Services (OLCOS), a project under the European Union's eLearning Program, has carried out some research, in Europe and beyond, to define a roadmap for leveraging educational practices that could help equip teachers, students and workers with the competences to participate successfully in the knowledge society (Ferran et al. 2006). OLCOS saw that for a better alignment of lifelong learning with the requirements of the knowledge society, it is essential to innovate and to implement new educational paradigms. OLCOS perceived a critical lack of education innovation for learner-centred and collaborative learning practices and processes in which it is more likely that competences are built up and proven. Educational changes were foreseen as a critical need to enhance IRC.

To incorporate innovative learning practices in educational institutions, teachers must change their role from dispensers of knowledge to facilitators of individual and collaborative learning and knowledge development. This means a transition from an educational model based on established information channels to a new model where there are infinite and diverse channels (Benito Morales 2000). Other implications of this paradigm shift are discussed in this book in Chap. 2.

Breivik states that IL is an essential enabler for the goal of learning (2000) and she believes that IL is essential for moving from the dominant paradigm of pre-packaging information to a new model of learning that will empower learners, and give them the capacity to engage in self-directed lifelong learning outside the walls of the formal educational process (Breivik 1998; Bruce 2002). "Textbooks, workbooks and lectures must yield to a learning process based on information resources available for learning and problem solving throughout people's life-times" (Breivik 1998). It is not a new information studies curriculum what is needed but restructuring the learning process and include IRC in every needed subject since they can be characterized as being methodological and transversal.

5.5 IRC for Students and Staff

Huge efforts had been made to identify the competences that a student should have and with the design of learning programs to acquire the competences related with information, a clear framework for embedding IRC across HE curricula will be provided together with examples on how to assess learners. Basically, these can be approached through pedagogical models (such as Seven Faces of Bruce, SCONUL Pillars, Big Blue or Big6) and standards (ACRL/ALA, CAUL or ANZIL).

The academic library sector that has led these developments comes from the United States, United Kingdom and Australia-New Zealand. The first initiative to establish standards for IL in HE was the "IL Standards for HE" by the Association of College & Research Libraries (ACRL), a division of the American Library Association (ALA) in 2000. Later on, the Society of Collage, National and University Libraries (SCONUL) published standards related with the Seven Pillars model and their standards by the Council of Australian University Librarians (CAUL). These standards provide the basic characteristics that an information liter-ate student should have.

These features can be grouped, following the IFLA standards, in three basic IL components: access, evaluation and use (Lau 2006). Then, learners basically should be enabled to master content and extend their research work, become more self-directed and assume greater control over their own learning. An information literate individual in HE is able to:

- Determine the extent of information needed.
- Access the needed information effectively and efficiently.
- Evaluate information and its sources critically.
- Incorporate selected information into their own knowledge base.
- Use information effectively to accomplish a specific purpose.
- Understand the economic, legal and social issues surrounding the use of information, and access and use this information ethically and legally" (ALA-ACRL 2004).

SCONUL added two additional standards to these:

- Classify, store, manipulate and redraft the information that is collected or generated.
- Recognize IL as a prerequisite for lifelong learning (SCONUL 2003).

These standards can be used as guidel ines for measuring the acquisition of IRC as they are complemented with a list of performance indicators related with each competence; that is to say, a range of outcomes for assessing student progress in relation with IRC are established.

Nevertheless, the greatest emphasis should be placed on managing information and evaluating it rather than finding information as the results coming from the CIBER's Google Generation study (Rowland et al. 2008) show.

Regarding the role of educational institutions in providing support to the enhancement of IRC, library associations recommend the establishing of partnerships between academics, staff developers, learning advisers, librarians and administrators that can be summarized as:

- "Through course materials, lectures and by leading face to face or online discussions, academics establish the context for learning. They also inspire students to explore the unknown, offer guidance on how best to fulfil information needs, and monitor student progress.
- Librarians coordinate the evaluation and selection of intellectual resources for programs and services; organize and maintain collections and points of access to information and provide advice and coaching to students and academic staff who seek information.
- Teaching advisers how to develop generic and course specific materials to support student learning and provide a range of services related to the transition to university and academic literacy reading, writing, listening and speaking in a university setting, time and task management and learning in an online environment.
- Administrators and staff developers facilitate opportunities for collaboration and staff development among academics, learning advisers, librarians and other professionals who provide students with opportunities to develop their IL according to their developmental level, mode of study and information needs (CAUL 2001).

So that, IL is important beyond the domain of libraries and librarianship but librarians can function as change agents to help to develop and put IL policies, programs and projects in place. "Librarians should play a consultative role to help other departments and units within the enterprise develop their own IL programs" (Lau 2006).

Furthermore, librarians provided a good example on how to promote IRC in the education community and how to deal with the delivery of course materials and information support in the "Information support for eLearning" of SCONUL. Its aims are ensuring that teachers, designers and administrators of eLearning courses are aware of the information support issues that arise in providing eLearning, and the ways in which libraries can help with them. IL is seen as one of the principles in which institutions should apply to enrich the educational experience of eLearners and to ensure that courses are supported by appropriate information resources. IRC should not only ensure that learners "can fully exploit information resources for their eLearning course, but also provides them with a life skill, and with mechanisms for updating their knowledge after the course has ended. It is important that you work with your librarians to embed IL training into the delivery of support for the course" (SCONUL 2003).

Adding to that, the point of view of OLCOS is that the role of teachers becomes more important in the new education paradigm as they are challenged to think out more complex learning opportunities for themselves and students. Teachers would need to stimulate and moderate active, constructive and collaborative learning processes. Then teachers are required to be aware of emerging technologies for information and communication, be capable of identifying the most important new literacies that each requires and be proficient in knowing how to support their development in the classroom (Gesser 2007).

At institutional level, teachers could be stimulated to acquire new competences and therefore play the new needed role through the existing recognition and reward systems of the HE community. For instance, in the case of the promotion of open educational resources, it was foreseen as essential to adopt institutional policies that encourage the opening of educational content and valuing the creation of such materials including in tenure and promotion processes (UNESCO IIEP 2005).

There is a great deal of evidence available regarding the fact that the university is increasing its level of acquisition of information competences of students and teachers. Librarians, teachers and students have clear ideas about their implication and responsibility over the learning process of information competences. Furthermore, teachers and librarians are working in a coordinated and collaborative way to adjust the acquisition of IRC to individuals of different learning rhythms, from different study areas, etc. (Webber and Johnston 2006). This collaboration can generate different proposals for the acquisition of IRC. One can be a transversal subject for all students on IRC, especially for novice students. Another option is the integration with existent subjects with content, activities and assessment that included IRC. And finally tutorials, portals, repositories, etc., for self learning of IRC.

But still the success of IRC acquisition depends on the enthusiasm of librarians to reach a grade of collaboration with teachers with the aim of involving students in the process of searching and using information. Furthermore, the complete success of an IRC program depends on the commitment at the institutional level. Therefore, information professionals must devote time to create the relevant strategies to convince and sell the benefits of IL to institutional leaders to get their support (Lau 2006).

5.6 Final Recommendations

After reviewing several educational initiatives in the final report "OLCOS Roadmap 2012," some recommendations with regard to the required competencies and skills for the knowledge society were established. In this sense, the recommendation for teachers was to understand the great importance of education and lifelong learning in the knowledge society and clarify their professional role, appropriate approaches and required skills to facilitate learning and developing learner's knowledge and competencies. This new professional understanding is far from trivial given that it should include the requirement that teachers regularly question, evaluate and improve educational practices and content. Furthermore, it should also involve the sharing of practical experiences, lessons learned and suggestions on how to better foster the development of student's competencies among a community.

On the other hand, the recommendation for students from the OLCOS observatory was that learners should demand that educational institutions and teachers help them in acquiring the competencies to successfully participate in the knowledge society. They should ask for educational approaches that ensure that learning experiences are real, rich and relevant such as those related to the addressing of real world problems, working collaboratively, using new tools and information services, and critically discussing content and study results.

References

Advisory Committee for Online Learning. (2001). *The e-learning e-volution in colleges and universities: A Pan-Canadian challenge*, from http://www.cmec.ca/postsec/evolution.en.pdf.

ALA (American Library Association). (1998). *A progress report on information literacy: An update on the American Library Association Presidential Committee on Information Literacy: Final Report*. Chicago: American Library Association. Retrieved October 15, 2005 from http://www.ala.org/ala/acrl/acrlpubs/whitepapers/progressreport.htm.

American Library Association. (2004). *Information literacy competency standards For higher education*. Retrieved November 13, 2008 from http://www.ala.org/acrl/.

Anderson, J., Reder, L., & Simon, H. (1996). Situated learning and education. *Educational Researcher*, 5, 5–11.

Anttiroiko, A.-V., Lintilä, L., & Savolainen, R. (2001). Information society competencies of managers: conceptual considerations. In: E. Pantzar, R. Savolainen, & P. Tynjälä (Eds.), *In search for a human-centred information society* (pp. 27–57). Tampere: Tampere University Press.

Bawden, D. (2001). Information and digital literacies: A review of concepts. Journal of Documentation, 57(2), 218–259.

Benito Morales, F. (2000). "Nuevas necesidades, nuevas habilidades. Fundamentos de la alfabetización en información", in Gómez Hernández, J.A. (Coord.), Estrategias y modelos para enseñar a usar la información: guía para docentes, bibliotecarios y archiveros, KR, Murcia, pp. 11–75.

Boekhorst, A. K. (2003). Becoming information literate in the Netherlands. *Library Review*, 52(7), 298–309.

Breivik, P. (1998). *Student learning in the information age*. Arizona: ACE, Oryx Press.

Breivik, P. S. (2000). *'Information literacy and lifelong learning: The magical partnership'* in *lifelong learning conference*, papers for the inaugural International Lifelong Learning Conference Yeppoon Queensland Australia (pp. 1–6), July 17–19, 2000 from http://www.libraryinstruction.com/information-literacy.html.

Bruce, C. S. (2002). *Information literacy as a catalyst for educational change: A background paper*. White paper prepared for UNESCO, the U.S. National Commission on Libraries and Information Science, and the National Forum on Information Literacy, for use at the Information Literacy Meeting of Experts. Prague: The Czech Republic. Retrieved January 10, 2003 from http://www.nclis.gov/libinter/infolitconf&meet/papers/bruce-fullpaper.pdf.

Bundy, A. (2003). *One essential direction: Information literacy, information technology fluency.* Paper presented at eLit 2003: Second international conference on information and IT literacy held at Glasgow Caledonian University June 11–13, 2003 from www.library.unisa.edu.au/papers/papers.htm.

Candy, P. C. (1998). Repairing the plane in flight: Developing information literacy in professional practice. In D. Booker (Ed.), Information literacy: The professional issue, Proceedings of the third national information literacy conference conducted by the University of South Australia Library and the Australian Library and Information Association Information Literacy Taskforce, 8 and 9 December 1997, Adelaide: University of South Australia Library.

Castells, M. (1996). *The information age: Economy, society and culture*, Vol. 1, The rise of the network society. Oxford: Blackwell Publishers.

CAUL (2001). *Information literacy standards* (1st ed.). Canberra, Council of Australian University Librarians.

Cheetham, G. & Chivers, G. (2000). A new look at competent professional practice. Journal of European Industrial Training, 24(7), 374–383.

Christensen, C. M. et al. (2008). *Disrupting class: How disruptive innovation will change the way the world learns.* New York, NY: McGraw-Hill.

CILIP (2005). *Information literacy: Definition.* London: CILIP. Retrieved October 30, 2005 from http://www.cilip.org.uk/professionalguidance/informationliteracy/definition/.

Christensen, C. M., Horn, M. B., & Johnson C. W. (2008). *Disrupting class: How disruptive innovation will change the way the world learns.* New York, NY: McGraw Hill.

Conole, G. (2004). E-Learning: The hype and the reality. A wealth of resources and new forms of communication and virtual communities. *Journal of Interactive Media in Education*, 2004 (12) [www-jime.open.ac.uk/2004/12] Published 28 Sept 2004 ISSN: 1365-893X. (Designing and Developing for the Disciplines Special Issue), No.12.

Correia, A. M. R. (2002). *Information literacy for an active and effective citizenship.* White paper prepared for UNESCO, the U.S. National Commission on Libraries and Information Science, and the National Forum on Information Literacy, for use at the Information Literacy Meeting of Experts. Prague, The Czech Republic. Retrieved January 10, 2003 from http://www.nclis.gov/libinter/infolitconf&meet/papers/correia-fullpaper.pdf.

Delors, J., Al Mufti, I., Amagi, I., Carneiro, R., Chung, F., Geremek, B., Gorham, W., Kornhauser, A., Manley, M., Padrón Quero, M., Savané, M.-A., Singh, K., Stavenhagen, R., Won Suhr, M., & Nanzhao, Z. (1996). Learning: The treasure within. Report to UNESCO of the International Commission on Education for the Twenty-first Century. Paris: UNESCO.

European Ministers of Education (1999). *Bologna declaration. The European higher education area.* Bologna: The National Union of Students in Europe.

Ferran, N., Minguillón, J., & Geser, G. (2006). *The OLCOS roadmap 2012 for the further development of open educational practices and resources*, Book of Abstracts. Online Educa Berlin 2006, 12th International Conference on Technology Supported Learning & Training (pp. 111–113). Nov.-Dec. 29-1, Berlin, Germany.

Ferran, N. (2010). *Towards a personalised virtual library.* Saarbrücken, Germany: VDM Verlag Dr. Müller. ISBN 978-3-639-24575-2.

George, R., & Luke, R. (1995). *The critical place of information literacy in the trend towards flexible delivery in higher education contexts.* Paper delivered at the learning for life conference, Adelaide, 30 November – 1 December, 1995.

Geser, G. (Ed.) (2007). *Open educational practices and resources – OLCOS roadmap 2012.* Open eLearning Content Observatory Services. Accessible at http://www.olcos.org/english/roadmap/.

Goff, L. J. (2007). United States and Canada information literacy state-of-the art report. In *Information literacy: An international atate-of-the art report.* Second draft, May, 2007. Retrieved January 10, 2008 from http://www.infolitglobal.info.

Harrison, R., Reeve, F., Hanson, A., & Clarke, J. (Eds.). (2002). *Supporting lifelong learning: vol. 1: Perspectives on learning.* London: Routledge.

Hinchliffe, H. J. (2001). Information literacy as a way of life. *Research Strategies*, 18(2), 95–96.

Horton Jr., F. W. (Ed.) (2008). *Understanding information literacy: A primer.* Paris: UNESCO. http://unesdoc.unesco.org/images/0015/001570/157020e.pdf.

Johnston, B., & Webber, S. (2003). Information literacy in higher education: A review and case study. *Studies in Higher Education,* 28(3), 335–352.

Keen, K. (1992). Competence: What is it and how can it be developed? In J. Lowyck (Ed.), Instructional design: Implementation issues (pp. 111–122). Brussels: IBM International Education Center.

Kirchner, P. A. (1999). *Using integrated electronic environments for collaborative teaching/ learning.* Keynote speech presented at the 8th annual conference of the European association for research on learning and instruction (EARLI 99), Gothenburg, Sweden, August 26, 1999. Retrieved January 16, 2002 from http://www.ou.nl/otecresearch/publications/wetpub/ EARLI%20keynote%20in%20artikelvorm3.PDF.

Kirschner, P., Vilsteren, P., van Hummel, H., & Wigman, M. (1997). A study environment for acquiring academic and professional competence. *Studies of Higher Education,* 22(2), 151–171.

Klausegger, C., Sinkovics, R. R., & Zou, H. (2007). Information overload: A cross-national investigation of influence factors and effects. *Marketing Intelligence & Planning,* 25(7), 691–718.

Koper, R. (2000). *From change to renewal: Educational technology foundations of electronic learning environments.* Heerlen: Open University of the Netherlands, Educational Technology Expertise Center.

Kuhlthau, C. (1993). *Seeking meaning. A process approach to library and information services.* Norwood, NJ: Ablex.

Lau, J. (2006). *Guidelines on information literacy for lifelong learning: Final draft (60p). Veracruz.* México: Universidad Veracruzana. http://www.ifla.org/VII/s42/pub/IL-Guidelines2006.pdf.

Lewis, D. (1996). *Dying for Information?* London: Reuters Business Information.

Lloyd, A. (2003). Information Literacy: The meta-competency of the knowledge conomy? An exploratory paper. *Journal of Librarianship and Information Science,* 35(2), 87–92.

Lloyd, A. (2005). Information literacy: Different context, different concepts, different truths? *Journal of Librarianship and Information Science,* 37(2), 82–88.

Lloyd, A. (2006). Information literacy landscapes: An emerging picture. *Journal of Documentation,* 62(5), 570–583.

Lupton, M. (2004). The learning connection. Adelaide: AusLib Press.

Lyman, P., & Varian, H. R. (2003). *How much information.* Retrieved April 9, 2008 from http:// www2.sims.berkeley.edu/research/projects/how-much-info-2003/.

Misko, J. (1998). Do skills transfer? An empirical study. In VET research influencing policy and practice: Proceedings of the first national conference of the Australian Vocational Education and training Research Association (pp. 289–300). Sydney.

Muir, A., & Oppenheim, C. (2001). *Report on developments world-wide on national information policy.* Prepared for resource and the library association by Adrienne Muir and Charles Oppenheim with the assistance of Naomi Hammond and Jane Platts, Department of Information Science, Loughborough University. London: Library Association Retrieved February 10, 2006 from http://www.la-hq.org.uk/directory/prof_issues/nip/.

Rowlands, I. et al. (2008). The Google generation: The information behaviour of the researcher of the future. *Aslib Proceedings: New Information Perspectives,* 60(4), 290–310.

OECD. (2006). *Think scenarios, rethink education.* Paris: OECD.

O'Sullivan, C. (2002). Is information literacy relevant in the real world? *Reference Services,* 30(1), 7–14.

Reuters. (1996). *Dying for information.* London: Reuters Business Information.

Savolainen, R. (2002). Network competence and information seeking on the Internet. *Journal of Documentation,* 58(2), 211–226.

SCONUL. (2003). *Information support for eLearning: Principals and practices.* http://www. sconul.ac.uk/publications/pubs/info_support_elearning.pdf.

Shapiro, J. J., & Hughes, S. K. (1996). Information literacy as a liberal art: Enlightenment proposals for a new curriculum. *EDUCOM Review,* 31(2), March/April. Retrieved July 11, 2003 from http://www.educause.edu/.

Spira, J., Goldes, D. 2007. *Information overload: We have met the enemy and he is us*. Basex.

Todd, R. (1995). In D. Booker (Ed.), Information literacy: A sense making approach to learning. In the learning link: Information literacy in practice. Adelaide: Auslib Press, 1995, PP. 17–26. ISBN: 1 875145 38 9.

UNESCO. (2003). *The prague declaration: Towards an information literate society*. Accessible at: http://portal.unesco.org/ci/en/files/19636/11228863531PragueDeclaration.pdf/Prague Declaration.pdf.

UNESCO – International Institute of Educational Planning/Albright, Paulv. (2005). *Internet discussion forum: Open educational resources – Open content for higher education (24 October – 2 December 2005)*. Final forum report, http://www.unesco.org/iiep/virtualuniversity/media/forum/oer_forum_final_report.pdf.

Virkus, S. (2006). Development of information-related competencies in European ODL institutions: senior managers' view. *New Library World*, 107(11/12), 467–481.

Virkus, S. (2004). Information literacy and learning. In P. Brophy, S. Fisher, & J. Craven (Eds.), *Libraries without walls 5: The distributed delivery of library and information services* (pp. 97–109). Proceedings of an international conference held on September 19–2, 2003, organized by the Centre for Research in Library and Information Management (CERLIM), Manchester Metropolitan University. London: Facet Publishing.

Virkus, S. (2003). Information literacy in Europe, a literature review. *Information Research*, 8(4). Available online from http://informationr.net/ir/8-4/paper159.html.

Webber, S., & Johnston, B. (2006). Working towards the Information Literate University. In G. Walton & A. Poe (Eds.), *Information literacy: Recognising the need* (pp. 47–58). Oxford: Chandos.

Webber, S. (2007). Editorial. *Journal of Information Literacy, 1*(1), Retrieved April 30, 2007 from http://www.informationliteracy.co.uk/upload/jil/vol1issue1_editorial.pdf.

Waddington, P. (1997). *Dying for information? A report on the effects of information overload in the UK and worldwide*. London: British Library and Innovation Centre (British Library Research and Innovation Report 78).

Wurman, R. S. (1989). *Information anxiety*. New York. Doubleday.

Chapter 6
Copyright Issues in E-Learning

Raquel Xalabarder

Abstract Among the several legal issues involved in the production and exploitation of e-learning contents, copyright and intellectual property deserve special attention, not only because of its strategic and economic importance in any e-learning project, but mainly because of the intricacies that may derive from the different domestic laws involved as a result from the ubiquitous nature of the Internet. For a successful and peaceful production and exploitation of e-content, one needs to take into account the copyright laws, any pitfalls they may generate and adopt the best contractual practices to avoid them. This chapter will identify these issues and examine the existing legal framework from an international perspective.

Legal issues involved in any e-learning project may be of different kinds. Just to mention a few, one can easily think of *image rights* (i.e., the recording of a professor giving a lecture is later posted on an e-learning platform), *users' privacy concerns* (personal data protection involved in the registration of students, tracking of their use, etc.), *competition law* (anti-trust law applied to technological issues such as platforms, interoperability, etc.), *access to government information* (conditions to access data, statistics, etc.; for instance, the European Directive 2003/98/EC[1] allows governments to set authorization and access conditions to the information generated by them) and, last but not least, *ISP liability* (to what extent may an e-learning platform or institution be exempt from liability of any infringements – of any nature, such as libel, defamation, etc. – committed by their users?): on the one hand, e-learning platforms and institutions may somehow "contribute" to any infringement occurring on the Internet and, under general liability rules, be held liable for the infringements committed by their users, and on the other, they may also qualify

---

[1] See Directive 2003/98/EC of the European Parliament and of the Council of November 17, 2003, on the re-use of public sector information.

R. Xalabarder (✉)
School of Law and Political Science, Universitat Oberta de Catalunya, Barcelona,
Catalonia, Spain
e-mail: rxalabarder@uoc.edu

N. Ferran and J. Minguillón (eds.), *Content Management for E-Learning*,
DOI 10.1007/978-1-4419-6959-0_6, © Springer Science+Business Media, LLC 2011

as "Internet Service Providers" (ISP) and be exempt from such liability under the "*safe-harbors*" requirements provided in national laws.[2]

Copyright is just one more, but it is proving to be the most troublesome so far. In terms of copyright, *e-learning* must face at least *two major obstacles:*

- *Ownership of works created by professors/teachers* (lessons, course-packs, exercises, comments, debates, etc.). e-learning puts pressure on an issue that has been traditionally neglected by universities: copyright policy. Leaving patents aside, universities have not shown much interest in claiming any copyright in the materials created by their faculties for teaching and research purposes. Now, digital media offers new opportunities of a higher potential economic gain and a larger exploitation market (also for minority language universities). Such opportunities require a higher investment (than traditional "publishing") and universities are starting to reconsider their copyright policies.
- *Use of pre-existing works as part of e-learning instruction.* Since teachers cannot produce all the digital content they use in their courses, online teaching – as in all types of teaching – requires the use of pre-existing material. In order to secure the lawful use of pre-existing works for teaching purposes, two options are available: rely on *a statutory exception to copyright*, or *obtain a license* from the copyright owner. Neither one – as they stand now – are completely satisfactory to address the needs of online teaching.

On the one hand, *copyright exceptions* traditionally provided for educational and teaching purposes in domestic laws are ill-suited to cover teaching uses conducted through the Internet; on the other, the *differences among domestic laws*, combined with the territoriality of existing copyright choice of law and jurisdiction rules – basically designed for a physical world – threaten to become a *de facto* impediment for the development of e-learning within a lawful copyright framework.[3]

As a result of the slow (and counteractive) development of laws to successfully address these issues, e-learning has turned to a more flexible tool: licensing, and mostly, *open licensing*. Nevertheless, some practical problems may derive from the

---

[2]For instance, both the Digital Millennium Copyright Act of 1998 (US) and the Directive 2000/31/CE on e-commerce (EU) list safe harbors for the provision of services of mere conduit, caching and hosting and (at least, the DMCA) of search engines and links. Among the requirements specified for the application of the safe-harbors, the lack of "actual knowledge" or "awareness" about the infringement is paramount. It means that the ISP is not obliged to monitor (control) its users' web pages and actions (i.e., infringements) but that as soon as the ISP knows about the infringement, it must act expeditiously to remove or to disable access to the illegal information or activity in order to benefit from the exemption. Failure to meet these requirements does not directly assign liability upon the ISP for the infringement committed by its client/user, but will make it ineligible to benefit from the exemption. Safe harbors are only a "filter"; liability will be ultimately established according to the general rules on liability of domestic laws.

[3]In fact, failing a harmonized and secure playground for exempted teaching uses, an online university has two options: either face a myriad of possible infringements in different countries (under different applicable laws) or start a "mission impossible" search for worldwide licenses.

use (and correct understanding) of open licensing systems. As we will see, the multiple versions and language of the existing licenses as well as the difficulties for their interoperability may end up further complicating the development of e-learning projects. It may not be easy to live in a copyrighted world, but a variety of open-licensing systems may complicate it even more.

This article endeavors to examine these issues. But before doing so, it is necessary to briefly examine the foundations of the copyright regime and its special implications for e-learning.

6.1 What is Copyright?

Intellectual Property is a very broad concept that comprises different regimes of exclusive rights, such as patents, trademarks, and copyright. These systems have two issues in common:

- The rights granted confer *exclusivity* (the power to authorize and, let's not forget it, to prohibit)
- The pursuing of *a common goal to promote creativity and innovation* (ultimately, to provide some benefit for society)

As for the rest, they are very different in their scope and terms of protection:

- *Patents* are difficult to obtain (novelty, non-obviousness, and industrial application is required) but they grant strong exclusive rights, for a very short time (usually 20 years).
- *Trademarks* are easier to obtain, and grant exclusive rights limited to a specific product or service within a market, for a short period of time (i.e., of 10 years) which can be renewed *ad perpetuam.*
- *Copyright*[4] is the easiest to obtain (protection is automatically granted as long as it is an original creation), but the exclusive rights granted are not very strong (they are expressly limited in specific cases (that we call *limitations* or *exceptions*) for purposes such as free speech, access to information, education, private use, etc.) and are granted for a limited non-renewable time (i.e., of 70 years *post mortem auctoris*).

As we mentioned before, all these IP systems have a common goal: to promote further investment in creativity and invention. Article I, Section 8 of the US Constitution offers a good example:

Congress shall have Power… *to promote the Progress of Science and useful Arts*, by securing for limited Times to Authors and Inventors the *exclusive Right* to their respective Writings and Discoveries

---

[4]In this chapter, we will use the term copyright to refer, in general, to the rights granted to authors as well as to the "other" related rights granted – in some jurisdictions – to artists and producers.

Of course, it is not easy to explain that the "public interest" (the common good) is fostered by means of an exclusive right, a "private property." Yet, it would be too simple (and wrong) to oppose private property to common good.

Property (of any kind) calls for boundaries. And so does intellectual property. Copyright is inherently limited by the concept of work, by the definition (scope) of the exclusive rights and their limitations and by the term of protection. Let us see them all.

6.1.1   The Concept of "Work"

Copyright is limited by the very definition of work: not everything is protected. What is protected by copyright is only the *original expression/creation* that results from an intellectual effort: the writing, the painting, the sculpture, the movie. No more, no less. Neither the *ideas, nor the information, or the facts* that lay behind a work will be protected by copyright.

It is never easy to *distinguish between protected expression and non-protected ideas (or information).* In fact, recent copyright developments tend to dilute such a distinction: for instance, in the EU, the maker of a database is granted *a sui generis* right (so as not to call it a "copyright") to authorize and prohibit the substantial extraction and re-use of its contents (facts). Nevertheless, the idea/expression dichotomy is paramount to understand the subject-matter of copyright.

Copyright protection is automatically granted.[5] No need to comply with any formality (i.e., publication with © notice) or registration: a work is protected from the very moment of its creation. This *prohibition of formalities* is one of the fundamental principles of the Berne Convention of 1886,[6] and precisely one of the reasons why the USA (among other countries) refused to sign it until very recently.

6.1.2   Exclusive Rights

Copyright consists of a bundle of *exclusive rights* granted to authors, so that they can (directly or through licensees) exploit their works and obtain some economic income in return. These rights are usually the following:[7]

---

[5]Some important exceptions to this rule may be found in the USA, which required registration and first publication with © notice until 1989 (despite being one of the founding members, the USA only signed the BC in 1989, that is, more than a hundred years later), and in Spain where registration was required for protection until 1987.

[6]See Berne Convention for the Protection of Literary and Artistic Works, of September 9, 1886, as revised at Paris on July 24, 1971 and amended in 1979 [hereinafter, Berne Convention or BC]: http://www.wipo.int/treaties/es/.

[7]It should be pointed out that the specific nomenclature and qualification of the exclusive rights granted by copyright may vary according to each domestic law or international instruments. For instance, some jurisdictions prefer to refer to *distribution* also in digital online contexts (i.e., the USA).

- Reproduction (make copies of the work)
- Distribution (put "tangible" copies of the work in the market)
- Communication to the public – which includes making it available over the Internet[8] (make the work available to the public without distributing "tangible" copies)
- Transformation or adaptation (modify the work: translate, adapt, make a new "derivative" work, etc.)

In addition, some laws grant *"moral" rights* aimed at protecting the author's "personality-related" interests in the work (rather than his or her economic interests in it). These moral rights generally include attribution, integrity, first divulgation, access to the only copy of the work, and withdrawal from the market. Despite moral rights are typical from *"droit d'auteur"* systems, they are not completely unknown in *"copyright"* systems.[9][10]

6.1.3 Limitations: Terms of Protection and Exceptions

As already outlined, copyright is also *limited in time*. At an international level, the minimum term of protection that countries are obliged to afford to foreign authors under the Berne Convention is 50 years *post mortem auctoris*.[11] In order to avoid cutting foreign authors a better deal than to national ones (since the BC does not apply to protect "national" authors and works, *ex* art.5(3) BC), all national laws have introduced, at least, the term of 50 years *post mortem auctoris*, and many of them provide for longer terms. This is the case in Europe, where the harmonized term of protection (in all EU countries) is 70 years *post mortem auctoris*[12] (in the case of a joint work – created by two or more authors, the term lasts for 70 years after the last surviving author's death).

---

[8]However, we usually refer to "distribution" (following the US approach) to refer to online delivery of works since, at the end, a tangible copy is made (i.e., a print out).

[9]The distinction between "copyright" and "droit d'auteur" systems was used to explain why the IP protection granted in Anglo-Saxon (common law) systems focused mainly in the exploitation rights (disregarding any "moral" right of the author), for shorter a shorter term of protection, and maintained formalities as a condition of protection; while in European continental systems, the protection was more "favorable" to the author's personal (non-economic) interests, offered longer terms and did not require any formalities in order to grant protection. Such a distinction has been losing significance in recent times, so we will refer to "copyright" in general.

[10]For instance, the USCA sec.106A which grants attribution and integrity rights to the authors of works of visual art. In addition, in common law systems, these "personal" interests tend to be protected beyond the copyright statute, by means of publicity and privacy rights, consumer protection, contracts, defamation, etc.

[11]According to art.7 BC, a country member of the Berne Union must protect, within its territory, the works of foreign authors (from other member countries) for a minimum term of 50 years PMA. In addition, a complex system of comparison of terms (between the term of protection according to the law of the country of protection and that of the country of origin of the work) is envisioned in its art.7.8 BC.

[12]The harmonized term of protection was set by Directive 93/98/EC of October 29, 1993, later consolidated by Directive 2006/116/EC of December 12, 2006.

Once the term of protection has expired, the work enters *the public domain*. Since creation does not happen in a vacuum, the public domain is paramount for the cultural and artistic evolution of a society. In fact, one might defend that the public domain is the "natural" context for work, while copyright is but a temporary exception to the public domain: a monopoly that is tolerated because (and only to the extent that) it is useful and beneficial for the community: by promoting further creation and investment in creation.

In any case, the *public domain* should be distinguished from the concept of the *commons*. As can be seen, by granting an "open license" the author is not placing his work in the public domain[13]: the work will remain protected until its formal entering into the public domain (that is 70 years after the author's death).

In addition to time, copyright is also limited by specific purposes, called *limitations or "exceptions."*[14] National laws, as well as international instruments, expressly establish some specific cases (circumstances) where authors are not allowed to exercise their "exclusive rights" to either prohibit or authorize the use of their work. Such limitations tend to be narrowly defined (and interpreted) and respond to specific interests (usually other "fundamental" rights granted in national Constitutions) that are deemed worthy of protection, such as freedom of expression (i.e., parody, quotations), access to information (i.e., news reporting and public speeches) or access to culture (i.e., teaching purposes and research, libraries, archives, and museums, etc). In these specific cases, provided some specific requirements are met, the use of the work need not be authorized and thus cannot be prohibited by the author.

Of course, education never fails to be mentioned as a limitation/exception to copyright in all international instruments, as well as in national laws, as a fundamental right to be balanced against the authors' exclusive rights. Nevertheless, domestic laws fail to grant a uniform and complete treatment of education as a copyright limitation. As will be observed, the extent and conditions of the exceptions provided for educational purposes vary, sometimes widely, among domestic laws. The lack of statutory consensus is far more acute when digital formats and online teaching are considered, since most national exceptions envisioned for educational and teaching purposes are not meant to cover online (or digital) use. As already mentioned, this un-harmonized ground may become an important obstacle for the development of e-learning projects in a lawful context.

---

[13]Not all jurisdictions allow for the author to dispose of his copyright; where copyright is public mandatory law, works enter the public domain only by virtue of the law (by expiration of the term of protection).

[14]Usually, a distinction is made between "limitation" to refer to non-voluntary (compulsory) licenses which are remunerated, and "exception" to refer to free uses. We will not make such a distinction here, and will use the term exception or limitation without distinguishing between free or remunerated uses.

6.2   Who Owns the Copyright in Original Work Used in E-Learning?

In addition to lacking clear IP policy rules, universities have traditionally relinquished to their faculties any claim to copyright in the teaching and research materials they produce. Partly, because it serves as an economic incentive (especially in countries where professors are not highly remunerated); partly, because the economic value of this work (patents aside) is not too high; and finally, because most universities are not in the publishing business. Now, e-learning offers new opportunities to enlarge the market for academic works; but, at the same time, such opportunities require a higher investment: e-learning projects and platforms are not cheap to produce and maintain.

National laws are not of much help allocate copyright ownership in teaching academic work and, as usual, they vary widely. The basic rule, accepted as a principle in all laws, is that authorship and initial copyright ownership vest with the *original creator*. Beyond the general principles, differences arise. Most national laws provide for some specific rules to determine the allocation of, at least, copyright ownership of *work created under employment*, but solutions do not always coincide.

* Some countries have *work made for hire provisions* (or similar ones) which convey all copyright in the work created by the professor to the university (or employer).

For instance, according to sec.201 (b) USCA,

> In the case of a work made for hire, the employer …is considered the author …and, unless the parties have expressly agreed otherwise in a written instrument signed by them, owns all of the rights comprised in the copyright.[15]

And according to sec.101, a "work made for hire" is

1. A work prepared by an employee within the scope of his or her employment or
2. A work specially ordered or commissioned for use as a contribution to a collective work, as a part of a motion picture or other audiovisual work, as a translation, as a supplementary work, as a compilation, as an instructional text, as a test, as answer material for a test, or as an atlas, *if the parties expressly agree in a written instrument* signed by them that the work shall be considered a work made for hire.

This means that *if the author is an employee* and assuming that the writing and posting of e-learning material is part of the scope of his/her employment, all copyright in it will belong to the university or institution. Instead, *if no employer–employee*

---

[15] A similar imperative "work made for hire" provision may be found in sec.11 of the UK Copyright Act: "where a literary, dramatic, musical or artistic work is made by an employee in the course of his employment, his employer is the first owner of any copyright in the work subject to any agreement to the contrary."

relationship exists, the Institution can only claim copyright in the e-learning project if the work was commissioned (as an instructional text) and agreed – in a written instrument – that it was "made for hire." Failing that, the copyright belongs to the Author. As we will see, it is paramount to take these provisions into account in order to identify who is allowed to grant any license on the teaching or research material created by a professor.

- In a European context, the assignment of copyright to the university or institution operates through softer rules which tend to distinguish between works created under employment and works created under commission.

- Most national copyright laws tend to "presume" that copyright in *a work done by an employee* within the scope of his/her employment belongs to the employer, unless the parties have agreed otherwise. This "presumption of transfer" in favor of the employer is similar to the work made for hire provision but is subject to the parties' agreement to the contrary.

For instance, art.51 Spanish Copyright Act reads:

> In the absence of a written agreement, it shall be presumed that the exploitation rights have been granted in exclusive to the employer, with the scope necessary for carrying on the activity that was usual at the time the work made by virtue of the said employment relation was delivered.

The interpretation of this kind of provisions is not an easy task. On the one hand, we need to decide what "the usual activity" of the University is (is it only teaching? also research? the writing and publication of treatises? all of them?) and whether it applies to all kind of academic work produced by their faculties and staff (teaching materials, academic writings, syllabus, treatises, etc.?). On the other, there is also room for doubt about whether the presumption also applies to non-employment relationships: whether it also covers "public" universities and institutions, where faculty and most teaching staff are not employed but "civil servants." Legal doctrine agrees that this presumption also applies to work created by civil servants (be it professors, teachers, etc.) because they are created according to the same patterns that exist in an employment relationship: non-spontaneous creation (the work has been directly or indirectly requested by the employer), subordination (the employer has set the rules and patterns for it to be done), and alienation of the result (the employer is the one exploiting the result of the labor).

In other countries, lacking a specific statutory provision, the courts have interpreted the existence of an "implicit" assignment of copyright in favor of the University (i.e., as the French courts have interpreted *ex* art.L111.1 French Copyright Act).

And a few national laws adopt a presumption of authorship (not merely of ownership): the employer is deemed to be the author (and copyright owner) of the work created under employment (i.e., see art.7 Dutch Copyright Act).

This is so as far as academic work created under employment (or under similar circumstances) is concerned.

– When the work was created under a specific *commission*, European laws are reluctant to provide for a transfer (or a presumption of transfer) of copyright in favor of the commissioning party. In general terms, unless the parties have agreed to a license, the author (commissioned party) retains all copyright in the commissioned work.

The same applies when the *work is a result of external funding*. Therefore, in order to avoid any doubts and problems down the road, the allocation of copyright should be clearly decided in the funding Agreement by the Government Agency or Private Institution granting the funds.

In short, the authorship and copyright ownership in e-learning materials will depend on the national copyright law, on the kind of institution that develops the e-learning project and on the specific terms of the contract (or relationship) between the teacher/professor who creates the material and the Institution. The allocation of ownership being a matter of contracts and bargaining power of the parties, the *need for good contracts and clear IP policies becomes paramount*.

6.3 Exceptions for Teaching Purposes

As we have seen, when using pre-existing academic work for e-learning purposes, one may either benefit from the coverage of a statutory limitation/exception or seek a license from the copyright owner. Let's examine the first option.

Domestic laws (as well as supranational and international agreements) provide for different exceptions applicable for teaching-related use. Depending on the specific language and scope, these exceptions may or may not cover e-learning use.

Use involved in e-learning projects may include anything from the simple reproduction of a work (to prepare for the lesson or to use it in the course of the instruction as compulsory reading or as part of debates, exercises or exams, etc.), its translation or adaptation (transformation) into a new derivative work, or its further dissemination (communication to the public) to students, regardless of how this is done (i.e., linked to the course syllabus, sent via e-mail, posted on message-boards or on the "classroom e-reserve" website). Thus, except for the right of distribution (which, as we saw, is usually limited to "tangible" copies), all exploitation rights may be involved in e-learning activities.

Works used in e-learning projects may be of all kinds: chapters of treatises and books, scholarly articles, poems, images, lyrics, musical works/recordings, etc., and even the recording of a live lecture. Instead, materials that are not part of the teaching or instruction, itself (for instance, personal web-pages or blogs and private e-mails, etc., posted on the university website) should not be considered as e-learning use, despite being done in an e-learning context.

Most domestic copyright laws provide for exceptions to allow the use of copyrighted work *for the purpose of teaching*. Although most of them fail to expressly mention e-learning, some are broad enough to cover distance learning activities and even digital ones. We will focus on these exceptions. Furthermore, *quotation exceptions*, which traditionally exempt the reproduction or use of a work (or at least, a part of it) for criticism and scientific research, will play an important role in allowing some e-learning use (a role that will be especially significant in those countries where no specific exception is provided for teaching purposes or where the existing teaching exception is not applicable to the digital world). On the other hand, private use/*private copying exceptions*, which allow to reproduce a work for the private use of the copier (for instance, for research and study) may "supplement" the teaching exceptions, for example, where the teaching exception does not cover the reproduction or use made by students in the course of the instruction; In many countries, private copying is subject to equitable remuneration of the author, operated by means of collecting societies. Finally, some domestic laws contain very detailed provisions regarding the free reproduction and further use of academic work by *libraries*, archives, and museums. Although assessing the impact of these exceptions with regard to e-learning activities[16] is far beyond the scope of this study, it is important to keep in mind the interaction between the several exceptions. Last but not least, in some countries (i.e., sec.107 USCA), the *fair use doctrine* offers a flexible and technology-neutral exception to copyright that may easily apply to e-learning, although its scope in that field remains to be fully seen according to the specific circumstances in each case.

Having said this, let us now focus on the specific limitations provided for teaching purposes in national copyright laws as well as in international instruments.

Educational purposes were already present in the first version of the Berne Convention of 1886 and have remained there (although under revised language) ever since.[17] Also the WIPO Copyright Treaty of 1996[18] expressly referred to education in its Preamble, when "recognizing the need to maintain a balance between the rights of authors and the larger public interest, particularly *education, research and access to information.*" More recently, the EU Directive on Copyright in the Information Society[19] stressed its goal "to promote learning and culture by protecting works and other subject-matter while permitting exceptions or limitations in the public interest *for the purpose of education and teaching*" (Recital 14).

---

[16]That is, whether users can get digital copies covered by library exceptions, whether digital copies may be made for preservation purposes and to e-reserve collections to improve the services they render, whether digital copies may be provided through interlibrary loan, etc. On this subject, see Laura Gasaway, *Values Conflict in the Digital Environment: Librarians Versus Copyright Holders*, 24 COLUM.-VLA J.L. & ARTS 115 (2000).

[17]The same may be found in the Universal Copyright Convention signed in Geneva in 1961: "*Teaching, scholarship or research*" purposes are envisioned as a limitation to the translation licensing scheme provided for in Art.V*ter*.

[18]See WIPO Copyright Treaty of December 20, 1996 [hereinafter, WCT]. A parallel clause can be found in the Preamble of the WIPO Performances and Phonograms Treaty of December 20, 1996 [hereinafter, WPPT].

[19]See Directive 2001/29/EC of the European Parliament and of the Council of May 22, 2001, on the harmonization of certain aspects of copyright and related rights in the information society, 2001 O.J. L-167/10 (22.06.2001) [hereinafter, EUCD].

Furthermore, the 1948 UN Universal Declaration of Human Rights[20] acknowledges as a *fundamental right* not only the author's right,[21] but also education[22] and access culture.[23]

6.3.1 The Berne Convention and the EUCD

The Berne Convention has hosted an *exception for educational purposes* since its birth. The Berne Act of 1886 reserved "the liberty of extracting portions from literary or artistic works for use in publications destined *for educational or scientific purposes*" to national legislation. The Brussels Act of 1948 changed the matter reserved to national law under Art.10(2) as "the right to include excerpts from literary or artistic works *in educational or scientific publications.*" At the 1967 Stockholm Revision, the proposal of a minor amendment that only affected the English text (to replace "excerpts" with "borrowings") resulted in a major amendment as current *Art.10(2)*:

> It shall be a matter for legislation in the countries of the Union, and for special agreements existing or to be concluded between them, to permit the *utilization, to the extent justified by the purpose, of literary or artistic works by way of illustration* in publications, broadcasts or sound or visual recordings *for teaching, provided such utilization is compatible with fair practice*

There is no doubt that the BC language is aimed at covering any new means of exploitation that may be used to convey distance education, hence, digital means and the Internet. However, it is worth pointing out that by substituting "education" for "illustration for teaching"[24] the scope of this exception may have been severely reduced. The interpretation of "illustration for teaching" is ultimately a matter for national laws and courts, so one can only hope that the current language is not interpreted restrictively, but wisely and fairly so as to fully address e-learning needs.

---

[20] See Universal Declaration of Human Rights, General Assembly of the United Nations, Resolution 217 A (III) of 10 December 1948 [hereinafter, UNUDHR], http://www.un.org/Overview/rights.html, accessed November 13, 2006.

[21] See Art.27.2 UNUDHR: "Everyone has the right to the protection of the moral and material interests resulting from any scientific, literary or artistic production of which he is the author." However, we should never forget that while every human being has a fundamental right to education and to participate in cultural life, only authors – those who create – enjoy copyright. This should not be read so as to diminish the importance of the copyright as a fundamental human right, but it should always be kept in mind in order to find the right balance between these fundamental rights in our copyright laws.

[22] See Art.26.1 UNUDHR: "Everyone has the right to education."

[23] See Art.27.1 UNUDHR: "Everyone has the right freely to participate in the cultural life of the community, to enjoy the arts and to share in scientific advancement and its benefits."

[24] The Stockholm Conference proceedings show that this major amendment went through completely unnoticed.

Furthermore, unlike the quotation exception (in art.10 (1) BC), the teaching exception of art.10 (2) BC is not mandatory for Berne Member States: each State will choose whether to introduce it or not in its copyright law.

The *EU Copyright Directive of 2001* also provides for a specific exception for illustration for teaching under *art.5 (3)(a) EUCD*:

> use for the sole purpose of *illustration for teaching* or scientific research, as long as the source, including the author's name, is indicated, unless this turns out to be impossible and to the extent justified by the non-commercial purpose to be achieved.

This exception is technologically neutral and clearly intended to apply to both face-to-face and distance education, including by digital means. Recital 42 of the EUCD expressly includes *"distance learning"* within that exception, and the Commission's Explanatory Memorandum accompanying the initial proposal of December 10, 1997 (COM(97) 628 final) further confirms that the teaching exception is intended to apply to *"the new electronic environment."*

Furthermore, art.5 (3)(a) EUCD allows for a broad use for teaching purposes:

- It may cover the reproduction and communication to the public (and perhaps also transformation)[25] of the whole work – provided that this is justified by the teaching purpose
- It does not discriminate between private or public institutions (according to Recital 42, the "organizational structure and means of funding [are] not decisive") as long as the "non-commercial nature of the activity" remains assured
- Although it does not require equitable remuneration (of the copyright owners) for the exempted uses, member States are free to require soIn short, most online teaching use could be covered under this exception. However, like the rest of limitations listed in art.5 (2) and (3) EUCD, the teaching exception is not compulsory: Member States are not obliged to implement it. Unfortunately, as we will see, European legislators are not paying enough attention to the needs of e-learning.

6.3.2 Teaching Exceptions in Domestic Laws

Not all *teaching exceptions existing in domestic laws* will allow the carrying on of e-learning projects or platforms without the authors' consent.

The teaching exceptions provided for in European countries offer (despite being in a mostly "harmonized" context) a good example of what goes on elsewhere: *teaching exceptions are varied in scope and some of them clearly failing to cover online teaching uses.*

---

[25] Art.5.3 EUCD does not cover the right of transformation, since this right was not harmonized by this Directive. However, Member States may choose to implement it (together with the other exploitation rights) under each of the listed statutory exceptions. As we will see, some countries have extended the teaching exception to the transformation right, others have not.

1. Some States have opted for an almost *verbatim* implementation of art.5 (3)(a) EUCD and, as a result, intend to *cover online teaching uses*.[26] They allow reproduction, distribution, and communication to the public (including the making available online) of works for teaching purposes, and some also allow for their translation.[27]

    However, some specific language as to the nature and amount of works covered by the exception may reduce its scope. For instance, some laws expressly limit the exception to *"fragments" or "parts" of works*[28]; or set specific amounts for specific kinds of works.[29] Others expressly exclude works primarily intended for education.[30] Other visible disparities concern the kind of *institutions that may benefit* from the teaching exception. Most laws have opted for the EUCD open-ended eligibility clause based on the *"non-commercial purpose"* of the teaching use or activity,[31] but others have added specific language[32] such as *"schools and universities (higher education institutions) and non-commercial institutions of further education and of professional training,"*[33] establishments *"officially recognized or organized – for that purpose – by public authorities,"*[34] or *"institutions which are not aimed at obtaining a direct or indirect economic or commercial advantage."*[35]

    Finally, some laws establish remuneration in favor of authors[36]; others expressly allow the teaching use for free,[37] while a few remain silent.[38]

2. A second group of domestic teaching exceptions is clearly *unfit to cover online teaching use* because it only covers reproduction and photocopying,[39] or because when communication to the public is included, the specific language reduces the exception to "live" teaching (such as plays, recitals or showings in front of a real audience or teaching within a "classroom").[40]

---

[26] This is the case of *Belgium, France, Germany, Italy, Luxembourg, Portugal, Poland, the Netherlands, Hungary,* as well as *Switzerland* (despite not being a E.U. Member).

[27] Either by expressly mentioning it (i.e., *Poland* and *the Netherlands*) or by simply referring to "use" (i.e., *Switzerland*).

[28] For instance, *Italy* and *Portugal*.

[29] For instance, *Germany* and *Belgium*.

[30] This is the case of *France* and *Germany*.

[31] See *Italy,the Netherlands* and *Luxembourg*.

[32] Therefore, in disregard of the specific explanation in Recital 42 EUCD.

[33] See *Germany*.

[34] See *Belgium*.

[35] See *Portugal*.

[36] See *Belgium, France, Germany, Switzerland* and *the Netherlands*; the specific remuneration schemes are left for Government regulation.

[37] See *Hungary*.

[38] See *Luxembourg, Portugal* and *Italy*.

[39] This is the case of *Austria* and the *UK*.

[40] This is the case of *Ireland, Greece* and *Spain*.

3. In *Nordic countries*, teaching uses tend to be subject to remunerated *extended collective licenses* and it is expected that online teaching (and digital uses) will soon be covered by them. It remains to be seen whether the scope covered by extended collective licensing will fully satisfy online teaching needs.[41]
4. Beyond the European scenario, it is worth mentioning some recent efforts made in the USA[42] and Australia[43] to adopt specific legislation aimed at fostering the use of pre-existing works in online teaching, as well as in Canada, where the topic is currently being considered as an amendment to its Copyright Act.[44]

Within this *non-harmonized scenario*, it is easy to foresee why *copyright may be an important obstacle for the lawful development of e-learning projects*: something that can be lawfully done according to the law of one country but cannot be safely done online and thus failing the author's consent.

6.3.3 Conclusions

In principle, both the BC and the EUCD would allow Member States to exempt the use for e-learning purposes, of lawfully disclosed works, provided that:

---

[41] For instance, in Denmark the extended collective license managed by COPY-DAN already covers scanning, printing, storage, e-mail transmission, upload in a password protected intranet and download, in all kind of educational institutions (schools – at all levels, universities, etc.), in exchange of a fixed amount per student, per year. However, a vestige from the reprographic licenses limits the copying to a maximum of 20% or 30 pages of a work, whichever is less.

[42] In the *USA*, the TEACH Act of November 2, 2002 which amended the Copyright Act of 1976 (see http://www.copyright.gov/title17/) was adopted to transport the instructional exceptions already existing under sec.110 (that covered both face-to-face teaching uses and distance-teaching uses by means of radio and TV broadcasting) into a digital environment. If there is one criticism to be made to the TEACH Act is its narrow scope, which may be somehow excused by its non-remunerated character, but which makes it clearly unsatisfactory to cover the needs of online teaching. However, when examining the US scenario for teaching uses, two other facts remain fundamental: the general *fair use* defense of sec.107 USCA and a voluntary – but widely accepted – licensing remunerated systems that allow for the compilation of material for teaching purposes, also in digital format [see, for instance, the Copyright Clearance Center, http://www.copyright.com/ among others].

[43] In *Australia*, the Copyright Amendment (Digital Agenda) Act 2000, No.110 (see http://www.austlii.edu.au/au/legis/cth/consol_act/caaa2000294/) provides for a statutory collective licensing regime for the digital reproduction and communication to the public of all kind of works (from digital sources, only) for educational uses (in broad terms, from use as part of the instruction to the making of e-packs and e-reserves), by all kind of educational institutions (primary or secondary institutions, universities, and assimilated institutions). It is all managed by only one collective society; the remuneration fee is agreed by the parties (or, by default, set by the Copyright Tribunal) according to several parameters, such as the nature of the institution, the kind of work, the students, and so on. This statutory collective license does not preclude the possibility that authors and institutions negotiate individual licenses.

[44] Under a broader Copyright Act reform [Bill C-61, An Act to Amend the Copyright Act *see* http://www.parl.gc.ca/], *Canada* is considering the introduction of a limitation for teaching uses similar to the U.S. TEACH Act.

- The work is used *only to the extent necessary* for the teaching purpose
- Reasonable effort (including DRMs, if necessary) is undertaken to *restrict access to registered students and to prevent misuse* (minimize infringements)
- Authors are *duly credited* (including the source) and – where necessary – *receive fair compensation*[45]

Unfortunately, national laws are far less favorable to exempt e-learning use. Furthermore, significant differences existing in national laws fragment the EU internal market and generate legal uncertainty. This legal uncertainty is enhanced by the unresolved question of choice of law: which law applies to regulate online uses?

Fragmentation and legal uncertainty benefits nobody. On the one hand, it forces extra-cautious institutions to seek licenses for e-learning use that need not be licensed; and on the other, it explains why scared owners set *unreasonable prices and conditions* to license online use or, simply *refuse to license* their work for e-learning projects. The public interest (of society at large) is poorly served when laws fail to grant learning (and e-learning) purposes the statutory recognition they deserve.

Recent voices have arisen at an international level claiming for a higher respect of public interests within the copyright laws. For instance, both the current discussions for a WIPO Development Agenda,[46] as well as other projects[47] which attempt to bring some more "balance" and flexibility into copyright laws, refer to education as a primary concern not only as part of developing countries preferential treatment (as is the case in the Berne Convention Annex[48]), but as a fundamental interest that copyright laws should acknowledge and respect.

---

[45] Fair compensation should take into account the nature of the work (works primarily intended for teaching may be excluded from the exemption, so as not to unnecessarily prejudice the legitimate interests of the author), the specific teaching use (not all teaching uses should be compensated and compensated equally), the nature of the educational establishment and/or program, and the existence of technological protection measures implemented.

[46] On September 28, 2007, WIPO member states adopted a Development Agenda, consisting of a series of recommendations to enhance the development dimension of WIPO's activities. The recommendations include a set of 45 agreed proposals covering six clusters of activities including Technical Assistance and Capacity Building; Norm-setting, Flexibilities, Public Policy and Public Knowledge; Technology Transfer, Information and Communication Technology (ICT) and Access to Knowledge; Assessments, Evaluation and Impact Studies; Institutional Matters including Mandate and Governance. See the Draft Report of July 17, 2006, on the existing Proposals concerning the WIPO Development Agenda at http://www.wipo.int/edocs/mdocs/mdocs/en/pcda_2/pcda_2_4_prov.pdf. Before that, see also the "Treaty on Access to Knowledge" proposed by the *Consumer Project on Technology* (see Draft of May 9, 2005 at http://www.cptech.org/a2k/consolidatedtext-may9.pdf).

[47] See *Copyright and Access to Knowledge – Policy Recommendations on Flexibilities in Copyright Laws*, by Consumers International at http://www.ciroap.org/A2K.

[48] APPENDIX "SPECIAL PROVISIONS REGARDING DEVELOPING COUNTRIES" to the Berne Convention, http://www.wipo.int/treaties/en/ip/berne/trtdocs_wo001.html.

An internationally mandatory exception for online teaching use (if necessary, by means of a compulsory license) could help solve this problem. In the meantime, authors and users must turn to licensing schemes.

6.4 Licensing: "Traditional" or "Open"?

If the specific e-learning use that we need to carry out is not covered by an exception, we need to obtain the authorization of the copyright owner.

6.4.1 Traditional Copyright Licensing

Traditional copyright licenses are granted directly by the copyright owner or by means of the collective societies which are empowered by the copyright authors and owners (either via a license or a mandate) to grant such licenses. Obtaining a license to reuse pre-existing contents (sometimes produced by the same universities) for teaching activities in e-learning platforms is, nevertheless, not an easy task. Difficulties are of a different nature: identifying and locating the owner, obtaining timely responses, unreasonable terms and prices and even the refusal of license (let us not forget that exclusivity grants a right to authorize but also to prohibit the use of the work). On the other hand, collective societies are not always helpful in providing licenses for e-learning purposes since in many cases they do not manage the digital rights of their members yet (authors and owners being afraid to grant collective societies the management of their rights in online means of exploitation). For all these reasons, traditional licensing for e-learning purposes is far from being a reality in most countries.

6.4.2 Open Licensing

Open licensing was developed as an alternative to the failure of "traditional" copyright to successfully address the needs of e-learning and of a networked society. However, as we will see, open licensing is only a limited solution.

The open licensing system is very simple: the *author* chooses a license and attaches it to his/her work posted online. *Users* will be able to identify the conditions set by the author to allow usage of his/her work. *The user becomes a licensee* when he/she re-uses the work, and implicitly accepts the terms of the license set by the author. So, it is essential to bear in mind a distinction between mere users (passive users) and re-users (active users) who become licensees.

Open licensing is often used in e-learning platforms and projects to deal with copyright issues because it allows the building up of a body of *licensed works* (the "commons") that can be used for further teaching purposes online.

It is no surprise that open licensing is strongly rooted in academic contexts. On the one hand, it alleviates the frustration of the academic community when faced with the lack of sound IP policies of their universities.[49] In 1998, the *Open Content* project was created as an attempt to translate Richard Stallman's *Free Software* principles onto the educational community. Prof. David Wiley (Center for Open and Sustainable Learning[50] at Utah State University) drafted the *Open Content* license which authorized the reproduction, redistribution, and modification of any "contents" designed for teaching (education) subject to attribution and *copyleft* (the resulting derivative work was to be subject to the same license).[51] Shortly after, the MIT *Open Courseware Project*,[52] as well as other OER projects,[53] started to use *Creative Commons* licenses to post their teaching materials online. In 2004, the *Open Content* license was dropped in order to benefit from the widespread use of CC licenses which allowed to cover all kind of works, not only educational ones, and afforded a larger pool of works to choose from, also for teaching purposes.

It is worth mentioning that despite its widespread acceptance, the *Creative Commons* licensing system is only one among the many different existing "open licensing" systems.[54]

6.4.3 *Creative Commons Licenses*

In 2002, Prof. Lawrence Lessig, at that time at Harvard University, created the *Creative Commons* Project, as a tool to "rebuild" the balance, the fairness, that the US Copyright Act had lost in recent years (as a result of the US joining the

---

[49]To make a long story short: the academic production (both research and teaching results) is "appropriated" by publishers (and database producers) and universities end up subscribing (and, usually, paying high fees) to have access to their own production; the need for alternative digital repositories is obvious.

[50]See C()SL at http://cosl.usu.edu.

[51]The original "Open Content" license is available at http://opencontent.org/opl.shtml. A new version of the license is currently under consideration: http://opencontent.org/blog/archives/355.

[52]*Open Courseware* (OCW) is an educational Project of "open" teaching materials developed by the MIT, and sponsored by the William and Flora Hewlett Foundation. See http://ocw.mit.edu/index.html.

[53]The expression Open Educational Resources (OER) was used for the first time in 2002, within a UNESCO forum to evaluate the impact of the MIT OCW in developing countries. OER stands for all the educational material or resource which is offered to the general public, for free, subject to an "open license" which allows its use, transformation and reuse. See Fitzgerald, B. (2007). *Open Content Licensing (OCL) for Open Educational Resources*, available at http://www.oecd.org/edu/oer.

[54]See Liang, L. (2004), Guide to open content licenses: http://media.opencultures.net/open_content_guide/.

Berne Convention in 1989),[55] which were perceived as significantly restricting the "public domain."[56] The project intends to ensure a *"commons"*; a pool of works available to all users, for free and without any copyright restrictions (either because their authors have licensed the exploitation rights to the general public or because they are already in the public domain after the term of protection expired).

The basic CC license authorizes any reproduction, distribution, transformation, communication to the public of the work, in any means and format, for commercial and non-commercial purposes, for free, forever. From there onward, the author can "restrict" his/her license by choosing to:

- Exclude commercial uses
- Exclude the making of derivative works or
- Allow the making of derivative works under the condition that they be subject to the same license

These combinations result in six different licenses, which are easily identified with user-friendly icons[57]:

Attribution (by)
Attribution (by) – No derivatives (nd)
Attribution (by) – Non-commercial (nc)
Attribution (by) – No derivatives (nd) – Non-commercial (nc)
Attribution (by) – Share alike (sa)
Attribution (by) – Non-commercial (nc) – Share alike (sa)[58]

We do not have time to examine all the implications that these licenses may have for e-learning uses, but will simply point out some fundamental issues.

- *Who can grant a CC license?* Only the original copyright owner can grant such a license: the author, artist, musician, producer of a recording. And even this may

---

[55]This changes consisted, basically, in dropping the formality of first publication with © notice to obtain copyright protection (which ultimately permitted authors to decide whether their works would be in the public domain or protected) in favor of automatic protection upon creation; the introduction of the moral rights of integrity and attribution for the works of visual art (sec.106A); and the 20 years extension of the term of protection effected by the *Sony Bono Term Extension Act* (Public Law 105–298) of 1998 to "catch up" with the E.U. 70 years *post mortem auctoris* term. This Act was challenged for unconstitutionality (alleged to infringe Art.I, Sec.8 U.S. Constitution of 1787), but the Supreme Court confirmed its validity. See *Eldred v. Ashcroft*, 537 U.S. 186 (2003), 239 F.3d 372, *affirmed:* http://supct.law.cornell.edu/supct/html/01–618.ZS.html.

[56]See Lessig, L. Cultivating the Public Domain – Creative Commons White Paper: http://wiki.creativecommons.org/Cultivating_the_Public_Domain.

[57]Each license consists of three different layers of reading: the *Commons Deed* (for straight comprehensible reading – this is where the characteristic CC icons are visible); the *Legal Code* (for legal purposes); and the *Digital Code* (for computers reading).

[58]Of course, (*nd*) and (*sa*) are incompatible.

vary depending on the jurisdiction and language of the CC license, since as we have observed, domestic laws may provide for different results as to authorship and initial ownership of works created under employment or commissioned.

Although CC licenses grant a *prima facie* statement of lawfulness, there is no mechanism to control that the one who is posting and licensing the work is the real author or copyright owner. The CC project does not intend to do so (neither should it do so). This is a question for courts and evidence.

- *What contents may be subject to a CC license?* Only what is protected by copyright can be subject to a license; that is, original works, performances and recordings.

CC licenses should not be attached to non-protected works (i.e., works in the public domain) or to material which does not qualify as a work. This would be an unnecessary as well as an incorrect licensing practice. Both authors and users should be well aware of what is copyrighted (and can be CC licensed) and what is not.[59]

We should always bear in mind that an e-learning project may be using all kind of contents: syllabi, lectures, exercises, exams, videos, readings, etc., and that this may include academic work protected by copyright but also facts, information, work in the public domain, etc. We should therefore be vigilant! Not all material used for e-learning purposes will need a copyright license; or, a copyright license granted for an e-learning project may not cover all its contents (there may be data, factual information, work in the public domain, etc., that will not be governed by the license). The license will only affect the copyrighted contribution of the author who is granting it.

In short, CC licensing is not a substitute of copyright law.

- *It is a license, not a registry.* Quite often users and authors (as well as institutions) believe that CC licensing offers some kind of "formal" protection of their academic work! Copyright Registries (public or private) – where existing – may be helpful since registrations provide *prima facie* evidence, but CC licenses do not have this purpose.
- *Moral rights.* The contractual obligation to grant attribution (credit) to the author is especially important in some jurisdictions where the Copyright law does not recognize an attribution right to all authors.[60] In most other countries (i.e., European ones), the obligation of attribution derives directly from the copyright laws (and regardless of any license), as a moral right that all authors are granted and cannot waive or transfer.

---

[59] Nevertheless, the distinction between what is an unprotected idea, what is an original expression, and what is a derivative work (and what, if not authorized, is an infringement) is proving to be one of the most complex legal issues in copyright.

[60] This is the case of the USA (where CC licenses were born): sec.106A USCA grants moral rights of attribution and integrity to authors of works of visual art only.

Furthermore, the CC licenses' silence on other moral rights (such as the moral right of integrity) does not mean that the author who is granting a CC license is forsaking or waiving them. Regardless of any license allowing for derivative work, the author can always oppose a modification that is prejudicial to his/her honor and reputation (and the court will decide whether there has been an infringement of the moral right of integrity or not).[61]

- *Exploitation rights.* CC licenses cover all the exploitation rights except for adaptation (transformation) which may or may not be licensed by the author. In addition, these exploitation rights may be granted for any purposes or limited to non-commercial purposes. In short, not all CC licenses are the same and the user should always check its specific scope, before transforming its contents for use in an e-learning project. For instance, the CC license used in the OCW project excludes both commercial use and the making of derivative academic work. And when the teaching use includes work licensed under different licenses (some more restrictive than others), such use should always comply with the most restrictive one. In short, the author will be always able to exercise any rights granted by law that are not part of (or excluded from) the license.

- *Forever, for free and in any format.* These three basic factors that are embedded in the license and cannot be excluded or "tuned" by the author.

  - Everybody can use the work for free. Yet, the author may enter any other copyright contracts ("traditional" or otherwise) with publishers, producers, or musical editors, etc. – as long as they accept to pay for a non-exclusive license of rights on the work and do not mind competition (by the public at large). Furthermore, CC licenses do not affect any compensation or remuneration rights granted by law to authors and artists as unalienable rights: such as the compensation for private copying.[62]
  - CC licenses authorize not only digital uses but also "analogue" ones, use in the "real world" (paper, CD and DVD, broadcast, theater play, etc.). It is fundamental to take this into account when deciding whether to include commercial or non-commercial use under the license. Furthermore, the original CC license covers any format, now known or available in the future, which is not valid in some jurisdictions (mostly in EU countries) and may be an example of possible interoperability problems of a same license from different jurisdictions.

---

[61] Of course, by excluding the making of derivative works from the license, the chances of an infringement of the integrity right may be reduced (and if so, it would amount to a triple infringement: of the moral right of integrity and of the transformation right, in addition to a infringement of the contract/license).

[62] Version 3 of the CC license has already addressed and solved this issue by distinguishing between statutory non-waiveable remunerations (which remain unaffected by the license) and those derived from voluntary (collectively or individually) licenses, which are expressly waived under the license.

– CC licenses are granted *ad perpetuam*, as long as the work is protected by copyright.[63] The author can change the license and also cancel it, but its effects and previous re-uses will continue to be effective, available, and re-usable.

- The author can choose to exclude *the making of derivative work* (i.e., translations, dramatizations, musical arrangements, film adaptations, or any other transformation of the work). Of course, the author may choose to authorize any of such uses on an individual basis. When the making of derivative work is licensed, the author can choose to subject them all to the same license: this is the strict concept of *copyleft (sa)*.[64]

- The author can *exclude commercial uses*. Such an exclusion severely restricts the scope *of* the licensed exploitation rights. Although a first distinction between commercial and non-commercial use is done by explaining the former as "primarily intended for or directed toward commercial advantage or private monetary compensation," this is one of the trickiest issues posed by these licenses. In case of doubt, it is advisable to contact the author for authorization: at any time, and subject to any new condition, he/she can authorize a commercial use excluded from the license.

- *No license can derogate from a statutory exception*. Regardless of the kind of license granted (if any), *users* may use works according to the terms allowed by the copyright law under the exceptions: *quotations, parodies, teaching purposes, information, etc*. In that sense, open licenses are precious for the "commons," because they increase the amount of works available without DRM and indirectly reinforce the scope of free use granted by law (not only by licenses). For instance, anybody is allowed to make quotations (also for commercial purposes) of a work licensed only for non-commercial use.

- In case of *infringement*, the author must go to court – as under any other license or non-license-related infringement. However, as the chain of re-use grows, the more complicated it will be to trace and sue infringers down the line, to the extent that it will be useless to do so.

- *Users become licensees*. For *mere consumers* (those who only use licensed work) the effects of CC licensing are only beneficial, no strings attached: it enlarges the number of works available for consumption and they are "slightly" bound by the license.[65] Yet, *re-users* (those who create a derivative work) are obliged by the license terms, and it may not always be easy to keep up with them. They should be always aware of the obligations they have accepted by using CC licensed material and the complexities derived from the realm of contracts – which may be more difficult than copyright itself.

---

[63] Once the work enters the public domain, the license becomes useless and ineffective.

[64] Over half of the CC licenses granted worldwide include the *copyleft* clause: $(by - sa)$ o $(by - nc - sa)$.

[65] In fact, they could probably do the same without the license, by virtue of the exceptions and limitations embedded in the copyright law.

- Interoperability problems may arise with other "open licenses" but also among CC licenses from other jurisdictions. For instance, the problem of excluding commercial or derivative use from CC licenses may make it incompatible with contents licensed in other platforms, such as Wikipedia or GNU Documentation Licenses (the GPL version for "documents"). Furthermore, the fact that CC licenses are adapted to different copyright laws (of different jurisdictions) may also cause problems of cross-border interoperability – even within the same type of license.[66]

6.4.4 Some Final Comments on "Open Licensing"

CC licenses have proven to offer an alternative and easy means to ensure the development of e-learning projects, and to counterbalance what is considered a restrictive copyright regime, by allowing authors to give back to society what the law is granting them in exclusive.

However, there may be some unexpected dangers in promoting the *"commons"* by means of private legal instruments (i.e., licenses) based on exclusive rights (copyright). Some scholars[67] point out that the *Creative Commons* strategy based on property and licensing will not only fail to create an alternative to the copyright regime but also lead to unintended consequences: by making copyright licensing easier, it is making copyright stronger!

It may well be true that by only focusing on licensing practices, works end up deemed protected only when published with a CC license (or any other license); and, paradoxically, a tool intended to enhance the lawful use of works, may become a tool to strengthen the protection of the exclusive rights.

Copyright is a complex subject matter. Faced with the "threat" posed by digital technologies, our copyright laws have been losing *"balance."*

Licensing (open licensing) is proving to be a flexible solution to promote e-learning and to restore the public interest in the use of copyrighted works. But it can only take us so far. It is within the copyright law that the balance needs to be restored (through the statutory exceptions). And on this matter, nothing has been done so far. It would be wise to take advantage of the "thrust" of the open licensing movement to achieve that goal.

6.5 Final Remarks

This chapter tried to identify several copyright issues that e-learning projects may have to face to ensure the success of e-learning projects.

---

[66] We mentioned above that in most EU countries the CC licenses will only cover the means of exploitation known at the time it was granted, while in other countries, such as the USA, a license may include means of exploitation unknown at the time of the license.

[67] See Elkin-Koren, N. (2005). "What contracts cannot do: The Limits of Private Ordering in Facilitating a Creative Commons", 74 *Fordham Law Review* 375.

Despite very favorable and flexible international – and supranational – umbrellas (namely, the BC, WCT and EUCD), domestic laws are far more restrictive when exempting e-learning use. The significant differences existing in these laws fragment the market and may generate legal uncertainty, especially when taking into account that, as a result from the "territoriality" approach of copyright choice of law rules,[68] several copyright laws may apply to regulate one e-learning use, depending on where the students are located. Legal uncertainty and fragmentation benefits nobody and forces us all to find alternative tools, such as licensing and specifically, open licensing.

Licensing for e-learning purposes is not an easy task. Additional difficulties exist in locating the owner, obtaining timely responses with reasonable terms and conditions; while collecting societies are not of much help because they do not always have licensed digital rights in the work they manage. Open licensing is proving to be an important and useful tool for the development of e-learning; yet it poses complex issues that we should all be aware of.

As I pointed out, there may be some risks involved in focusing only on open-licensing systems to foster e-learning projects and platforms. I contend that educational purposes should be rebalanced first within the copyright law, by means of strengthening the exceptions for educational purposes that already exist in national and international instruments and making them compulsory for Member states to implement.

One may argue that no exceptions would be necessary if a solid licensing system were available, and that efforts should be devoted to building such a system instead of to the "old-fashioned" legal technique of limitations. However, this reasoning forgets that exclusive rights granted to authors call for boundaries and that education and culture deserve to act as a limit to these exclusive rights and also in a digital context.[69] E-learning purposes need be fully acknowledged as a fundamental limitation to copyright. The legislator should see to it that the proper exceptions exist for that purpose.

If we fail to do so, copyright law will remain foreign to e-learning and vice versa. E-learning efforts should not only rely on altruism – of individuals and/or institutions – and licensing, they should also be sanctioned by the copyright laws. If the current copyright laws are not well adjusted to the new technological means and needs, we simply need to re-adjust them. Education (including e-learning) and access to culture is too important a public good not to try.

---

[68] Vid. Art.5(2) BC: *lex loci protectionis*.

[69] We should not forget that the distinction between face-to-face and online teaching will soon be obsolete, as digital formats and networked environments spread also in the teaching realm, and that the public interest that justifies copyright exceptions for teaching purposes is the same regardless of the means used to conduct that teaching.

Part II
Case studies and Practical Issues

Chapter 7
Survey on Learning Content Management Systems

Josep Maria Boneu

Abstract This chapter describes the most relevant standards for content management within the e-learning context. The first part of this chapter is devoted to the concept of Learning Object, which is presented and studied as a way of management learning content inside e-learning environments. The central part of the chapter is an introduction to e-learning technical standards, where the principal actors in e-learning standardization efforts are presented, together with the main areas of standardization and the most important initiatives in progress. The final part describes the most popular content management standards and specifications, such as IEEE LOM (Learning Object Metadata), SCORM (Sharable Content Object Reference Model) and IMS Content specifications (IMS Content Packaging, IMS Question and Test Interoperability Specification and IMS Digital Repositories Specification).

7.1 Introduction

In recent years, we have witnessed the development of the Learning Content Management Systems in the Web (Content Management Systems or CMS). These are tools that allow creating and easily maintaining a Web, performing some of the most tedious tasks which until now took the time of web administrators. The background and foundations of the concepts discussed in this chapter can be found in Chap. 1.

The Content Managers provide an environment for the update, maintenance and extension of the Web with the collaboration of multiple users. In any virtual environment, this is an important feature, as it strengthens the cohesion in community, enabling users to participate in a more collaborative manner.

The Learning Process cannot stay away from technological innovation; therefore TIC learning (referred to from now on as e-learning) is the latest step in the evolution

J.M. Boneu(✉)
Department of Computer Science, Centre d'Estudis Politècnics, Barcelona, Catalonia, Spain
e-mail: jboneu@uoc.edu

N. Ferran and J. Minguillón (eds.), *Content Management for E-Learning*,
DOI 10.1007/978-1-4419-6959-0_7, © Springer Science+Business Media, LLC 2011

of remote education. E-learning provides the opportunity to create student-focused learning environments, which are in addition interactive, efficient, easily accessible and very suitable for self-disciplined students, learning on their own or with a tutor's support.

According to the analysis of Khan (2001), an e-learning scenario must consider eight fundamental aspects: the institution, pedagogical criterion, technological design, interface, evaluation, management, support and ethical use. This way *e-learning* does not only offer a computer-based course, but a combination of resources, interactivity, support and structured learning activities.

7.2 CMS and E-Learning

The Content Management Systems or CMS are software mainly used to facilitate both internet and intranet web management, this is why they are also known as Web Content Management or WCM (Robertson 2003a). It is necessary to consider, however, that the application of CMS is not limited only to webs, and in the case of e-learning, the management is not centred in the Web but also in the educational contents [reusable learning objects (RLOs), resources, documents, assessment, among others].

The CMS evolution towards e-learning systems demands specific requirements that a general CMS not always meets, or if it does, it does not offer the same facilities a tool created to perform this function would have.

The contents and the systems of communication along with the e-learning platforms are the elements comprising an e-learning system, in which the main element is the platform.

The e-learning platform is the server software which deals mostly with:

User management: registration, learning monitoring and reports generation, among other tasks.

Course management: record of user's activities, both of the test results and all assessment types made, and of sequencing and access to the educational material.

Communication services management: forums of discussion, chats, video conferences, workshops, blogs and wikis among others, which must be programmed and offered when necessary.

With respect to the contents, these have become nowadays a fundamental part of all the process, in constant change thanks to the application of the Web 2.0 new techniques in which the consumers of contents are simultaneously producing them, and in which the content takes priority over the format (O'Really 2005).

The contents or courseware are the learning material available for the student. The contents can take several formats, depending on their adjustment to the different subjects. The most common one is the WBT, online courses with interactive and multimedia elements that allow the user to keep progressing on content, and assessing their learning. However, in other cases it can be a "virtual" lesson through video conference and supported by a presentation in the form of slides, or in explanations on a "digital board". At other times, the content does not adapt to a multimedia presentation, and so it is best to use document form materials that can be unloaded and completed with online activities, such as discussion forums or talks with the tutors. Really, any type of representation of the contents can be combined with the others and all make up the same e-learning system.

Therefore, the contents reusability and interoperability on different platforms require firstly standard-based courses, and secondly that the platforms may support such standard, making both courses developed by the own organization or by others easier to use. More on standards and specifications can be found in Chap. 9.

Nowadays, there is not just one standard in the market, but they are all trying independently to solve these problems. The widely accepted LOM (Learning Object Metadata) standard developed by IEEC LTSC (Institute for Electrical and Electronic Engineers Learning Technology – Standards Committee), allows the description of a learning object through metadata. AICC (Aviation Industry CBT Committee) was the first organization created to develop a set of rules allowing the CBT courses exchange. The description of educational itineraries is possible thanks to the resources description frameworks, RDF (Resource Description Framework), or through IMS LD (IMS Learning Design, based on Educational Modelling Language), and the ADL (Advanced Distribute Learning) SCORM (Shareable Content Object Reference Model) standard, widely accepted and used, allows the organization of contents supporting the educational itineraries description, the contents sequencing, the packaging of contents for their convenient distribution and the learning process monitoring; as such, SCORM encompasses the initiatives of other standards (Fig. 7.1):

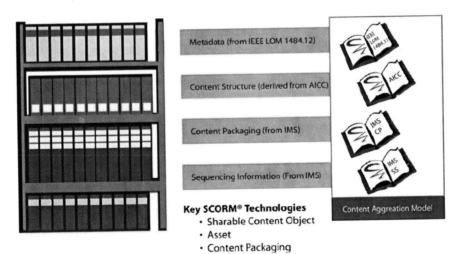

Fig. 7.1 The SCORM Content Aggregation Model book as part of the SCORM bookshelf. *LOM* learning object metadata. (Source: SCORM 2004 (3rd ed.) Content Aggregation Model)

- The IMS course description system,
- Information exchange though an AICC API (Application Program Interface)
- The IEEE LOM learning objects description.

7.3   The CMS Evolution Towards E-Learning

The CMS evolution during the past few years has had three stages, which have had an increased influence over the contents creation speed, cost, flexibility, learning personalization, student's attention quality and competitive advantages for the organizations using e-learning solutions.

- *First stage*: The CMS (Content Management System or Course Management System) are the most basic e-learning platforms, which allow the generation of dynamic web sites; the objective being the creation and management of online information (texts, images, graphics, videos, sound, etc.). They are also characterized by not having elaborate interaction tools (forums, chats, diaries, etc.), nor real-time support. They are also called Authorware and the functional centres are normally the courses, or groups of courses and groups of students, in which it is not possible to manage co-relativities, prerequisites, learning plans, evaluation of relations, among other functions. They are generally used in vertical projects, when the client organization does not have a learning administrator, and it is necessary to enable a group in specific contents in a very short time. Due to their characteristics, they can be easily implemented and at low cost.
- *Second stage*: The LMS (Learning Management System) are created from the CMS I, which provide an environment that makes possible the web update, maintenance and expansion with the cooperation of multiple users. LMS are learning-oriented and provide tools for the academic contents management, improving the competences and intercommunication of course users; they can adapt learning to the business demands and to one's own professional development. They have tools to distribute the courses, resources, news and contents related to general learning. They are usually called LCMS (Learning CMS). The names LMS and LCMS are generally used as synonymous, even when they are not so. The LMS are the virtual component of traditional education, the software that provides teachers and students with training administrative and academic functions, by which they can communicate, transfer information, assess and be assessed, and pay, among other functions. They are integrated, not isolated, interface systems and are based on open and not owner standards (Table 7.1).
- *Third stage*: The LCMS (Learning Content Management System) are platforms integrating the CMS and LMS functionalities, including the contents management for personalizing each student's resources, in which the companies become easily, quickly and efficiently their own content editors, and thus help solve the problems of former platforms: difficulty in generating materials, flexibility, adaptability to changes, learning control and updated knowledge maintenance.

Table 7.1 Comparative summary between LMSs and LCMSs

Uses	LMS	LCMS
Target users	Course managers, training administrators, teachers or instructors	Content designers, instructional designers, project managers
Provides	Courses, capacitating events addressed to students	Learning contents, support to development and users
Classroom management, teacher-based Training	Yes (but not always)	No
Administration	Courses, capacitating events students	Learning contents, support to development and users
Competences–skills analysis	Yes	Yes (in some cases)
Participants performance during training	Main focus	Secondary focus
Users collaboration	Yes	Yes
Keeps users profiles database	Not always	Not always
Events agenda	Yes	No
Contents creation tools	No	Yes
Reusable contents	Not always	Yes
Integrated assessment tools for making exams	Yes (most LMS have this capacity)	Yes (most have this capacity)
Workflow tools	No	Yes (sometimes)
Shares student data with ERP (enterprise requirement planning)	Yes	No
Dynamic assessment and adaptive learning	No	Yes
Content distribution, navigation control and student's interface	No	Yes

They add knowledge management techniques to the LMS in structured environments, designed so that the organizations can implement their processes and practices better, with the support of courses, materials and online contents. They can be very efficiently created by their developers, expert collaborators or instructors taking part in the contents creation. The LCMS present the following characteristics:

– They are simple tools that facilitate contents creation by means of WYSIWYG editors.
– They are based on a reusable "content objects" model, in which the content is reused throughout the courses, curricula, and can be transferred among organizations.
– They have tools available for the system's administration, in terms of registering, learning monitoring, initial, formative and global assessment, sequencing, user tracking, contents adaptation and assessment, among others.
– The content is not subject to just one presentation pattern, but can be edited in various formats in which the contents are not limited to a series of navigation controls.

- The content is stored in a centralized database and can be located through several criteria, including several formats.
- They usually include an engine that helps to adapt the content to different user groups with different profiles, providing in some cases different environments or visualization forms.
- They provide tools for the collaborative communication and learning, both by using synchronous and asynchronous resources which facilitate a simple communication between students and teachers.
- They must allow sharing knowledge resources and team work.
- They provide mechanisms for the stored knowledge security and protection, establishing different levels of privileges according to each user's functions.
- They provide simple tools that help the contents migration to facilitate the adaptation to the different educational needs and situations that may take place.
- They must facilitate connectivity to other LMS following the current standards XML, IMS, AICC and SCORM, making the edition of materials in various formats and platforms more flexible (Hernandez 2003).
- The installation process should be simple enough, not requiring further adaptation, localization, personalization and such other processes, which result in an increased cost and delay the installation.

Considering the use of these tools implies saving costs, and the low cost of their development, it would seem they should be very expensive. While this is true for certain commercial products, powerful LCMS are available with open source code licenses, so they can be accessed freely.

A common trend in use for platforms is their capacity to interact with other trust platforms on the net. This platform networking allows users of a given platform to access the resources and contents stored in another platform by a single-on access. Likewise, platforms are becoming integrated within current social nets, obtaining resources and contents for their use.

7.4 Functional Division of LCMS

A division of LCMS functionality is proposed into four categories: content creation, management, publication and presentation.[1]

7.4.1 Content Creation

L/CMS provide tools for designers without technical knowledge in web pages to be able to focus on content, leaving presentation aside, as normally two different people deal with each of these two areas. Information is made up by assembling

---

[1]http://www.programming-pool.com/blog/web-content-manangement-system-structure.html

pieces of content called "components", which may be independent from one another and most importantly they are reusable.

Most commonly, a text editor WYSIWYG[2] is provided (Robertson 2003b), in which the user can see the final result while writing, in the style of commercial editors, but with a limited text format range. This limitation makes sense, as the objective is to enable the creator to emphasize certain points, without modifying much the website's general style; there are other tools such as the XML document editing, office computer systems applications integrating L/CMS, existing documents import, and editors that allow to add marks, usually in HTML, to indicate a document's format and structure.

For the creation of the site itself, L/CMS provide tools which define the structure, page format visual appearance, patterns use, and a modular system which may include functions not planned originally.

With respect to the administration and information distribution, besides the contents designers and page-makers, the editor is in charge of approving the information to be published and of retiring it once a piece of news or a component's life cycle is over. As for the visibility of the information, the reusable components allow to personalize it as the user consumes it.

The implementation of the LMS platform does not guarantee the means for the creation and adapted generation of the necessary courses for the organization, but it simple acts as a distribution platform in which the minimum instructional unit is the course itself.

7.4.2 Content Management

The created documents are placed in a central database which can also store the rest of the web data such as data related to documents (versions done, author, publication and expiration dates) and users preferences, web structure, etc.

The web structure can be configured with a tool that normally presents a hierarchical organization of the site and allows modifications, like assigning a group to each area, people in charge, editors, authors and users with different permits. This is essential to facilitate the work flow of the edition process which goes from the author to the final person responsible for the publication. The CMS allow the communication among the group members and keep a record of every work flow step.

7.4.3 Publication

Any approved page or resource is automatically published on the deadline, and when it expires, it is archived for future reference. The pattern applied to the

---

[2]WYSIWYG (What You See Is What You Get), referred to contents edition, it means working on a document which already has its final appearance. Editing an HTML page with an editor other than WYSIWYG implies working with the codes that indicate the format it will have, without seeing the final result.

publication is the same defined for the whole web or for the specific section where the site is, so that the resulting web site pages show a consistent appearance. The separation between form and content allows modifying the visual appearance of a web site without affecting the already created documents, saving the authors worrying about the final design of their pages.

7.4.4 Presentation

A CMS can automatically manage the web's accessibility, with the support of international standards such as WAI, and adapt to the preferences and needs of each user. It is also compatible with the different navigators available in all the platforms (Windows, GNU/Linux, Mac, Palm, among others), and by its internalization capacity, it can be adapted to the language, measure systems and culture of the visitor.

The system can manage many other aspects such as the navigation menus, or the hierarchy of the current page within the web, adding links automatically. It also manages all the internal or external modules the system may include. Thus, a news module would, for instance, present an animated advertisement or message, while another forum module would show on its home page the title of the last messages received, in all cases, with the corresponding links, and following the pattern created by the designers.

7.5 Basic Characteristics of E-Learning Platforms

There are four basic and essential characteristics that any e-learning platform should have (Berlanga and García Peñalvo 2004):

- *Interactivity*: They make users aware of their central role in their own learning process.
- *Flexibility*: Group of functionalities that allow the e-learning system to be easily adapted to the organization where it must be implanted. This adaptation refers to the following aspects:
- Capacity to adapt to the organization's structure.
- Capacity to adapt to the organization's learning plans.
- Capacity to adapt to the organization's contents and pedagogical styles.
- *Scalability*: Capacity to function both for a small or great number of users.
- *Standardization*: Using standard platforms means using courses developed outside the organization, so courses can be available not only for the organization that created them but also for others that meet the standard; it also guarantees the durability of courses, as they are being constantly updated, and finally, the students' behaviour during the course can be monitored.

Meeting the standard, on the one hand, guarantees an institution the investment feasibility in an e-learning system, not relying solely on one technology will ensure the courses continuation in case of technological changes, while on the other hand, more courses can be offered, which reduces the purchasing costs and facilitates their exchange.

7.5.1 Other Important Characteristics of E-Learning Platforms

There are other general characteristics of e-learning platforms:

- *Open code*: We refer to "Open Source" software when it is distributed with a license to see and modify the application's source code. Many times the license can also be available to redistribute the code. However, Open Source does not necessarily mean that an application should be for free; therefore, the platform's version downloaded may be modified and developed up to the wished extent.
- *Free platform*: The use of the platform will not involve any purchasing or license costs. On the other hand, there are pay platforms developed by groups or companies which simply sell a product. The GPL (General Public License) Open Source which can be found in the market offers the platform developers support in the installation and other services.
- *Internationalization or multilingual architecture*: The platform should already be translated, or should be easy to translate, so that users may become easily familiarized with it. In some cases the software is localized, in other cases documentation, tutorials and other materials are available in multiple languages. This problem does not exist in pay platforms, as whatever is needed is paid for and developed.
- *Technology used:* These are the more common programmes used: PHP, Java, Perl and Python, Open Source languages, very appropriate for developing dynamic Webs and used largely for GPL platforms. ASP programming language is mostly used in pay platforms.

In the database fields, GPL platforms use more frequently GPL databases, such as Mysql and PostgreSQL. Some GPL platforms use Oracle, although this use is more limited to pay platforms. However, there are also cases in which e-learning platforms are used simply as questionnaire generators and do not use databases.

With respect to the server chosen, most GPL platforms use Apache rather than IIS, while pay platforms are mostly based on IIS solutions and Windows 2000 Server.

And finally, the selection of the server's operating system follows the same criteria: GPL platforms tend to function commonly on UNIX systems: MAC, Solaris or Linux, although it is stated they also work well on Windows, which is the most common system used by pay platforms.

- *Wide community of users and documentation*: The platform must count with the support of dynamic communities of users, forums, developers, technicians and experts. It must be backed up by appropriate documentation which facilitates its installation, administration and use.

These are good indicators of the product's updates, monitoring, continuity and quality.

7.6 CMS Functionalities Oriented Towards E-Learning, LCMS

The current e-learning platforms offer many functions (CUE 2003), which can be grouped as follows:

7.6.1 Learning-Oriented Tools

- *Forums*: Discussion forums permit the exchange of messages during a course (or the time the instructor considers appropriate). Forums can be organized chronologically, by categories or topics of conversation (threads); they may allow or not to attach files (of a certain size) to the message; they also allow an asynchronous communication among all the course users and promote team work. There are also talk forums with the same aims as the written ones.

The forum may behave in different ways: as a notice board where only the instructor can write, or where the student can only provide feedback to the instructor's input (but cannot put forward any topic of discussion), or forums where the student can see what other colleagues have written only after s/he has entered his/her own comments, or they may not be restricted and anybody may start a debate and answer messages. The forum can be configured through the users' roles, accepting other possible configurations.

The forum is a key element in communities based on constructivist and collaborative learning and may be an assessed activity.

- *Forum search*: This helps select and localize the messages among all the debate topics which include the search pattern entered.
- *E-portfolio*: Digital or electronic portfolios allow to monitor the participants' learning process, from their assignments and other training activities realized, irrespective of their formats (images, documents, spreadsheets, or others). Some e-portfolio platforms are integrated as (and with) learning platforms, such is the case of Mahara.[3]
- *Files exchange*: This allows the users to load files from their computers and share them with the instructors or other students in the course.
- *Multiple format support*: The platform must offer support to multiple file formats such as HTML, Word, Excel, Acrobat, among others.
- *Synchronous communication tools (chat)*: Used for exchanging messages among participants.

---

[3]Mahara is an open source e-portfolio, weblog, resume builder and social networking system, connecting users and creating online learner communities. Mahara is designed to provide users with the tools to demonstrate their life-long learning, skills and development over time to selected audiences.

- *Asynchronous communication tool (electronic mail or messenger)*: An e-mail can be read or sent within a course. E-mail tools permit to read and send messages only from within the course or alternatively they make it possible to communicate with external mail addresses, enabling course users to communicate more easily.
- *Multimedia presentation services (videoconference, video, digital board, etc.)*: This refers to the use of videoconferencing for communication between the system and the user, or between two users; a digital board can be used by the instructor in a virtual lesson, as a synchronous communication service between students and teachers, as the applications sharing and voice chat.
- *Blogs/online logs*: Tools that allow students and teachers to write notes on a log, which take several forms in their educational sense, known as edublogs:

    - Subject weblogs, in which the teacher logs comments, asks for students' opinions, proposes activities, calendar, etc.
    - Individual student weblogs in which students are asked to enter periodically monitored and supported not only in terms of the topics or contents but also in relation to copyright, style guidance, quoting sources, etc.
    - Group weblogs, in which students acting as an editorial team edit entries related to the established topics, styles and procedures.

Blogs, weblogs or binnacles are most likely the greatest exponents of the new Web 2.0 (De la Torre 2006) which allows individual or group writing in internet periodically very easily and for free, allowing debate or comments on each of the topics covered or messages received.

- *Wikis*: Tools that facilitate the elaboration of online documents in a collaborative manner.

Wikis have become an alternative source of knowledge to the classical ones, adding a wider range of connotations which make knowledge more subjective. A clear example is Wikipedia, an internet encyclopaedia made up by the contributions of any of its visitors willing to share their knowledge. Being built by everyone may on the one hand lead to find erroneous information in it, but on the other hand this very fact is being considered as positive for the learning process, as it fosters the students' rational and critical awareness in their approach to information, contrasting the different sources.

- *Database*: These are tools to help fill in database tables in a collaborative way to share information. The creation of databases with a structure defined by the trainer and the registers filled in by the students in tables allows fill-in a database with formatted information according to the typified structure of the database.

7.6.2 Productivity-Based Tools

- *Personal notes or favourites*: Bookmarks help the student easily get back to a web page visited. Such marks may refer to a course or to any other topic, but in any case they are personal and private even when they can be shared with the teacher, colleagues or the whole class.

- *Calendar and progress review*: Calendar utilities that allow the student to plan ahead in time the course activities.
- *Help in using the platform*: Guidance and help in the use of the learning system for the participants, which normally include tutorials, user's manuals, and online, telephone or e-mail help.
- *Course browser*: To help select and find courses by entering a search criterion.
- *Synchronization mechanism and offline work*: Students may work disconnected from the platform, once they have downloaded the course partially or completely and work on it. The next time they connect, the point at which they stopped working online will be synchronized or updated. Alternatively, the course content may also be found in a CD-ROM linked to the online course contents.
- *Edition control, expired pages and broken links*: These tools edit pages when the deadline is met, so they are not accessible afterwards; they also run tests to locate and correct links to nonexistent pages.
- *Site news*: Tools to keep users informed of the latest platform's news.
- *Updating notices, forum messages and automatic delivery*: Every time a platform event concerning its users takes place, an automatic message is generated informing them, so they do not need to spend time to find out such relevant events.
- *Content syndication support (RSS, News, PodCast, etc.)*: These allow including in the platform syndicated contents, offered from outside or inside the platform, or even creating contents that may syndicate from other platforms. Thanks to the aggregators or feeds readers (programmes or sites that read RSS sources), summaries of the wished websites can be obtained from the operative system desktop, e-mail programmes or through web applications acting as content aggregators. RSS (Really Simple Syndication) usually refer to textual contents, while PodCast refer to multimedia contents downloads (image and/or sound) through syndication, which in both cases is done using XML files.

7.6.3 Student Involvement Tools

- *Work groups*: These can organize a class in groups so the teacher can assign the corresponding tasks or projects to each of them.
- *Self-assessment*: Such tools let students practise or revise online tests and their score on them, which are not part of the teachers' assessment.
- *Student's corner (Study groups)*: Common areas for students to get together in study groups, clubs or collaborative working groups.
- *Student's profile*: Common areas where students may make themselves known: show their work, put up their photos, personal preferences, topics of interest, or other personal data.

7.6.4 Support Tools

- *Users' authentication*: Process by which users gain access to their course entering a user's name and a password. It also refers to the process responsible for creating and maintaining such user names and passwords.
- *Assignment of privileges according to user's role*: These are the utilities to assign access privileges to a course, to its contents and tools, according to the user's role, for example: student, teacher, course creator, assistant professor, administrator, etc.
- *Registration of students*: The registration of students to a course can be done in different ways: teachers can include students to the course or students can register themselves or delete the registrations, if such options are available, or registrations can be read in a database.
- *Audits*: These allow consulting all the actions done by the platform participants, and obtain statistics on its use; they also provide administrators with information on the use of the system.

7.6.5 Course and Content Editing Tools

- *Automated tests and results*: These allow teacher create, administer and assess the tests done, which can be auto-corrected, showing the solution or comments, as the teacher prefers.
- *Course administration*: The course administration tools not only allow teachers to monitor the progress of students through the course material, but they also allow students to check their own progress through different assignments and tests.
- *Course creator support*: Help and support to the course creators for administering them. These may be in forums, online, by telephone, or e-mail.
- *Online assessment tools*: Teachers' help tools to monitor the students' progress during the course.
- *Student's monitoring*: These provide an additional analysis of the course materials use.

7.6.6 Tools for Study Programmes Design

- *Conformance with accessibility*: This means conformity with standards that allow people with disabilities to access online information (Krug 2001).
- *Reusing and sharing contents*: This refers to which contents can be shared with another teacher, in another course and in a different centre. The system should allow sharing open content files and repositories.
- *Course templates*: Tools for creating an online course.

- *Curriculum administration*: This provides a customized curriculum to students based on the educative program prerequisites or activities, on previous assignments or on test results.
- *Environment's customization (look and feel)*: Personalizing the system allows to modify the graphic appearance of courses presentation, so they may show the organization's image.
- *Educative design tools*: Help tools for course designers to create learning sequences, templates or assistants.
- *Conformance with educative design*: Conformity with standards IMS, AICC and ADL to share learning materials with other e-learning platforms.

7.6.7 CMS Knowledge Management

Most of the multiple existing Knowledge Management (KM) definitions involve the gathering, organization, classification and distribution of knowledge understood as the result of an information treatment process and the interaction of the group of users interested in such information.

The technology of knowledge must consider computer methods and techniques which facilitate the interaction and collaboration of users by means of a robust support structure and efficient users' communities for the storage and treatment of information, which should also meet the social, financial and academic needs of the users (Cobos et al. 2002).

The existing KM tools differ in the importance given to their goals; therefore some show particular emphasis on collaborative work towards the generation of knowledge for the community, while others give priority to generating knowledge structures. Depending on their priorities, they can be classified as follows:

- *Knowledge integral systems*: These provide both collaborative work mechanisms and internal organization of common memory mechanisms. The knowledge units managing these tools are documents in any format, including web pages and normally represent the knowledge structure hierarchically, in what is known as the knowledge tree, but also through hierarchical networks of connected nodules which facilitate interaction and collaboration among users by means of forums, or discussion groups. Some examples of this system are Meta4, KnowNet, Microsoft SharePoint Portal Server, KnowCat (Knowledge Catalyser), a system developed by the Universidad Autónoma of Madrid and KnowNet of the ESPRIT project (Alaman and Cobos 1999).
- *Systems focused on generating knowledge structures*: This group comprises three big groups of systems:

  - *The mediator information system:* Their main aim is to provide users with an interface for consultation, normally through a particular dominion on the web, with heterogeneous and disseminated sources, though it looks like a homogeneous and centralized system. Knowledge collection and integration is processed a priori without allowing the final system's users interaction. The description and indexation of the knowledge sources and content are realized in languages that allow connecting information, such as the standard RDF,[4] an example of these systems is WebKB developed by the School of Information Technology of the Griffith University of Australia. These types of systems focus on creating a virtual structure that relates and facilitates knowledge clearly, not giving much importance to the interaction among users.

– *Digital libraries*: Systems comprising the digital communication and storage of information technologies to reproduce emulate and extend the service provided by conventional libraries, such as gathering, cataloguing, administering and distributing bibliographic information. These systems can collect information from distributed information sources and allow users to make up their own digital libraries. An example of such systems is COSPEX (Conceptual SPace Explorer), a system for creating a private digital library, and DSpace and Eprints, systems to make up a digital library with open source software.

– *Ontology-based systems*: The first application of ontology in computer systems was in Artificial Intelligence systems. Later on they have been used in diverse computer systems, and are the basis of diverse knowledge management systems, such as business fields, in the intelligent management of news (Caldwell et al. 2003) or for wider uses such as the definition of conceptual models, among others. In such systems, the dominion's structure is known a priori, and therefore they support automatic search and facilitate the decision-making process by applying an inference search engine to ontologically structured databases. Cyc OpenCyc is an example of such systems.

• Systems focused on knowledge collaborative work: These systems give particular importance to the community, the user and their characteristics, and can be classified as follows:

– *Shared spaces*: These offer a shared space for user interaction to share knowledge or create new knowledge in a collaborative manner, through the following functionalities:

  (a) Communication tools: messenger, forums or chats.
  (b) Content teaching tools: files, contacts, or links.
  (c) Tools for joint activities: Wikis, group calendars or digital boards.

An example of these systems is BSCW (Basic Support for Cooperative Work).

– *Recommendations systems*: Systems made up from the collaborative screening of information, so the user may receive that information most relevant to their

---

[4]RDF: Resource Description Framework, this is a W3C recommendation (World Wide Web Consortium) which provides a technology for metadata description in the Web, the language syntax is based on XML (Extensible Markup Language), which is based on SGML (Standard Generalized Markup Language). RDF is a metadata language for describing resources, a syntactical proposal to define relations and descriptions which can be exchanged and automatically processed by computers.

interests, likes and preferences. These systems refer both to systems recommending lists of products, and those helping users to evaluate such products. The system included in Amazon is a good example, the knowledge-oriented NewKnow developed by NewKnow Network. This tool classifies knowledge in categories and offers the possibility of establishing relations among documents, originated from the users' consultation of the documents.

– *Collaborative learning*: Learning, as a social activity implies that a community of users, students, may share knowledge and acquire new knowledge through the so-called social construction of knowledge (Jonassen et al. 1993). The learning process in these systems is developed by means of integration, administration and distribution mechanisms of knowledge among users, students and teachers. These systems are characterized by having:

(a) An environment for the students' community with a collaborative toolkit available to facilitate their continuous work, as well as the exchange of ideas and knowledge.
(b) Knowledge structured in themes, sequences, or discussion forums, in which the units of knowledge are not only the documents, but also exercises, workshops, tests, notes, etc.

Examples of this system are Moodle and ATutor, Sakai among others.

7.7 E-Learning-Oriented KMS

Digital resources like texts, videos, images, audio and their combinations are really widely used within the traditional educative models and e-learning, but the diversity of formats and the lack of information about the resource reduce the extent to which this material can be used and reutilized. In order to promote the learning resources, these must be conceived as learning objects (LO). LO are small pieces of content used to back-up learning, which may be used in different contexts as they are described by metadata. LO must be created with functional requisites such as accessibility, reusability and interoperability, and with two basic principles: granularity and composition.

For resources to be easily searched, used, reused and shared, they should be centralized in object repositories (LOR), accessible through the internet, which act as portals with a web-based user interface, and having search and resources cataloguing services. LOR also offer the possibility of performing federate searches over other LOR. CAREO, MERLOT and ARIADNE are good examples, among many others. Chapter 2 describes the use of learning object repositories in virtual learning environments.

The LOR catalogue is made up from each LO metadata, although in some deposits the object is only linked and stored in another Internet site. If a LOR meets the e-learning standards, it will be technologically capable of communicating data and contents, both to LMS and to LCMS, export or import content packages to be used in a course.

The potential use of LOR to manage learning content and prepare it to be processed in other applications provides a relevant meaning to content development and improvement. Thus, the application of ontology in resource description standardises a semantic nucleus, which facilitates the search and recovery of learning objects in e-learning content deposits and in the semantic web, since even if the resources are created and described by metadata, it is still very difficult to find and recover resources; this is specially so for those systems helping users find information contained in the Web, as the linguistic problem, the inconsistent use of terminology, and the limitation of search engines to "understand/interpret" what human minds mean and want, result in recovering irrelevant information.

The semantic web is a proposal to structure the resources available, v them to their semantic meaning, so later on software agents will be able to analyse and execute search operations with better results (Santacruz-Valencia et al. 2004).

7.7.1 Recommendations for Creating LORs

In the creation of a reusable learning object, the developers should consider its double function, on the one hand it will take part of a bigger unit (in one or more courses), and it must also be independent with its own granularity level. The following are a few specifications developers should consider during the learning object generation process:

- Use appropriate formats for information presentation, for easy reading and comprehension must outweigh other considerations.
- A learning object must be self-contained and highly reusable, and external references to the very object are not allowed, this information must be included by the integrator the moment the course is contextualized.
- The use of language must be consistent, avoiding synonyms that may lead to confusion.
- The language should be appropriate for a large audience, avoiding excessive specialization always according to the content level.
- Avoid presenting dense texts which may be difficult to read on the screen, since most learning objects will be consumed via web.

References

Alamán, X., & Cobos, R. (1999). KnowCat: a web application for knowledge organization. Proceedings of the World-Wide Web and Conceptual Modeling (WWWCM'99) Papers' Case Studies.

Berlanga Flores, A. J., & García Peñalvo, F. J. (2004). Introducción a los Estándares y Especificaciones para Ambientes e-learning. Tendencias en el Desarrollo de Aplicaciones Web. *Páginas* 25–37. Departamento de Informática y Automática de la Universidad de Salamanca. ISBN 84-688-7872-3. http://zarza.fis.usal.es/~fgarcia/doctorado/iuce/Estandares.pdf

Caldwell, N., Clarkson, J., & Huxor, A. P. (2003). Web-based knowledge management for distributed design. IEEE Intelligent Systems, Vol. 15, 3, pp. 40–47.

Cobos, R., Esquivel, J. A., & Alamán, X. (2002). Herramientas informáticas para la Gestión del Conocimiento: un estudio de la situación actual. Novatica 155 pp. 20–26.

CUE (2003). Learning management systems for the rest of us. Corporate University Enterprise. http://www.uv.es/ticape/pdf/CUE-LMS%20White%20Paper.pdf

De la Torre, A. (2006). Web Educativa 2.0. Edutec. Revista Electrónica de Tecnología Educativa, 20. http://www.uib.es/depart/gte/gte/edutec-e/revelec20/anibal20.htm

Hernandez, E. (2003). Estándares y Especificaciones de E-learning: Ordenando el Desorden. Universitat de Valencia. http://www.uv.es/ticape/docs/eduardo.pdf

Jonassen, D., Mayes, T., & McAleese, R. (1993) A manifesto for a constructivist approach to uses of technology in higher education. In T.M. Duffy, J. Lowyck, & D.H. Jonassen (Eds.), Designing environments for constructive learning. Springer-Verlag, Heidelberg, pp. 231–247.

Khan, B. H. (2001). Web-based Training. New Jersey: Educational Technology Publications.

Krug, S. (2001). No me hagas pensar. Madrid: Prentice Hall.

O'Really, T. (2005). What is Web 2.0: Design patterns and business models for the next generation. http://www.oreillynet.com/pub/a/oreilly/tim/news/2005/09/30/what-is-web-20.html

Robertson, J. (2003a). So, what is a content management system? Step Two. http://www.steptwo.com.au/papers/kmc_what/index.html

Robertson, J. (2003b). Looking towards the future of CM. Step Two. http://www.steptwo.com.au/papers/cmb_future/index.html

Santacruz-Valencia, L. P., Aedo, I., & Delgado Kloos, C. (2004). Objetos de aprendizaje: Tendencias dentro de la web semántica. http://www.rediris.es/rediris/boletin/66-67/ponencia18.pdf

Chapter 8
E-Learning Standards for Content Management

Salvador Sánchez-Alonso, María Gertrudis López, and Dirk Frosch-Wilke

> *Historically, the success of automation has relied on two factors. The first is an understanding of the assembly process, first discovered and performed by hand, then captured, studied, and expressed in a technology. The second factor is the standardization of component properties [...] that creates a marketplace in which many vendors can create components competitively. The broad availability of inexpensive standardized components makes assembly processes easier to express in concrete terms.*
>
> David Wiley

Abstract This chapter demonstrates that standardization is a very important subject in an e-learning context. Many e-learning systems and resources have emerged during the last decade. Thereby often economical as well as technical problems became significant due to missing standards. Economical reasons (e.g., high costs for producing learning material) often demand for reusability of learning resources. This in turn immediately requests for technical aspects like interoperability between systems of different vendors and discoverability of learning content.

For this reason a multiplicity of initiatives have been started to define standards in different e-learning areas (e.g., learning content, learning processes, students' data, and repositories) in the past.

Based on the fundamental concept of learning objects, this chapter describes many of these standardization efforts, their correlations, and the main actors in detail.

8.1 Introduction

The British Standard Institute defines standard as "a published document that contains a technical specification or other precise criteria designed to be used consistently as a rule, guideline, or definition. Standards are created by bringing together

S. Sánchez-Alonso (✉)
Computer Science Department, University of Alcalá, Alcalá de Henares, Henares, Spain
e-mail: salvador.sanchez@uah.es

N. Ferran and J. Minguillón (eds.), *Content Management for E-Learning*,
DOI 10.1007/978-1-4419-6959-0_8, © Springer Science+Business Media, LLC 2011

the experience and expertise of all interested parties such as the producers, sellers, buyers, users and regulators of a particular material, product, process or service."

A good example of a standard is the formats and measures for electrical pins and plugs that allow to fit plugs into the sockets (both usually made by different manufacturers) at the time of connecting an electrical device to the electrical supply network. This example also explains the difficulties that involve the lack of normalization. In this sense, most of us have experienced the frustration (during a travel to another country) of seeing how our electrical device plugs do not match with the local sockets. In this case, the problem is due to the existence of many different local-scope plug standards: three mixed pins in the United States, three gross flat pins in the United Kingdom, two gross round pins in the European Union, three fine round pins in Switzerland, etc. Unfortunately, the universal consensus permitting to use the same plugs around the world is still pending (Fig. 8.1).

The elaboration of a standard is a process that involves time and participation of many different people and organizations. In the first place, the generalized use of a product generates different partnerships and associations of users. These are the first organizations that after a period of use, sometimes disordered, promote the normalization, producing technical documents to achieve interoperability between the products of its members. These documents, frequently of internal character, are usually named specifications, and even though they cannot be considered standards, they are frequently the roots of a later standard. Therefore, specifications do not cover the needs of all the users, but only those of the users in the consortium where the standard is formulated. It is important to remark that a specification is always associated with committees not accredited for the publication and formal diffusion of standards, such as IETF (*Internet Engineering Task Force*), OMG (*Object Management Group*), or W3C (*World Wide Web Consortium*).

From one or more specifications over the same kind of products, certification entities such as IEEE,[1] CEN,[2] or ISO,[3] with the aid of experts in the matter, improve the specification to cover the necessities of all their users and potential manufacturers of the product. The full task of creating a standard begins with the composition of a first draft, which is gradually refined, each version of it being distributed and improved. When the current version of the evolving draft is considered mature, it is transformed

Fig. 8.1 Electrical plugs standards in the EU, United Kingdom, Switzerland and the USA

---

[1] http://www.ieee.org

[2] http://www.cenorm.be

[3] http://www.iso.org

Table 8.1 Differences between specifications and standards

Capture the approximate consensus	Capture the general acceptance
Evolve quickly	Evolve slowly
Facilitate	Regulate
Manage the risk on a short term basis	Manage the risk on a long term basis
Experimental	Conclusive

into a standard proposal and submitted to a certification entity for acceptation (in fact it might be the same entity that managed the preparation of the drafts). If the proposal is finally accepted, it is formally recognized as a standard, officially published and its diffusion and adoption promoted.

The following table summarizes the differences between standards and specifications (Table 8.1).

In the case of e-learning, standardization becomes necessary because of the availability of a greater number of educational materials in digital format, but also because of the development of a real market for learning and content management platforms. The major advantage of e-learning compared to the previous concept of education based on courses, and the exhaustion of the traditional high-cost courses, have promoted the emergence of this new approach, frequently based on the fragmentation of educative resources commonly known as "learning objects."

8.2   Learning Objects and Reusability

From the beginnings of the application of information and telecommunication technologies to learning and teaching processes, experts in the field have been involved in a great controversy over the "learning object" concept. The different visions that each author or institution have about what is (or must be) a learning object are sometimes so different that it often becomes very difficult to give a shared definition. In this section, we will analyze some of the more widely used definitions to finally provide our own as a summary of them. Additional discussion about this concept can be found in Chapter 3 "Learning objects, content management and e-learning."

Among the many definitions of learning object, the one given by Mills (2002) defines learning object as:

> "An object or set of resources that can be used for facilitating intended learning outcomes, and can be extracted and reused in other learning environments"

This definition suggest that the use of learning objects allows to reuse contents created for a certain educational experience in different learning contexts, probably unknown to the original author. Another definition, in fact one of the most referenced and consistent with other definitions provided by other authors, describes a learning object this way:

> "An independent and self-standing unit of learning content that is predisposed to reuse in multiple instructional contexts" (Polsani 2003)

Another widely known definition is that included in the IEEE learning object metadata (LOM) standard. For this standard, a learning object:

"Any entity, digital or non-digital, that may be used for learning, education or training"

However, it is important to mention the digital nature of learning objects, since the existing definitions often obviate this characteristic. The digital character of learning objects is enforced in the definition by Wiley (2002):

"Learning object is any digital resource that can be reused to support learning"

It is important to observe that the resources considered as learning objects should be described by external descriptions called metadata. These metadata are descriptions about the learning objects (although the term metadata is not exclusive for learning objects) with the following characteristics:

- Metadata "says something" about the learning object, in a general sense.
- Metadata are physically external to the educational resource; they can be in a separate file or be obtained from a different service.
- Metadata use a technical format for their expression and for their interchange, often languages defined over XML.
- A series of descriptors, fields or standardized elements allow metadata to obtain a certain level of interoperability between different systems.

As a summary of the preceding discussion, we propose a learning object definition that not only combines harmoniously several of the previous definitions, but also has a clear orientation toward certain management operations of educational resources, such as search automation and educational resources composition, functions that are considered very important by many authors. This is the definition of learning object that will be used in this chapter:

"A learning object is an educational unit in digital format, independent, self-content, persistent and predisposed to be reused in different educational contexts thanks to the inclusion of self-descriptive information in the form of metadata"

8.2.1   Learning Objects Reusability

The idea of learning resources reusability is not new. It is in fact as old as education itself. Books and other materials have always been reusable resources. However, the zero costs of reproduction of digital materials, and the global scope of computer networks, make possible a different kind of digital resources reusability. Today, digital resources can be reused again and again to compose more complex resources which are, of course, cheaper to produce than traditional courses. Therefore, the creation and publication of an educational experience in digital format implies creation, discovery, and/or composition of learning objects. The reusability of these units, and the possibility of assembling them at will to construct more complex materials, is one of the more outstanding and attractive characteristics of current e-learning technologies.

The term reuse can be formally defined as "to use something, either with its original functionality or with other purposes." However, the simple use of a previously existing Web content is not new. In fact, this form of reuse started with the Internet and the rest of similar systems of digital distribution. Therefore, it makes sense to think about the differential qualities that justify a new paradigm, the learning objects paradigm, and not only the extension of existing reusability paradigm. At least two novel aspects differentiate learning objects reusability from the reusability of digital materials in a general sense:

1. Learning objects reusability is based on the creation and use of external descriptions of the proper resources called metadata. Without these metadata, there does not exist any novel aspect in the learning objects paradigm; we would be, instead, in the typical case of Web contents reusability, commonplace from the origins of the Internet.
2. Metadata, if provided in appropriate languages, allow developing new technological tools aimed at facilitating and improving learning object searching and management processes.

Therefore, metadata are essence and not a mere facility in the learning objects paradigm. Metadata are in fact a fundamental element of value. Consequently, a digital resource with an excellent pedagogical design will not be per se a good learning object: it will be a good learning object in proportion to the quality of its metadata. However, what is metadata quality? The answer is very simple: the capacity of metadata to provide information that helps improve the current technological Web tools to search and assemble learning resources. This implies the following assumption:

> "Learning objects metadata are (or must be) used to construct technology tools oriented to improve searching processes"

The preceding ideas clearly delineate what a learning object is, and the role of reusability in relation to LOM. Therefore, the new characteristics of learning object reusability as a scientific and technological endeavor must have a solid justification. In the following section, we will sketch two possible justifications of reusability (which are not mutually exclusive) from a pedagogical and technological perspective: the first one from an economic viewpoint, and the second one from a technical point of view.

8.2.2 Economic Justification of Reusability

As introduction to this section, let us examine the following reflection about reusability by Stephen Downes, one of the most influential authors in the e-learning field:

> "...there are thousands of colleges and universities, each of which teaches, say, 'Introductory Trigonometry.' And each trigonometry course in each of these institutions

describes, say, the sine wave function. Moreover – because the properties of sine wave functions remains [*sic*] constant from institution to institution – we can assume that each institution's description of sine wave functions is more or less the same as each other institution's. What we have, then, are thousands of similar descriptions of sine wave functions. Now suppose that each of these institutions decided to put its 'Introductory Trigonometry' course online [...] So now what we have are thousands of similar descriptions of sine wave functions available online. [...] The world does not need thousands of similar descriptions of sine wave functions available online. Rather, what the world needs is one – or maybe a dozen, at most – descriptions of sine wave functions available online.

The reasons are manifest. If some educational content, such as a description of sine wave functions, is available online, then it is available worldwide. So even if only one such piece of educational content were created, it could be accessed by each of the thousands of educational institutions teaching the same material. Moreover, educational content is not inexpensive to produce. Even a plain web page, authored by a mathematics professor, can cost hundreds of dollars. Include graphics and a little animation and the price is double. Add an interactive exercise and the price is quadrupled.

Suppose that one description of the sine wave function is produced. A high quality and fully interactive piece of learning material could be produced for, say, a thousand dollars. If a thousand institutions share this one item, the cost is a dollar per institution. But if each of a thousand institutions produces a similar item, then each institution must pay a thousand dollars, or the institutions, collectively, must pay a million dollars. For one lesson. In one course."

(Downes 2001)

There is not very much to add to Downes' eloquent description from an economic perspective. He emphasizes the "production cost" of learning materials, and the economies generated by the reusability. According to Longmire (2000), to model didactic contents in form of learning objects produces very important benefits in terms of cost, development time, and learning effectiveness. Among these benefits, it is possible to emphasize the following two:

- *Facility to update, search, and manage the contents.* LOM provides valuable information about the resources with no need to evaluate their content, thus facilitating their management. A typical analogy about this is a label yogurt: if it did not exist, it would be necessary to open all yogurts of a refrigerator until finding one with the desired flavor, since it is impossible to know its content otherwise. In this case, the yogurt metadata (flavor, expiry date, etc.) are in their label.
- *Increase of value.* From a business point of view, the value of the content created increases whenever a learning object is reused, as the design and development costs are simultaneously avoided. This allows an easier return of investment in the learning object and increases the possibilities of selling those contents that can be used in different contexts.

So far in this section, we have emphasized the cost benefits related to reusability. However, there are also technical criteria that complement and are associated to this point of view, as we will see next.

8.2.3 Technical Justification of Reusability

The use of learning objects allows reducing the time used in the search and access to the educational resources, thus facilitating the creation of new contents in electronic format. Therefore, it is possible to consider that, in addition to the economic reasons given in the previous section, significant technical reasons justify the design of educational resources in the form of reusable learning objects. Some of these are:

- *Flexibility.* If the resource is designed from the beginning to be reused in different contexts, it will be more easily reusable than other resources designed in a traditional way, as these would have to be adapted to each new context.
- *Personalization.* Those resources designed to be reused are ideal to build tailored educational materials. Reusable learning objects facilitate the fulfillment and planning of learning based on competences, a growing model that represents an alternative to the traditional learning model. This model proposes the acquisition of certain competences, regardless of the discipline. Let us explain this with an example. Imagine a programmer working for a company that develops financial software. Let us think that this programmer has been entrusted by his/her company to conduct a programming project, for which to make use of interpolation methods is needed. As our programmer does not have the knowledge about this particular issue, he/she will need to learn the fundamentals of numerical methods of interpolation (and only this). However, the "traditional" alternative would consist of following a standard course on numerical methods (if such course does exists) that probably would include other families of numerical methods different to the interpolation. It is even possible that such course would not deal with interpolation methods in enough detail. Unfortunately, that is not what our programmer needs and demands. Instead, a tailored course based on learning objects would provide the programmer with all the knowledge on this specific matter and only this, avoiding other related contents not relevant for the task assigned. In fact, to compare a personalized education based on competences to enrolling in a traditional course would be like comparing a tailored suit with the prêt a porter fashion at the department stores.
- *Uniformity.* Reusing learning objects helps an organization to keep their educational contents uniform regardless the course where a particular learning object has been integrated. Using the same learning object (e.g., one that contains biographical information on an historical figure) allows a company to guarantee that this information will always be the same regardless the training course followed by its employees (supposing that several training courses reference to the same historical figure).
- *Rapidity.* Making use of reusable learning objects accelerate the creation process of new contents because authors no longer create materials from scratch.

All the above emphasize the key element of learning objects: its predisposition for reusability. However, so far there exists no general acceptance for the capacity of a learning object to be reused. It is desirable, in any case, a certain commitment between the willingness of a learning object to be reused in different contexts and its capacity for effectively achieving its educational objectives in those contexts in which it is used.

8.3   An Introduction to E-Learning Standards

The new learning approach described, based on the existence, shared use, and reuse of learning objects, has great benefits. However, the use of learning objects is not sufficient for transforming traditional teaching into a new teaching approach providing all those benefits. Some bases of interoperability and compatibility are necessary to permit that components developed by different entities can interchange information and be used as a whole without modifications. Here is exactly where e-learning standards play a role, facilitating the learning object plugs to fit in the management platforms' sockets.

During the last decade, many electronic learning systems and resources have emerged. Their existence and sometimes-chaotic use raised problems of resources reuse or interoperability, just to mention some. To attain these problems, many organizations and international consortia have been encouraging and sponsoring numerous activities oriented to standardization, promoting the development of different recommendations about the use of learning objects and designs.

The existence of standards defining particular aspects such as the structure as well as the content of the metadata and the manner to pack learning objects or the content sequence is essential for the successful development of e-learning systems. The benefits derived of standardization have been profusely described and are commonly known as "–ilities" (*accessibility, affordability, durability, extensibility, discoverability, interoperability, manageability,* and *reusability*):

- Accessibility: the content will be available from anywhere at any time.
- Interoperability: components developed by different vendors can be used together and interchange information.
- Reusability: as discussed in the preceding section, a manner to save efforts when new educational contents are created, but also a solution to the so-called teacher bandwidth problem. *Teacher bandwidth* is a term coined by David Wiley to describe the number of students a teacher can service, which can be seen as a bottleneck that limits the number of people who can gain access to educational opportunities in traditional learning scenarios.
- Extensibility: understood as the capacity of easily creating new educational contents through the assembly and construction of module-based contents.
- Discoverability: facility to locate contents stored in repositories that use metadata as cataloguing form.
- Affordability: reasonable costs thanks to the standardization that reduces the development expenses.

- Manageability: facility to manage the contents since the design in small modules facilitates content changes and updates.
- Durability: standard content development avoids contents to become obsolete due to platform changes.

Additionally, standardization promotes communication and interchange, facilitating the organizations that generate contents to obtain additional benefits from their investments. Finally, the standardization promotes the development of automated tools for creation and management of standardized educational contents.

8.3.1 *Main Actors in the Standardization Efforts*

The efforts in the development of standards and specifications for learning objects and designs have been mainly promoted by North American and European organizations. Overall, these organizations carry out great investments in their employees' training (governmental institutions) or in their customers (universities, training companies, etc.) and they make an extensive use of educational software. Next, we will study the contributions of the institutions and organizations involved in e-learning standardization. The study does not try to be exhaustive nor to refer to every organization which has participated in some manner proposing, modifying, or writing up normalization models. For those interested in this subject, it is recommended to access to the much more exhaustive and updated work by the CEN/ISSS learning technology standards observatory.[4]

The IEEE Learning Technologies Standardization Committee (*IEEE LTSC*[5]) is one of the first organizations that were involved in the standardization process. Its main objective is the development of technical standards, practical recommendations, and guides for software components, tools, technologies, and design methods that facilitate the development, implementation, support, and interoperability of teaching as well as learning software systems. The IEEE LTSC works internally by means of tasks distribution in working groups (WGs). Each different group works either in needs exploration, compilation of draft documents, or in gathering experiences and expert opinions. Although years ago the WGs of IEEE LTSC used to work in all the aspects related to computer-based learning, now they have both transferred the study of several aspects to other institutions such as ISO and given up the efforts in certain areas. Currently, IEEE LTSC interests are focused in a few well-defined areas: the production and diffusion of a metadata standard for learning objects (WG12), the study of digital rights expression languages to support technology-aided learning (WG4), the production of a standard of computer-managed instruction functions (WG11),

---

[4]http://www.cen-ltso.net
[5]http://ieeeltsc.org/

and the definition of a standard for learning-oriented competency definitions (WG20).

As it was said before, the IEEE LTSC has begun to transfer a big part of its activity toward *ISO* (International Standards Organization), establishing a specific subcommittee denominated ISO JTC1-SC36 on Learning Technology. The works of this subcommittee began in 1999 with the objective of taking over all aspects relative to the standardization of teaching and learning technologies, as well as their interoperability. ISO's interest is not only at a technical level, but it also looks at the cultural and social aspects.

The Global Learning Consortium *IMS*,[6] a community of hardware and software manufacturers, education institutes, publishers, governmental agencies, system integrators, multimedia content providers, and other smaller consortia, constitutes today the most active initiative in the specification and standard development in e-learning area. IMS actively collaborates with many other organizations to guarantee the compatibility and quality of the specifications produced. The major efforts of IMS address the specification of a content package specification for digital resources, the definition of educational modeling languages (EMLs), questionnaires definition, as well as group and student information management. At present, IMS develops specifications that allow eliminating obstacles to use information technologies applied to teaching at a great scale. In Europe, the IMS UK Centre collaborates with other active projects in this area at European level. This centre, refunded as CETIS (*Centre for Educational Technology Interoperability Standards*), currently explores the potential impact of information and communication technologies over learning as in the proper educational system.

The *AICC*[7] (*Aviation Industry Computer-Based Training Committee*) develops guidelines for the aviation industry about the implementation, delivery, and evaluation of computer- and Web-based training and other related technologies. AICC, which has been serving the aviation industry since 1988, is one of the most important consumers of educational software at a global level. It maintains a close relationship with the ADL initiative of the United States Department of Defense.

Another major purchaser and consumer of both learning software educational resources materials is the United States Department of Defense, which develops specifications and standards that allow the reuse and interoperability of educational contents through an initiative called *ADL*.[8] ADL (*Advanced Distributed Learning*) deals with Web-based education, coordinating its activities with other organizations such as IEEE, IMS, and AICC. The more important work of ADL is the SCORM reference model, a proposal that encloses a reference model for learning objects, a runtime environment, and an aggregation content model oriented to the shared use of learning objects.

---

[6]http://www.imsglobal.org

[7]http://www.aicc.org

[8]http://www.adlnet.org

Simultaneously, many EU-funded projects have dedicated effort to the development of learning technology-related specifications. Some results were later used to elaborate specifications and standards. Among the most relevant EU-funded projects, we can name *Prometeus* (*PROmoting Multimedia access to Education and Training in the European Society*), *GESTALT* (*Getting Educational Systems Talking Across Leading edge Technologies*), and *Ariadne* I and II (later Ariadne Foundation). Current European Union policy toward e-learning is not to duplicate efforts already in course somewhere in the world, but also to coordinate both the research projects funded under the EU framework programs and the internal programs of member countries. The aim is mainly to find collaboration lines between projects and to reuse the results of previous projects. In this way, the European Agency for Interoperability of Educative Standards (CEN/ISSS) has been promoting the *CEN/ISSS Learning Technologies Workshop* since 1999 to encourage the reusability and interoperability of educational resources, as well as the collaborative education model, the creation, and use of metadata for educational contents and the educative process quality, always considering the European cultural diversity.

Outside Europe, other relevant projects are *GEM*[9] (*Gateway to Educational Materials*) which provides a framework for publishing and searching educational resources available on the Internet, and *EdNA*[10] (*Education Network Australia*), oriented to promote Internet as a tool for computer-based learning among the Australian educational community, from students to content providers.

8.3.2   Main Areas of Standardization

Current e-learning specifications and standards cover different areas, but mainly all target the interoperability between different elements related to the content, the students' data, or the proper learning process. Most efforts are involved in an interdependency network that requires the collaboration of all organisms involved.

8.3.2.1   Standardization of Content-Related Elements

Metadata are commonly defined as *data about data*. Furthermore, metadata are structured so that they facilitate the management and location of resources on the Internet. In the particular case of educational resources in digital format, a metadata

---

[9] http://www.thegateway.org

[10] http://www.edna.edu.au

record should be composed of a set of fields that includes information about the content of the resource, its copyright information, its location, and other relevant elements that make sense from an educational point of view. The European project ARIADNE promoted the definition of these elements for learning objects and its results submitted in 1998 to the IEEE LTSC, to serve as the basis for the elaboration of the *Learning Object Metadata* (LOM) standard. Other efforts have addressed the compatibility between LOM and Dublin Core,[11] a more general metadata standard, oriented to describe all types of resources and not only learning objects.

Another important field of standardization is the systematization of the aggregation and disassembly processes, as well as the methods to export and import resources to exchange content between Learning Management Systems. One key piece in this field is the *IMS Content Packaging* specification that normalizes the internal structure and organization of learning resources packages by defining how the content tree must be represented. IMS Content Packaging has served, since their initial versions, as a basis for *SCORM CAM*, the SCORM content aggregation model. Other elements that come from the AICC CMI (Computer Manager Instructions) Guidelines for Interoperability facilitate the integration in SCORM 2004 of content sequencing functions that depend on the student's behavior, associating "objectives" and "prerequisites" to content package units. SCORM 2004 has adapted its Content Aggregation Model (CAM) including a new version of IMS Content Packaging and the specification for content sequencing *IMS Simple Sequencing*.

Another very important aspect is to define communication protocols in a runtime environment. The AICC *CMI Guidelines for Interoperability* proposes a mechanism to launch contents in a Learning Management System, a data model, and a communication mechanism between both elements that permit the content to ask for and to write information in the Learning Management System (LMS). These elements have been incorporated to the SCORM Runtime Environment (SCORM RTE), and served as the basis for the creation of the *IEEE P1484.11 Computer Managed Instruction Standard*.

IMS Question & Test Interoperability defines interoperability rules for auto-evaluations. This specification is aimed at promoting the interchange of question sets (as well as the answers to these) among different Learning Management Systems.

In October 2006, the IMS Global Learning Consortium announced a new standard for digital educational content and e-Learning systems: *IMS Common Cartridge*. This specification combines three of IMS's most widely adopted specifications, Content Packaging, Question and Test Interoperability, and Metadata, with the IMS Tools Interoperability Protocol, which enables standards-based data exchange between learning management platforms and standalone learning tools, such as adaptive tutors or assessment engines. IMS CC is aimed at defining "a commonly supported content format, able to run on any compliant LMS platform." Digital educational content, learning management systems, and learning software tools incorporating this Common Cartridge interoperability standard are becoming increasingly available, which support also a number of other commonly used specifications

---

[11] http://dublincore.org/

including IMS Question & Test Interoperability v1.2, IMS Tools Interoperability Guidelines v1.0, IEEE LOM v1.0, SCORM v1.2, and SCORM 2004.

Finally, other important specification worth to comment is the *IMS Digital Repositories*, aimed at promoting interoperability among learning object repositories (LORs), for these services to offer similar interfaces and to facilitate federated searches. Additionally, the European Agency for educative standards on interoperability, CEN ISSS, promotes the *LOR interoperability* initiative to achieve interoperability among different LORs.

8.3.2.2 Standardization of Students' Data

Projects focused on students' data management aim at facilitating information interchange about students' abilities, performance, security parameters, preferences, e-portfolios, etc. The main purpose of IMS Learner Information Profile (LIP) is to define data collections that can be used to import and export data from a server according to LTSC specification Public and Private Information (PAPI), a joint effort of LTSC and ISO/IEC JTC1 SC36 WG3 that seek the students' data transfer among different systems.

8.3.2.3 Learning Processes Standardization

Another relevant group of initiatives is the standardization of learning processes. *EML OUNL* is an EML developed by the Open University of the Netherlands (OUNL) to describe a variety of instructional models. The idea underlying this specification is that, regardless the pedagogical model, a learning design is based on a method that defines both activities and teacher and student roles. The *IMS Learning Design* specification is a language to model "Units of Learning" (UoL) based on OUNL EML. To facilitate both the development and widespread use of the specification and its subsequent implantation, IMS LD has been divided in three parts, known as Level A, Level B, and Level C.

8.3.3 Other Standardization Initiatives

In this section, we will mention other projects not as widespread as the specifications and standards mentioned before, but promising enough to be included because they point out new development and research directions for the future.

First, those projects oriented to normalize the accessibility requirements for the educative technology will be analyzed. The objective of these projects is not limited to guarantee access to handicapped people to digital educational resources but also to promote the development of educational materials adapted to different learning styles. *IMS AccessForAll Metadata and Accessibility for LIP* (ACCLIP) specifications, an *IMS LIP* extension, looks for facilitating, through the combination of content data and student profile, the identification of educational materials adjusted to the student preferences or requirements (IMS Global 2003).

The definition of competencies is another domain where significant standardization efforts are in progress. Many educational organizations use or implement systems that allow to develop their syllabi based on competences. In addition, different organizations have created repositories to store competence definitions. Unfortunately, these systems are not based on interoperability standards. Several projects, such as the IMS Reusable Definition of Competency or Educational Objective Specification (*IMS RDCEO*), the European consortium for Human Resource information interchange (*HR-XML*), and the European model for Student Competences (CWA 15455) progress in this direction. Due to the complexity associated with creating a unique system able to represent several varied situations, the *TenCompetence* project adopts a different approach that is not based on the organization but instead on the individual. The main goal is to create and to test the Personal Competence Manager (PCM) in real contexts gathering competence information from several sources and show it in a context, structures, and format defined by the users.

The harmonization of vocabularies (controlled collections of terms) is another objective of several projects. Data interchange and service integration allow to improve educational systems' performance. However, this interchange is very complex due to cultural and sector differences. *IMS Vocabulary Definition Exchange* (*VDEX*) defines a grammar for the interchange of value lists readable by automated systems and their conversion in useful information for user searches (IMS Global 2004). CEN/ISSS promotes two active projects dealing with the harmonization of vocabularies related to e-learning, an extensive e-learning vocabulary (CWA 15453), and IEEE LOM vocabulary (CWA 14871).

Copyright management of digital media has been addressed by several projects. XrML (eXtensible Rights Markup Language) defines usage conditions for digital objects, having been selected as the standard for individual management in multimedia applications environment MPEG 21. *DOI* (Digital Object Identifier) defines a unique instance to locate a file regardless of its location on the Internet. *ODRL* (Open Digital Rights Language) is a language used by Content Management Systems, part of an international effort aimed at developing and promoting an open standard for rights expressions. The ODRL initiative has recently published a profile specification for Creative Commons licenses.

Finally, the identification of common components of different systems favors the design of subsystems and reusable components. *Learning Technology Systems Architecture* (LTSA) is an IEEE standard neither prescriptive nor exclusive that specifies the architecture and components of virtual learning environments.

8.4 The IEEE LOM Standard

Following the definition given in Section 2, learning objects must be described by external statements named metadata. The following example shows a learning object and a metadata fragment describing it. Figure 8.2 shows: (a) a fragment of

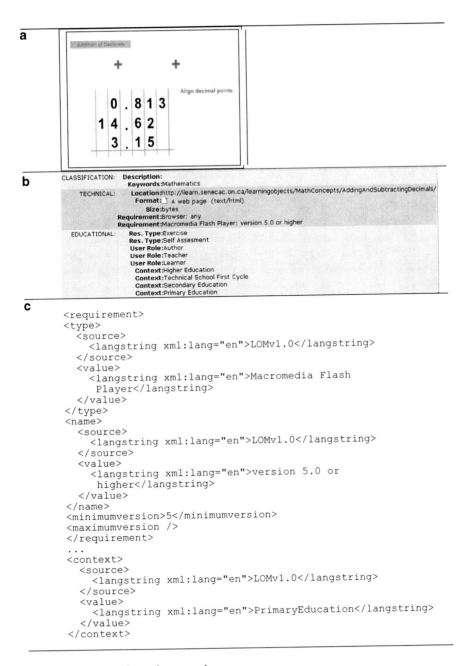

Fig. 8.2 Resource and metadata example

an educational resource consisting on an animation illustrating the sum of decimal numbers, (b) a fragment of its metadata in text format, and (c) a fragment of the same metadata in XML format.

According to the most common definition, metadata are "data about data." In our case, the resource that appears in Fig. 8.2a is described by the data that appear in

Fig. 8.2b, c. However, this definition cannot be considered complete, but a starting point that will serve as the basis for a more complete definition.

The previous example shows how metadata not only provide data related to the resource content, as the classification in the "Mathematics" category, but also provide additional data, for instance, about technical requirements to use the resource: "the Macromedia Flash software is required to execute this learning object." Other information gathered is about the possible contexts of use; in this case, it has been mainly oriented to "primary education." Therefore, metadata provide different types of information about resources, not only about their contents but also about other aspects that might be useful when managing, retrieving, searching, or storing the resource.

In 1998, the EU-funded project Ariadne developed, in collaboration with IMS, the initial metadata proposal that would be the germ of today's IEEE LOM standard. The main goal was to develop a metadata schema that could be used in a multicultural and multilingual environment, neutral in relation to the language used in the educational resource as well as in the metadata instance. IEEE LOM (*Learning Object Metadata*) is the metadata standard for learning objects by IEEE. It sets up a conceptual data schema that defines the structure of metadata records (called metadata instances) for learning objects. A metadata instance describes learning objects' characteristics grouped in nine categories: general, life cycle, meta-metadata, educative, technical, copyright, relation, annotation, and classification.

The use of this schema allows to learning object authors to specify what elements form a metadata instance, with the purpose of facilitating search, evaluation, acquisition, and use of learning objects by students, instructors, or automated systems, as well as their interchange and shared use, promoting the development of catalogs and inventories. Figure 8.3 shows the scheme of metadata categories in the IEEE LOM standard.

The inclusion of metadata instances together with the learning object gives standard information about its usage contexts, thus promoting its reusability. The following table shows part of a metadata record of a real learning object (Table 8.2).

8.5   IMS Learning Design

The learning object concept is frequently used in terms of "content," with a specific meaning of "the subjects or matters that treat in a written work." For information processing, "content" is synonymous of "document" in a general sense (including audio, video, etc.). All these imply a view of a learning object as a "document," a certainly restrictive vision of the concept.

Making use of the term "resource" in the definition of learning objects, we have a source of supply, support, or aid, specifically one that can be readily drawn upon when needed. However, not only static contents can be included in the category of those resources tagged as "learning objects." An important closely related subject

Category	Metadata elements
1. General	1.1 Identifier
	1.2 Title
	1.3 Language
	1.4 Description
	1.5 Keyword
	1.6 Coverage
	1.7 Structure
	1.8 Aggregation level
2. Life Cycle	2.1 Version
	2.2 Status
	2.3 Contribute
3. Meta-Metadata	3.1 Identifier
	3.2 Contribute
	3.3 Metadata Schema
	3.4 Language
4. Technical	4.1 Format
	4.2 Size
	4.3 Location
	4.4 Requirement
	4.5 Installation Remarks
	4.6 Other Platforms Requirements
	4.7 Duration
5. Educational	5.1 Interactivity Type
	5.2 Learning Resource Type
	5.3 Interactivity Level
	5.4 Semantic Density
	5.5 Intended End User Role
	5.6 Context
	5.7 Typical Age Range
	5.8 Difficulty
	5.9 Typical Learning Type
	5.10 Description
	5.11 Language
6. Rights	6.1 Cost
	6.2 Copyright and Other Restrictions
	6.3 Description
7. Relation	7.1 Kind
	7.2 Resource
8. Annotation	8.1 Entity
	8.2 Date
	8.3 Description
9. Classification	9.1 Purpose
	9.2 Taxon Path
	9.3 Description
	9.4 Keywords

Fig. 8.3 IEEE LOM metadata categories and elements

to learning objects is that of "learning designs," which can de defined as drawings, preliminary sketches, or plans of instruction. If we extend this definition to educational area, learning designs will be plans of activities that a designer (teacher, professor, etc.) decides appropriated to achieve specific learning objectives.

Table 8.2 LOM metadata for a learning object

LOM element	Information
1.1. Identifier	http://cvc.cervantes.es/aula/lecturas/
1.3. Language	English
1.4. Description	The Centro Virtual Cervantes website offers a collection of readings for Spanish students. The readings are classified as beginning, intermediate, and advanced levels
1.7. Structure	Collection
4.1. Format	HTML/text
5.5. Final user role	College
6.1. Use costs	No
6.2. Copyright and other restrictions	Yes

Learning designs are a kind of learning objects that determine a sequence of activities for a specific educational purpose. The basic elements of a learning design are:

- Targeted pedagogical objectives to achieve
- Sequence of activities and sub-activities
- Resources to be used in each activity and sub-activities
- Profiles and roles of participants in the activities and sub-activities

The creation of learning designs is neither a mechanical task nor a task with few alternatives. Many options exist, since the pedagogical design problem is a problem of opened rationality, where the options are neither predetermined nor conform to a fixed space. For example, if we want that some students learn computer programming from scratch, multiple alternatives of designing instruction are available: individual activities or exercises, teacher-guided activities, activities in pairs, in groups, etc. In addition, the sequences of activities accept many alternatives. However, let us go into another example. Given that the computer programming environment is related to the study of arrays and character strings, is it better to first study arrays and afterward to face the study of character strings or vice versa? All these decisions can be taken intuitively; they can be based on general pedagogical principles, or even on existing pedagogical knowledge. In any case, it is important to emphasize that the design description (the one we have outlined in the previous example) does not give information about what criteria or knowledge was used to make the decisions. Standards such as IMS LD (see below) do not provide normalized descriptors for that kind of information, but are of vital importance so that other people can understand how that design was made. For this reason, it is useful to include at least a brief associated description.

Another very important aspect of learning designs is that they do not fully define how an activity will be developed. Following a metaphor, it can be said that a learning design is like a "musical score", which has notes and times and silences. Nevertheless, as in score performances, both the director of the orchestra (in our case the teaching staff) and the musicians (the students) have a certain rank of freedom and creativity to interpret the musical piece (the learning design). This implies that

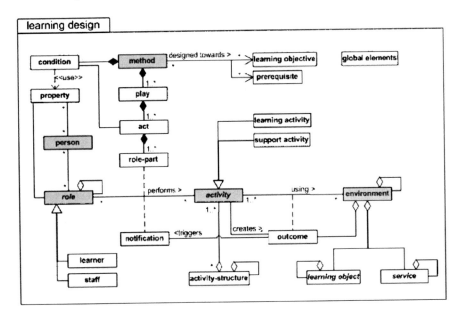

Fig. 8.4 IMS learning design: basic elements

two interpretations of the same piece, even though they should be recognizable and of course comparable, will not be identical and thus some will be considered better than others. In the same way, the structure established by a learning design can lead to several educational experiences, and the people in charge to apply them could give different courses depending on their skills or each specific context or situation.

IMS-LD (*Leaning Design*) specification allows to model learning designs. The language or model that it provides is shown in Fig. 8.4, where the following basic elements are depicted:

- The structure of activities: a method is a learning design structured in plays and acts, in a theatrical sense. Plays and acts are sub-activities. The plays are activities that can be performed in parallel (concurrent), whereas the acts are sequential activities. Each act can have different roles associated, which will be executed by participants (students or staff people). In an act, the role to be executed by a participant is represented by a role-part structure. For this, an act can have associated many role-part instances.
- The objectives (and their prerequisites) are associated to the concept of method.
- The roles (that will be associated to concrete people when the activity will be performed) allow a definition of properties for such. The concept "role-part" represents "the participation of a role in an activity," so that for the same activity different roles can have different participations.
- The resources are represented as learning objects and services (e.g., chat or forum) and are associated to the activities through environments.

It should be remarked that, in addition to the benefits associated with a common model of activity descriptions, IMS LD allows to register the interaction during learning, using IMS LD compatible systems. This opens the opportunity to study the results of different pedagogical strategies, and to identify interaction patterns of learners.

8.6 Shareable Content Object Reference Model

SCORM (*Shareable Content Object Reference Model*) is a set of specifications and standards created by different organizations, which is aimed at becoming the common model for learning objects. SCORM emerges from an activity promoted by the initiative of US Government ADL to unify efforts among groups with similar interests, thus creating a reference model that allows coordinating the emergent technologies and their commercial implementations, and facilitating, at the same time, the work of LMS and Learning Content Management Systems (LCMS) vendors.

SCORM only considers Web-based education. It is in fact an eclectic approach, based on the integration of the work by other standardization bodies with the objective to obtain a general reference model that allows creating objects that could be used in different platforms. Because this is the main goal of SCORM: to allow standard educational contents to be shared among different systems, to facilitate interoperability and to promote educational content reuse.

SCORM is a multi-part specification containing three main models: a Content Aggregation Model (CAM) for learning objects, a Sequencing and Navigation Content (SN), and a Run-Time Environment (RTE). Certain authors have compared SCORM with a library containing book sets, the different SCORM models. Inside a model, each specification or concrete standard would be equivalent to a library's book. Figure 8.5 shows this metaphor.

1) *SCORM* Content Aggregation Model (*CAM*):

- It defines how the learning objects must be.
- It specifies how to describe learning objects to facilitate search and location.
- It defines how to group and to pack learning objects together to create more complex units that can be transported among different systems.
- It specifies the rules to establish learning object sequences aimed at conforming more complex units (such as courses).

2) *SCORM* Run-Time Environment (*RTE*) describes the requirements of a SCORM-compatible LMS:

- It describes how the "content running" process must be made, as the set of operations to run so that the end users can see, can hear, etc. correctly in their computer a learning object.
- It establishes the communication model among different LMSs.

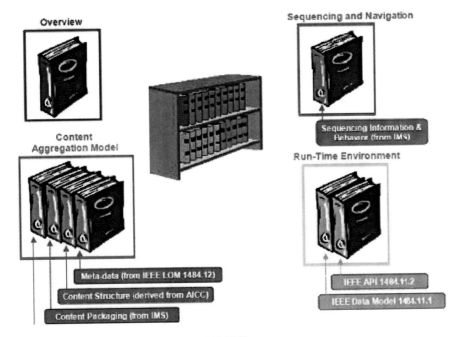

Fig. 8.5 The "books" that conform the SCORM library

- It defines a data model to obtain relevant information about the student and the educational experience. For example, the exact point in the course in which the student is, or the scores obtained in the evaluations.

All the preceding points have a specification or standard to support them. For example, to specify how learning objects must be described to facilitate their search, SCORM proposes to use IEEE LOM metadata standard previously analyzed.

3) *SCORM* Sequencing and Navigation Content (*SCORM SN*):

- Defines the content sequences for a user (generated by the learning management system or as consequence of the explicit user interaction).
- Defines how to interpret the sequencing rules associated to the contents.
- Is based on an activity tree navigation.

Figure 8.6 shows a SCORM operation schema, depicting how all the contents must be finally converted into a package before it can be distributed. This figure introduces several important concepts of SCORM:

- *Asset*: this is the more basic resource. Assets are simple contents such as texts, images, sounds, videos, or any kind of data a Web client can launch.
- SCO (*Shareable Content Object*): a learning object that can be included in a package and to be distributed by any SCORM-compliant system. SCOs are usually collections of one or more assets.

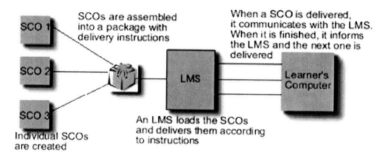

Fig. 8.6 SCORM model schema

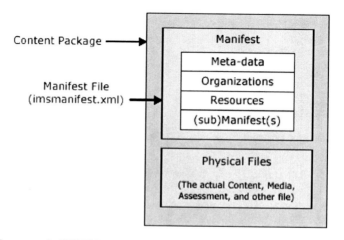

Fig. 8.7 Structure of a SCORM content package

- SCORM package: a unit composed of contents, metadata, and a complete list of package contents (something like its "invoice"). It usually contains one or more SCOs and its formal structure is shown in more detail in Fig. 8.7.

SCORM packaging is based on the Content Packaging IMS Specification that is based on the existence of a file denominated "manifest" and whose name is obligatorily "imsmanifest.xml." This file has four main sections:

- Metadata: metadata about the package itself, such as contents, size, etc.
- Organizations: it has one or more <organization> elements that can reflect different structures for the same contents (sequential, hierarchical, etc.).
- Resources: physical files stored in the manifest (either assets or SCOs), as well as references to external resources.
- Sub-Manifest(s): this element is necessary when the packages include aggregated contents, i.e., SCORM packages contained within others.

Finally, it is important to remark that SCORM also allows the existence of packages that only group not-related resources (called resource packages).

8.7 IMS Question & Test Interoperability

IMS Question & Test Interoperability (QTI) (IMS Global 2006) specification describes a data model for the representation of question and test data and their corresponding result reports. Therefore, the specification enables the exchange of items, tests, and data results between authoring tools, item banks, test constructional tools, learning systems, and assessment delivery systems. The data model is described in an abstract manner, using UML to facilitate binding to a wide range of data-modeling tools and programming languages, although a binding to XML has been provided for system data interchange.

The IMS QTI work specifically relates to content providers (that is, question and test authors and publishers), developers of authoring and content management tools, assessment delivery systems, and learning systems. The data model for representing question-based content is suitable for targeting users in learning, education, and training across all age ranges and national or cultural contexts.

Specifically, QTI is designed to:

- Provide a well-documented content format for storing and exchanging items regardless of the authoring tool used to create them.
- Support the deployment of item banks across a wide range of learning and assessment delivery systems.
- Provide systems with the ability to report test results in a consistent manner.

Sclater and Low (2002) argue that, in an attempt to avoid ambiguity, IMS QTI has developed its own terminology. In this regard, tests are known as assessments. An assessment has one or more questions. Before a question can be delivered, it is needed to have additional knowledge such as whether the score for getting it was correct, layout rendering information and what feedback should be given. Such questions, together with their associated data, are known as items.

It is often necessary to group a series of questions within an assessment. This is done using sections. It is possible to have a different section for each sub-topic and wish to know the score obtained for each section as well as over the assessment as a whole. In summary, an assessment can contain sections and/or items. A section can contain items and/or other sections. The person taking the test is called the participant. At the end of the assessment a results report is generated.

IMS QTI does not give support for a particular pedagogy or method of learning. On the contrary, it makes available a number of commonly used question types or item types. New item types and other proprietary extensions can be added if required by people building systems which implement the specifications.

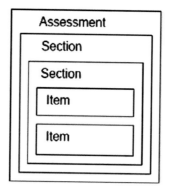

Fig. 8.8 IMS QTI ASI structure

There are two core structures within IMS QTI:

- ASI (Assessment, Section and Item): it is concerned with the content of the test (shown in Fig. 8.8)
- Results reporting: it is concerned with the results from the test. There are four constructs within the results reporting data model:

   ○ Summary: it contains data such as the maximum score and how many attempts have been made.
   ○ Assessment: it corresponds to the construct in the ASI model and can incorporate sections and items.
   ○ Section: as in the ASI structure.
   ○ Item: as in the ASI structure.

The IMS QTI specification is related to and can be used in conjunction with other IMS specifications. The specification is intended to be consistent with these in order to reduce redundancy and confusion between specifications. The related specifications are:

- IMS Meta-data Specification
- IMS Content Packaging Specification
- IMS Learner Information Packaging Specification

8.8 Standards for Digital Objects Repositories: IMS DRI

Learning object repositories are systems that provide access to learning object collections. However, many these repositories do not store learning resources, but instead they only store learning objects metadata. Therefore, it is possible that the same resource could be *found* in different repositories. The use of LORs as content management systems in learning environments is described in Chapter 2 "From content management to e-learning content repositories."

The fundamental functionality of a repository is learning object search, although several possibilities for their implementation exist:

- Interactive searching interfaces for end users.
- Query interfaces that can be used by software agents, e.g., through Web Services.

Nevertheless, sometimes the same search mechanism can serve for both uses. Finally, it has to be taken into account that traditional data retrieval methods (such as those provided by Internet search engines) must be complemented with a metadata-based search. The simplest form to make this kind of searching is to allow search by metadata fields.

However, those interfaces sometimes do not result satisfactory. New research approaches introduce advanced techniques that permit to use metadata domain knowledge by using ontologies. Nevertheless, since searching functionality is directly related to the concept of LOR, we will define this term as:

"A learning object repository is a software system that stores educational resources and their metadata (or only the latter) and has some kind of searching interface, either for human interaction or software system interaction, or both."

Additionally to searching functionality, another important function of the repositories is to intermediate with other repositories (something commonly known as *federated repositories*). This characteristic makes it possible to search in several distributed repositories at the same time through a single query, extending the possibility to find interesting resources, in a similar manner to the procedure followed by meta-searcher engines for the Web.

It seems logical to think that materials stored in an LOR should follow some metadata specification or standard such as IEEE LOM, to facilitate their classification, which would improve search results, thus facilitating retrieval. In fact, some authors argue that LOM originally was not developed in response to the practical necessities of people but instead to make up on line collections of reusable materials.

However, the standard specifically oriented to LORs is IMS Digital Repositories Interoperability (DRI). This is an important effort oriented to facilitate the interaction among repositories by means of standardization of the most common operations. This standard proposes a set of recommendations that "would have to be implemented through services to present a common user interface." One of the most interesting characteristics of this standard is that it does not introduce any new schema, but instead it tends to use existent schemes such as IEEE LOM for metadata or IMS specification about content packaging.

DRI specify functional interactions between the two layers defined in the "DRI functional architect": mediation layer and provision layer. These functions are the following:

- Search/Expose: definition of the searches of metadata associated with contents published in repositories.
- Gather/Expose: definition of the requests of metadata published in repositories and metadata aggregation for subsequent uses.
- Submit/Store: form in which a learning object is moved toward a repository from a certain site accessible through the Internet and how it is its representation to be accessed.

- Request: function that allows a system to ask for access to a learning object found after a metadata-based search.
- Deliver: it describes the answer of a repository that provides access to a given resource.
- Alert/Expose: alerting e-mail/SMTP services whose definition has not been deeply defined in the first phase of this specification.

References

Advanced Distributed Learning. (2004). *SCORM 2004* (4th edition version 1.1 Documentation). Retrieved August 23, 2010, from http://www.adlnet.gov/Technologies/scorm/SCORMS Documents/2004%204th%20Edition/Documentation.aspx

Downes, S. (2001). Learning objects: resources for distance education worldwide. *International Review of Research in Open and Distance Learning*. from http://www.irrodl.org/index.php/ irrodl/article/view/32

IMS Global. (2003). IMS *Learner Information Package Accessibility for LIP Access for All Use Cases* (Version 1.0 Final Specification). from http://www.imsglobal.org/accessibility/ acclipv1p0/imsacclip_usecasesv1p0.html

IMS Global. (2004). *IMS Vocabulary Definition Exchange Information Model* (Version 1.0 final Specification). from http://www.imsglobal.org/vdex/vdexv1p0/imsvdex_infov1p0.html

IMS Global. (2006). IMS Question & Test Interoperability. *Public Draft Specification* (Version 2). from http://www.imsglobal.org/question/qtiv2p1pd2/imsqti_oviewv2p1pd2.html

Longmire, W. (2000). A primer on learning objects, *ASTD Learning Circuits March*. from http:// www.astd.org/LC/2000/0300_longmire.htm

Mills, S. (2002). Learning about learning objects with learning objects. In *Proceedings of Society for Information Technology and Teacher Education International Conference* (pp. 1158–1160), Vol. 1, AACE.

Polsani, P. R. (2003). Use and abuse of reusable learning objects. Journal of Digital Information, 3(4). Retrieved August 23, 2010, from http://journals.tdl.org/jodi/article/view/89/88

Sclater, N., & Low, B. (2002). *IMS Question and Test Interoperability, CETIS Assessment Special Interest Group*. from http://www.scrolla.ac.uk/resources/s2/

Wiley, D. A. (2002). Connecting learning objects to instructional design theory: A definition, a metaphor and a taxonomy. In D. A. Wiley (Ed.), *The instructional use of learning objects* (pp. 3–24) Bloomington, IN: Agency for Instructional Technology and Association for Educational Communications and Technology. from http://reusability.org/read/chapters/wiley.doc

Recommended Lectures

Duval, E. (2004). Learning technology standardization: making sense of it all.*International Journal on Computer Science and Information Systems*, *1*(1), 33–43.

Fallon, C., & Brown, S. (2002). E-learning standards: a guide to purchasing, developing and deploy- ing standards-conformant e-learning.In K. Harman, & A. Koohang, (Eds.), *Learning objects: standards, metadata, repositories, and LCMS*. St. Lucie Press & Informing Science Press. from http://www.amazon.com/Learning-Objects-Standards-Metadata-Repositories/dp/8392233751

The MASIE centre. (2002). *Making sense of learning specifications & standards: a decision maker's guide to their adoption*. Industry Report. from http://www.staffs.ac.uk/COSE/cose- new/s3_guide.pdf

Chapter 9
Learning Object Evaluation and Reuse: A Hong Kong Experience

Jennifer Jones and Carmel McNaught

Abstract Learning repositories should be designed so that the content will be actively used by teachers. One of the key issues in learning repository design is the quality of the content. This chapter discusses a peer evaluation process that was developed for, and trialed on, Learning Objects funded by the LEARNet project in Hong Kong. The chapter begins with a discussion of Learning Objects and the need for evaluation. It then outlines the rationale for choosing peer evaluation in the Hong Kong context, how the peer reviews were conducted, the obstacles faced, and the resulting recommendations for future evaluations.

9.1 Learning Objects and Learning Object Repositories

With the importance of eLearning growing every year, producing and locating quality resources is a major focus of educational institutions and communities; but what is the most effective and cost-efficient way of answering this need? The expense of producing resources has led many educational communities to the idea of sharable Learning Objects (LOs) which, according to Downes (2001), not only reduce the economic burden on individual institutions but also provide sharing institutions a competitive edge over those institutions which do not share their resources. LOs are of interest for both education and training because they are flexible and have been designed to answer an educational need for tailored, adaptable online learning (Gibbons et al. 2000). As pointed out by Friesen "governments around the world are spending large sums of money on initiatives that promise the development of learning objects, learning object metadata and learning object repositories to store both this data and these objects" (Friesen 2004, p. 59). Over recent years, a number of eLearning and LO digital repositories have been created to help educators catalogue and find available resources in their field. We will use the term Learning Object Repositories

C. McNaught (✉)
Centre for Learning Enhancement and Research (CLEAR), The Chinese University of Hong Kong, Shatin, N.T, Hong Kong, China
e-mail: carmel.mcnaught@cuhk.edu.hk

N. Ferran and J. Minguillón (eds.), *Content Management for E-Learning*,
DOI 10.1007/978-1-4419-6959-0_9, © Springer Science+Business Media, LLC 2011

(LORs) to describe these collections. Well-known examples are MERLOT in the US (http://www.merlot.org/), the eduSourceCanada network in Canada (http://edusource. netera.ca/), and the Ariadne Foundation in Europe (http://www.ariadne-eu.org/). The well-publicized move of the Massachusetts Institute of Technology to make its online courses available as learning objects for others to use (MITOpenCourseWare; http:// ocw.mit.edu/) has made the link between discrete learning objects and whole course units much more real. A recent Australian initiative, ALTC Exchange, combines an LOR repository with a professional development network for higher education (http://www.altcexchange.edu.au/). A table of some common LORs is given in the Appendix at the end of the chapter.

It is important to clearly differentiate between Learning Content Management Systems (LCMSs) and LORs. LCMSs, such as Blackboard (http://www.black-board.com/) or Moodle (http://moodle.org/), are systems designed to organize static learning resources (e.g. notes, PowerPoints and URLs), interactive learning resources (e.g. quizzes, games and simulations), and a whole range of synchronous (chat) and asynchronous (forums) communication functions into an online learning environment which students can use during a particular course of study. LORs offer teachers a strategy for sourcing discrete learning resources that can be used when designing and putting courses together in a LCMS. Because the learning resources in an LOR are discrete stand-alone learning resources, they are called Learning Objects. In order to reassure teachers that it is worthwhile for them to spend time searching through LORs in order to find suitable LOs, it is imperative that these LOs be clearly described and of high quality. Rigorous evaluation of LOs in an LOR can give this reassurance. So, high quality LOs, accessible through a LOR, can offer teachers an opportunity to enhance the quality of the online and blended learning environments they build for their students.

Hong Kong's LEARNet project was set up to encourage both the development and sharing of quality LOs among Hong Kong's tertiary institutions. These LOs were catalogued within the Learning Resource Catalogue (later called Learning Resource Community, LRC), and were to serve as exemplars within the Hong Kong context – ideally seeding further development and sharing of resources among Hong Kong universities. The LEARNet project was set up with a government grant. The project used an existing database (LRC) which had been developed by staff at the University of New South Wales in Australia for the Universitas21 consortium of universities (http://www.universitas21.com/). The LRC is described in Koppi and Hodgson (2001) and Koppi et al. (2004). A LEARNet production fund provided small grants to local developers to develop new LOs or repurpose existing legacy materials.

Learning Objects are defined in the literature in numerous ways. IEEE's definition of an LO as "any entity, digital or non-digital, that may be used for learning, education or training" (2002, p. 6) attempts to cover a variety of learning resources; however, in doing this it encompasses almost all learning resources and misses some of the key qualities that are seen to make LOs unique. A more helpful idea is that LOs can be considered as reusable discrete units of learning which can both stand alone or be incorporated into larger units of learning. This dual functionality captures the essence of LOs. Wiley brings together the ideas of reusability, granularity and adaptability stating that LOs are "educational materials designed and created in small chunks for the purpose of maximizing the number of learning situations in which the resource can be utilized" (Wiley 2002, p. 2). LEARNet's description followed this more specific line while adding in the importance of metadata. The working definition was that learning objects:

- Are self-contained units of learning – each learning object can be taken independently.
- Are reusable – a single learning object may be used in multiple contexts for multiple purposes.
- Can be updated – as they reside on the Internet, revised versions are immediately available to users.
- Can be aggregated – learning objects can be grouped into larger collections of content, including traditional course structures.
- Are tagged with metadata – every learning object has descriptive information allowing it to be easily found by a search.

The initial focus of LO literature has overwhelmingly been on delineating the concept of LOs, their technical specifications and their metadata. This imbalance has led to a call for greater consideration of pedagogical purpose (Agostinho et al. 2004; Boyle et al. 2003; Jonassen and Churchill 2004; Wiley 2003), and reflective practice and evaluation (Laurillard and McAndrew 2003). The challenge for any LO project is to develop a reflective and evaluative culture that will not only help developers improve their products but also gives users confidence that a specific object is worthy of further investigation and potential reuse. While there are many accounts of small-scale successes (e.g. Weller 2004), most of the existing repositories are not used widely (McNaught 2007). The culture of reuse is not yet embedded into higher education.

McNaught et al. (2000) studied the adoption of technology across the Australian higher education sector. The study included five case studies of universities. The general response of the 81 participants in the case studies was that "existing databases were not particularly helpful in promoting or assisting those looking to adopt or make better use of computer-facilitated learning" (p. 175). The final report contained a strong recommendation that learning repositories needed to have a review mechanism as an integral part of their design if they are to be actively used by academics. These sentiments were echoed in a later Australian report on dissemination, adoption and adaptation of project innovations in higher education (McKenzie et al. 2005). Many of the Hong Kong academics who initiated LEARNet knew of these Australian studies and so evaluation was considered central to the project.

9.2 Background to Evaluation of eLearning

eLearning projects can greatly benefit from evaluation. Reeves and Hedberg (2003) suggested that the integration of evaluation into all technology-enhanced interactive learning systems is essential. Kennedy (1998) commented that formative and summative evaluation addresses a broad range of issues from interface design to student learning outcomes and is thus "fundamental in courseware development" (p. 375). There is a cyclic relationship (Phillips 1997) between evaluation and the other planning and implementation stages of an eLearning project: planning and implementation lead to evaluation, but evaluation also loops back into the planning and implementation stages by providing feedback and data for reflection.

eLearning evaluation takes place in different stages of the development and implementation of eLearning projects, usually with different purposes. Evaluation can be roughly distinguished into two main types of evaluation – formative and summative. Formative evaluation often co-occurs with development so that the eLearning product can be improved as it is being developed (Khan 2005). Summative evaluation, on the other hand, is usually conducted as the final assessment of the material or strategy. The distinction, however, should not be taken as a clear-cut dichotomy. Mandinach (2005) explained that supposedly summative evaluations can be formative, especially if the goal of evaluation is to provide constructive feedback and is linked into a model of evaluation based on continuous cycles of improvements and redevelopment.

There are diverse evaluation strategies involving both qualitative and quantitative methods. Very often multiple strategies are used in a single case to "triangulate results…thus enhancing the credibility of evaluation findings" (Breen et al. 1998 in Oliver 2000, p. 1437). Evaluation strategies for formative eLearning evaluation can include strategies such as checklists to confirm functions and accuracy, carrying out usability trials of product prototypes, or conducting pilot tests with a smaller number of subjects before using the online component in full scale. Summative evaluation strategies can range across open-ended comments from participants, structured closed surveys, focus-group meetings, investigation of the engagement in online activities through the web activity logs, and/or analyses of students' learning outcomes through monitoring, comparing and contrasting students' various forms of performance.

With such a diversity of evaluation purposes and strategies, benefits from evaluation are naturally also varied. For example, formative evaluation, of course, can assist the further improvement of learning materials before their actual use. A classic design for formative evaluation is that of Tschirner et al. (2006) who did three pilot tests with small groups of students (<30) focusing on the usability issues in online multimedia examinations in preparation for a later implementation on a larger scale. A valuable approach to summative evaluation is exemplified by McPherson (2004) and Levy (2003) who carried out evaluation studies as action research studies or practice-based research. Such studies are capable of providing rich descriptions of what works well in particular contexts.

Benefits from evaluation can also extend further than single individual eLearning projects. One example is the evaluation of learning object repositories. Nesbit and Li (2004), for example, proposed a system to evaluate a pool of learning objects in a repository. The learning materials were examined for content quality, learning goal alignment, feedback (perhaps in an adaptive form), motivation, and presentation designs. The evaluation of individual learning objects should benefit future users in selecting the most appropriate learning objects. However, as Jones and McNaught (2005) demonstrated, developing a robust and pragmatic evaluation system for learning objects does not ensure it will be used by other developers. Other broad evaluation designs include meta-analytic studies such as Lam et al.'s (2008) examination of 70 eLearning cases in Hong Kong universities in order to deduce the most popular eLearning strategies used in Hong Kong (in this study, fixed learning resources such as glossaries, notes and PowerPoints were the most popular).

9.3   What Kind of Evaluation for LO Repositories?

In considering what kind of evaluation we needed to undertake for the project, we drew on experiences and evaluation methods used by other LO repositories. Few of the catalogues or repositories we looked at had systematic quality controls but MERLOT has worked to establish quality measures and has put evaluation schemes into place. MERLOT has two systems of review for the learning resources described within its collection. The first is that of an informal system where any member of the MERLOT community can assign a personal rating and/or comments about the quality of the object. The second is a formal expert panel review which is modelled on the peer review processes used for scholarly publications such as journals or books. This process is, however, somewhat different in that any member may list or "publish" a resource before it undergoes review. This means that unlike a journal which reviews articles and then publishes only those which pass set criteria, MERLOT maintains a listing of the numerous learning resources and then chooses a subset of these resources for formal peer review. The chosen resources are evaluated by two members of a discipline-specific editorial board who look at the resource in terms of its "quality of content", "potential effectiveness as a teaching tool" and "ease of use" (MERLOT, 2010). If the results of the review are favourable (three stars or better), the review is posted to the site.

There is the possibility that an automatic system for LO evaluation may emerge over time. There is very interesting work being done in collaborative filtering. An example is that online bookstores such as Amazon and Barnes and Noble use collaborative filtering to track customers' patterns of book purchasing and use this information to offer customized sales catalogues to individual customers. This concept is being adapted to educational settings. For example, Ferran, Casadesús, Krakowska and Minguillón (in press) have used student survey data and the extensive access statistics they have at the Open University of Catalonia to develop typologies of students' habits in the online environment. This information can show which learning resources and activities are valued most highly by various groups of students. This type of rich, multidimensional data could then be fed back into the metadata describing the LOs in a LOR. This offers an additional avenue for evaluation in the future.

The aim of the LEARNet evaluation project was to develop and trial an evaluation scheme which the LEARNet project developers and potential users could utilize to determine the quality of LOs. There were three main goals for the evaluation. First, the evaluation needed to provide users of the LRC with credible information about the quality and potential usefulness of the LOs. Second, it needed to provide the developers with feedback and evidence from peers regarding the perceived quality and potential usefulness of their LOs. Last, it was to act as a practical and sustainable evaluative model which could be applied to subsequent LO development in Hong Kong. Given the increasing pressures that face higher education, an overriding consideration was the need to create a pragmatic model that could be carried out within a relatively short time frame. Taking these goals and needs into consideration three different evaluative models were considered – expert panels, user trials and peer reviews.

Setting up an *expert review* panel, much like the one set up for MERLOT, was considered. Having a panel of experts all familiar with the concept of LOs, the LRC and an agreed set of standards would be ideal. However, belonging to such a board would represent a significant commitment of time and, unlike similar editorial boards for academic journals, there would be little or no professional recognition from the board members' universities. It was noted by some LEARNet committee members that similar panels in Australia had great difficulty in recruiting and maintaining membership of such panels. For example, Taylor and Richardson (2001) were commissioned by the Australian government to develop an expert peer review system for ICT-based learning resources. After extensive consultation across the country, they produced a detailed proposal that, however, has never been properly implemented. Therefore, the LEARNet committee felt that the creation of such a panel might be a goal to aim for at some time in the future but was not a realistic option at that time. *User trials* were considered to be a supplementary step, which could be carried out by the users of the object; however, the time frame for such a trial is often a semester and so was deemed inappropriate as a sustainable model. With expert panel reviews and trials having been ruled out by the committee, the evaluation team turned to the idea of *peer reviews*. Peer reviews were seen to have the advantage of being less labour- and time-intensive and could create an evaluation model which developers could use themselves, while also trialing potential questions for a future LRC expert panel. Peer review is the also preferred evaluation mechanism for new LORs (e.g. Lefoe et al. 2009).

9.4   Developing a Peer Review System

Drawing on MERLOT's evaluation systems as well as the suggestions of Williams (2000), and Reeves and Hedberg (2003), a set of questions were initially drafted and distributed to the project developers for feedback and comment. This feedback allowed us to take in to account the evaluation needs of various LOs while still producing a set of evaluation questions that was both generic and robust.

During this process we discovered that the LOs seemed to fall into one of two groups – content LOs (in which the content was included in the LO) and LO tools (where the content was provided by the user of the object). In the evaluation project we evaluated 16 completed LO projects. Of these, five projects were of LO tools – an interactive graphing object, an ePortfolio tool, a matrix calculator, a metabolic calculator, and statistics simulation software. The applicability of these tools to several discipline areas was of especial interest to us. These LO tools, in particular, were designed to support adaptability which Parrish (2004) noted is one of the most challenging aspects of LO reuse potential. It should be noted that this chapter is focused on the process of evaluating LOs, and is not a report on the quality of the LOs themselves.

This distinction between content LOs and LO tools required different focuses within the question sets. In some cases, the LOs were a combination of both types (i.e. tools with sample content). The questions focused around four areas: *Design & Functionality* (the user friendliness of the navigation, the functionality of the LO's technical aspects, etc.), *Quality of Content* (this section was adapted for LO tools), *Learning Potential* and the *Quality of the LRC Record* (metadata). After the evaluation questions were set for each object, an evaluation website was created and sent to the peer reviewers who then evaluated the LO and its LRC record. Table 9.1 contains the basic set of evaluation questions that were customized for each context. A standard five-point Likert scale was used. Instructional notes were included with each section.

The peer reviewers were usually nominated by the LO developer; however, at times, the evaluation team also nominated reviewers. The original aim was to have six subject area peer reviewers volunteer to look at each LO or LO set. In practice, the projects averaged just over three reviewers each. Subject area reviewers were chosen over instructional design experts because we felt it was important that reviewers had a familiarity with the concepts being presented in the LO and with teaching such concepts to students. This would enable them to provide knowledge-able feedback on the Quality of Content and Learning Potential of the LO. The areas of Design & Functionality and the Quality of the LRC Record were not designed for instructional designers or metadata experts. Instead we wanted to get an idea of how 'comfortable' potential users, such as the peer reviewers, felt with the design and cataloguing of the LO (for example, was there enough information for them to find and use the LO, could they easily navigate using the LO's inter-face, etc.).

After the evaluation had been completed by all of the reviewers, the data were compiled into reports which showed the quality ratings (displayed as star ratings with one being the lowest and five being the highest) of the LO on the various scales. Sample reports are at http://www.cuhk.edu.hk/clear/learnet/index.htm Links to the reports were then placed in the LO's resource record in the LRC.

Table 9.1 Basic set of evaluation questions

Design and functionality

1. The navigation system is easy to use
2. The information, graphics, etc. are uncluttered
3. The Learning Object uses highly readable colours, fonts and text sizes
4. The [audio and video] operate smoothly. (Substitute as necessary – Flash programs, video, animations, PowerPoint presentations, etc.)
5. The [audio and video] are of good quality
6. Manipulating and entering content into the Learning Object is straightforward
7. The tool operates smoothly
8. The interface is easy to use
9. Comments about the Interface Design:

Quality of content

10. The Learning Object is free of spelling/grammar errors
11. The Learning Object is free of informational errors
12. The content of this Learning Object is up-to-date
13. The Learning Object has a clear set of instructions/help files that support the user's needs well
14. The Learning Object has made suitable reference to credible references
15. The content is well organized and all information can be easily located
16. Comments about the Quality of the Content:

Learning potential

17. The Learning Object could aid students' understanding of the concept(s) or topic(s) being presented
18. The Learning Object provides opportunities for higher-order thinking
19. Learners are required to use the Learning Object in an interactive way
20. The Learning Object provides the learner with appropriate and useful feedback
21. The Learning Object could be easily incorporated into larger collections of content (i.e. traditional course structures)
22. Comments about the Learning Potential:

Record in the LRC

23. An accurate web address to the Learning Object is given. (Or "Clear information about how to obtain a copy of the resource is given.")
24. The educational aims/goals described in the LRC record accurately describe those of the Learning Object
25. The educational level is clearly identified in the LRC record
26. The author has given enough information for users to use the Learning Object effectively
27. Overall, the information given in the LRC record accurately matches the Learning Object
28. Comments about the Resource Record:

Overall

29. Overall, I would rate this Learning Object highly
30. General Comments about the Learning Object:

9.5   Two LO Evaluation Cases

In order for LOs to be found and reused, academic teachers need to know, not only how to search for LOs, but also information on whether any LOs suit their needs. That is why we included an evaluation report with the LO's record within the LRC.

Unless a potential user had heard about the LO by word of mouth, the LRC record would be the first information they would receive about the LO.

9.5.1 Case 1: An Audiovisual Set of LOs – The Balinese Gamelan Kebyar

The Balinese Gamelan Kebyar (http://hkusua.hku.hk/~gamelano/) is a set of LOs produced partially with LEARNet funding. They are classified as content LOs. For cataloguing purposes the LOs in this project were considered to be 14 different learning objects but for the purposes of evaluation and this chapter we considered them together as a set.

The purpose of this set of learning objects was to introduce students to the Gamelan Gong Kebyar, a Balinese orchestra, its 11 instruments, their notations and sounds. The LO consists of 17 web pages linked by a simple five-item main navigation bar (see Fig. 9.1). Each of the 11 instrument's information pages are linked to each instrument's image. The student is then presented with another picture of the instrument along with a physical description, a brief explanation of how and with what it is played, and its musical role within the ensemble. The student can also listen to sound files of the different sounds the instrument can make, its part/track within the example ensemble piece, or the whole ensemble.

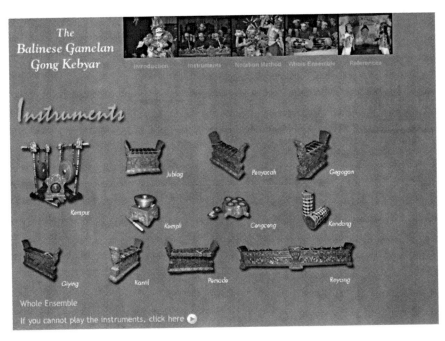

Fig. 9.1 Screen shot of the Balinese Gamelan's instrument page

9.5.1.1 The Evaluation of the Balinese Gamelan

The final version of the Balinese Gamelan's questionnaire consisted of 26 items, 21 Likert scale items and five open-ended items. Initially five subject area peers were nominated by the LO developer; then at a later date two more were added to the list. Of the seven nominated reviewers, four completed the review. The average rating for each section of the questionnaire is shown in Table 9.2.

In the area of Interface Design, which included questions about the ease of navigation, the layout of graphics/text and the readability of fonts and text colours, the reviewers gave a very high average rating of 4.8 (lowest rating = 1, highest rating = 5). The only comment that was made was that the instruments page could be divided into three "categories according to musical function (and thus further simplify the presentation)".

The Quality of the LRC Record was considered to be high by reviewers, whose average rating was 4.6. The only comment made came from reviewer 4 who pointed out the fact that dance was mentioned in the catalogue but "not described or represented in the site". This reviewer also commented on the vagueness of the metadata terms. Specifically, the reviewer felt "the phrase 'Typical students in the Student Level line' [was] vague...". It is of note that these descriptors are pre-determined within the LRC's metadata form.

Since this set of learning objects relies heavily on the sound files embedded within the content to demonstrate the various instruments to learners, it is important that the files work seamlessly on students' computers. Within the Quality of the Content section, a few problems were flagged for the developer, particularly with the operation of the files. Two of the reviewers indicated that the files had not run smoothly for them and one of them commented that she/he had not been able to open the ensemble audio file on her/his Macintosh computer even though the correct version of java was installed. As far as the sound quality was concerned, the ratings were high but also indicated there was room for improvement (Overall rating 4.3):

> It is a big challenge to balance the volume of so many audio files with such a wide frequency range, overall, well-done. However, some of the ensemble sections do not sound as clear as the solo, e.g. the 'gong' is barely audible, even on solo; another example is the kempli which produces noticeable artifacts (Reviewer comment).

Other items that were covered in the Quality of Content area focused on the text content. Within this area, accuracy of information, referencing, the organization of

Table 9.2 Summary of the compiled evaluation results for the Balinese Gamelan

Area	Average rating
Interface design	4.8
Quality of content	4.2
Learning potential	4.7
Quality of the LRC record	4.6
Overall	4.5

the content, were all rated highly, indicating that the LOs were well developed. One area that was still in need of improvement was that of spelling/grammatical accuracy. As this was seen somewhat as a developmental evaluation, items such as these could easily be rectified in the final/updated version of the LO. A final comment on the content of the LO was that while it was a valuable "tool for learning how to play in the ensemble" it could be "enriched" further. The reviewer's comment here seems to suggest that in terms of the definition of Learning Objects these LOs seem to have fulfilled their purpose. The reviewer may have been expecting more in-depth coverage of the ensemble. However, more depth might possibly affect the LO's reusability.

The Learning Potential section of the questionnaire probed whether there was a perceived value in the LOs, the level of interactivity required, the levels of explanation included and the portability of the LOs and the value it would add to courses on the topic. The results for the Balinese Gamelan were very positive (mean rating = 4.7). Encouragingly, evaluators responded with full marks for item 12, "The Learning Objects provide opportunities for developing an awareness of Balinese Gamelan Gong Kebyar instruments and their role within the ensemble". The evaluators also felt that the LOs could enhance courses on Balinese musical culture and would be easily incorporated in to course structures. Above all results show that these objects were viewed by the evaluators as being of high quality. In the reviewers' own words:

> An excellent idea. It has the potential to be a very valuable and easily accessible resource.

> I think it is perfectly self-contained, can stand on its own or be used with other materials

> Can be very useful in introducing the principle of gong kebyar musical organization to beginners. This, however, cannot take the place of actual music rehearsals in person.

The final general comments area received one comment on technical issues and two commending the developer's efforts and suggesting ways of adding to this resource. Here are two excerpts from the reviewers' final comments:

> Looks really great, a fantastic resource. It would be cool if there was a way to make-up your own songs, play around with the sound…

> Excellent! I suggest the content of the site be expanded with more music examples, including perhaps an illustration how dance movements coordinate with the music.

9.5.2 Case 2: A Customizable Tool – The Interactive Graphing Object

The Interactive Graphing Object (IGO) is an example of the second kind of LO evaluated – an LO tool. There have been a number of iterations of the IGO on the web (e.g. Kennedy and Fritze 1998; Kennedy 2004) and in a mobile version (Kennedy et al. 2004b). The theoretical framework of the IGO is explored in Kennedy et al. (2004a).

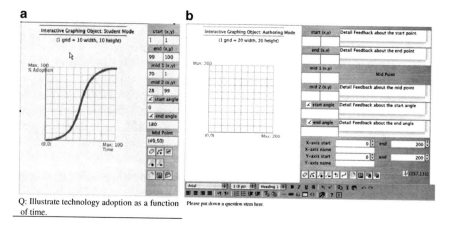

Q: Illustrate technology adoption as a function of time.

Student has graphed the answer to the Author mode question.

Fig. 9.2 Operation of the Interactive Graphing Object

The IGO is a LO tool which, in its student mode, provides an interactive space for learners to answer questions involving graphs (see Fig. 9.2a) and, in its author mode, a space for content experts and/or students to create graph questions (see Fig. 9.2b). In the student mode, learners are asked a question and then they use a mouse to estimate what the answer/graph might look like. The student can then 'fine tune' their curve by changing the numbers in the middle column or adjusting curve 'handles'. As the student works through the question, they may click on the checkmark icon to receive feedback or clues to help them complete the problem. Feedback on five aspects of the curve – start point, end point, mid point, start angle and end angle – can be built into the question by developers when they create the questions (see Fig. 9.2b).

9.5.2.1 The Evaluation of the IGO

The final version of the IGO's questionnaire consisted of 24 items, 19 Likert-scale items and five open-ended items. The IGO was one of the first LO tools we evaluated and we discovered the Quality of Content questions did not fit the nature of this LO. Therefore, we changed the section to focus on the Usability of the tool.

Four peer reviewers were nominated by the LO developer. Since the IGO was not a content-based or a discipline-specific LO, the developer chose reviewers from the area of instructional design and computer science. Three of the four nominated reviewers replied to the evaluation; however, one of the reviewers only submitted

Table 9.3 Summary of the compiled evaluation results for the IGO

Area	Average rating
Interface design	5.0
Usability (designing questions, etc.)	4.8
Learning potential	4.5
Quality of the LRC record	4.7
Overall	4.7

Table 9.4 Average ratings for Learning Potential for the IGO

Item	Average rating
1. The IGO can help improve students' understanding of the concept(s) or topic(s) being questioned	5.0
2. With appropriate question design, the IGO provides opportunities for higher-order thinking with students	4.5
3. Learners are required to use the IGO in an interactive way	5.0
4. The design of the IGO supports the development of innovative questions involving graphical answers to questions	4.0
5. The IGO supports and encourages the creation of highly customisable feedback for students	4.5
6. The Learning Object has Interdisciplinary applications (i.e. is flexible enough for a variety of content domains)	4.5
7. I would consider using this tool in the future for my students and/or recommend the IGO to colleagues	4.0
Rating for the Learning Potential	4.5

written comments and did not respond to the survey items. The average rating for each section of the questionnaire is shown in Table 9.3.

In the area of Interface Design, the respondents to the survey gave a rating of 5 on all items. The third reviewer commented that while the interface was "rich" and it "looks and feels attractive … the richness can itself be a problem. As with any rich interface the tricky problem is to make it simple for the users". The second area, Usability, also received a strong rating of 4.8. Reviewer One commented that "Usability needs to be tested with more authentic users – lecturers who will be likely users."

The results for the third area, Learning Potential (Table 9.4), were also very positive with a mean rating of 4.5. Evaluators responded very favourably to item 9, "The IGO can help improve students' understanding of the concept(s) or topic(s) being questioned" and item 11, "Learners are required to use the IGO in an interactive way". However, items 12 and 15 received mixed opinions from the reviewers (Reviewer One rating both items at 5 and Reviewer Two rating both items at 3). Reviewer Two's comment that "the learning tasks [built] around the IGO will be the critical elements in creating a high quality learning outcome", draws attention to the importance of the teacher's ability to develop engaging content for this tool.

The final area that this evaluation looked at was the Quality of the LRC Record. Overall the reviewers responded well to the LO (mean rating = 4.7). Here are a few excerpts from the general comments section:

Reviewer 1: This seems to be an exceptional peice [sic] of work. I hope it can achieve wide use.

Reviewer 3: Normally, lecturers simply impose their questions and materials on their students. My experience is that making these issues public, through collaborative development and sharing, opens up the whole issue of what is appropriate material. This is a very good thing. The question of composing good questions is implicitly opened up by the tool, which makes them public and exchangeable. Discussion on what constitutes good questions could be one very valuable spin-of from the tool.

9.6 The Evaluative Experience: Challenges

The LOs evaluated in this study all had funding for development or refinement. We therefore expected that the ratings would be quite high. Indeed, the lowest rating in the Interface Design section was 2.75, in the Quality of Content or Usability section was 3.25, in the Learning Potential section was 3.5, in the Quality of the LRC Record section was 3, and in the Overall section was 3. Several of the LO developers commented that they were pleased with the quality of the feedback, especially the open comments. However, this interest was "after the event" and it was very difficult to engage LO developers or their nominated reviewers at the outset. Indeed we identified a number of challenges related to project management, engagement of the LO developers, engagement of the peer reviewers, and evaluation tools. The challenges that we faced in this evaluation project are undoubtedly problems that many LO evaluations find. We will describe them now in the hope that other evaluators can learn from them.

9.6.1 Project Management

The project leaders had all received small grants to build or repurpose LOs, so as to fairly quickly populate the LRC with some high quality LOs. However, the speedy development and evaluation plan was not realized. In all, 36 LEARNet projects were funded in three stages – 17 in Round 1 (late 2002), 12 in Round 2 (mid-2003) and 7 in Round 3 (late 2003). At the time that the evaluation was conducted (mid-2004) several of these LO projects were not completed even though they had received funding a year or more previously. Nineteen of the 36 projects were completed by the evaluation cut-off in late 2004 and 16 had completed evaluations (Table 9.5).

Being involved in an evaluation process was a stipulated part of the grant. However, some of the project leaders were clearly not aware that they were obliged

Table 9.5 Number of projects completed and evaluated

	Total no. of new projects	No. of projects completed by cut-off	No. of projects evaluated
Round one	17	9	8
Round two	12	9	7
Round three	7	1	1
Totals	36	19	16

to evaluate their resource in some way. As the grant money had been dispensed and spent, we had little "hold" over the LO developers. For many, the evaluation phase was a very low priority, and several LO developers were slow in producing a list of reviewers and slow to giving feedback on the proposed questions. All this points to the need for clear and explicit project management and a tighter ongoing communication between any learning repository project team and individual LO developers.

As noted, once the evaluation had actually been completed, the project leaders were pleased with the reports they received. Perhaps our challenges with this process would be less in the future, as the "academic grape vine" spreads the word that our evaluation was useful.

9.6.2 LO Developers

The vision being put forth by the LEARNet project was one that many developers only superficially engaged with in order to get funding for their pre-existing projects. Few of the LO developers were interested in the idea of sharing their objects or receiving feedback from peers in a formal evaluation setting. They were producing these LOs for their own purposes. Once they obtained the funds, they appeared to just be willing to meet the bare requirements when it came to the evaluation. This attitude was also prevalent in the listing of the objects in the LRC where developers showed little interest in this important process. Tables 9.6 and 9.7 illustrate the variation in engagement with the evaluation process using data from the first six projects contacted. If it is challenging to set up evaluation when there is an evaluation officer to support the process, then it is not likely that it will occur voluntarily with just a set of evaluation protocols to refer to.

9.6.3 Peer Reviewers

As expected with something new, there was a great deal of email and phone contact with the peer reviewers in order to explain the method of completing the review. Despite having agreed to be reviewers, the actual response rate was lower than

Table 9.6 Response time for getting reviewer list from LO developer

Project	No. of days to suggest reviewers	Total no. of reviewers provided	Response when asked to provide six potential reviewers
a	3	3	Unable to provide more. Evaluation team found him one more
b	59	2	Asked evaluation team to contact other two other people who might to provide reviewers
c	20	11	N/A
d	30	2	Unable to provide more
e	59	5	N/A
f	70+	Still awaiting a response	N/A

Table 9.7 Response time for getting feedback on peer review questions from LO developer

Project	No. of days taken to provide feedback	Nature of response from LO developer
a	70+	No feedback ever given
b	31	Suggested a few additional questions
c	23	Said the questions were fine
d	30	Suggested one new question and a minor change
e	67	Requested deletion of some questions and suggested replacements
f	70+	Still awaiting a response

anticipated. It was noted that we had improved responses when reviewers were provided with a stricter timeline – being pleasantly assertive seemed to work! Table 9.8 showed just how much reminding was needed. Since the LO developers nominated their own peer reviewers, the evaluation process did not meet stricter blind review processes. It is possible that the openness of the review could have produced bias in the evaluation results.

9.6.4 Evaluation Tools

The initial goal was to set up the peer review within the LRC using the evaluation tools that were available within the LRC at the time. However, upon investigation of the available LRC review and evaluation tools, we discovered that they were not suitable for our needs and concluded that due to time constraints it would not be possible to wait for the LRC tools to be updated. This does point to the need for developers of LO repositories to consult educational evaluators when designing and building systems.

Table 9.8 Number of reviews submitted (snapshot at 22 August 2004)

Project	Review start date	No. of reviewers contacted	No. of reviews submitted
a	2 August 2004	4	1
b	Awaiting more reviewers	2	0
c	29 July 2004	6 of the 11 suggested	1 (+1 who did not follow directions)
d	6 August 2004	2	0
e	Awaiting site's final "bug" fix	5	N/A
f	Awaiting reviewers	0	N/A

9.7   Conclusion

We believe that evaluation is an essential aspect of LO development and sharing in order to ensure that we build up LO collections of high quality. However, as noted previously, the primary push of the LO community has been to define, create, catalogue and distribute LOs with limited attention given to evaluation. The goal of the peer review of the LEARNet LOs was, therefore, to gather evidence as to the quality of the LOs being developed within a short period of time and hopefully start a community evaluative approach where future users would feed back into the process. This project demonstrated that quality LOs can be developed and evaluated within the Hong Kong context. However, the development of an evaluation culture requires space and time for dialogue and reflection, space and time that LO developers did not have to give to the process.

There was little interest in sharing and academics felt there was little significance to doing so. Since the evaluation phase of the project, we have found that LO records in the LRC have only been accessed on a few occasions. The problem the LEARNet project has been left with is that there is a number of good quality LOs. These have been produced and catalogued but then not accessed. This is despite quite widespread advertisement for the LRC, through leaflets, emails, and several information and training sessions in Hong Kong.

McNaught (2007) has listed a number of criteria for successful learning repositories. They:

- Should be developed out of a genuine need within a community.
- Have a core of committed promoters whose enthusiasm is sustained over a number of years.
- Articulate a clear direction and focus.
- Consult with their user community(ies) to ensure that the resource collection is wanted and valued.
- Establish a good management process that ensures regular review and updating of resources.
- Are open access.
- Facilitate easy addition of resources.
- Have suitable granularity in the search mechanisms.

One key feature of these criteria is that of ownership. One possible way forward is not to assist LO developers with 'quick fix' evaluation strategies as we tried to do. This culture change may be better supported by a series of small action research projects involving teachers who are keen to gather evaluation data. Their LOs could be evaluated in peer reviews and in user trials, as seems appropriate, and the results well disseminated. Incremental change may seem slow but may well be the only truly sustainable evaluation strategy to adopt.

Acknowledgements Funding support from the LEARNet project to do this evaluation study is gratefully acknowledged. LEARNet was funded by the University Grants Committee in Hong Kong. The collaborative support of many of the LO developers and their peer reviewers is also sincerely appreciated. In particular the willing permission of Manolete Mora (Balinese Gamelan developer) and David Kennedy (IGO developer) to share their work is warmly acknowledged. This chapter draws on and significantly extends a paper published in the ED-MEDIA 2005 conference proceedings (Jones and McNaught 2005).

9.8 Appendix: A Selection of eLearning and Learning Object Repositories

Title of Repository	URL (accessed 6 March 2009)
ALTC Exchange	http://www.altcexchange.edu.au/
Apple Learning Interchange	http://edcommunity.apple.com/ali/
Ariadne Foundation	http://www.ariadne-eu.org/
DLESE (Digital Library for Earth System Education)	http://www.dlese.org/
EdNA (Education Network Australia)	http://www.edna.edu.au/
eduSourceCanada network	http://edusource.netera.ca/
IDEAS (Interactive Dialogue with Educators from Across the State)	http://ideas.wisconsin.edu/
MERLOT (Multimedia Educational Resource for Learning and Online Teaching)	http://www.merlot.org
MIT OpenCourseware	http://ocw.mit.edu/OcwWeb/
Wisconsin Online Resource Center	http://www.wisc-online.com/

References

Agostinho, S., Bennett, S., Lockyer, L., & Harper, B. (2004). Developing a learning object metadata application profile based on LOM suitable for the Australian higher education context. *Australasian Journal of Educational Technology, 20*(2), 191–208. Retrieved August 13, 2010, from http://www.ascilite.org.au/ajet/ajet20/agostinho.html

Boyle, T. (2003). Design principles for authoring dynamic, reusable learning objects. *Australian Journal of Educational Technology, 19*(1), 46–58. Retrieved August 13, 2010, from http://www.ascilite.org.au/ajet/ajet19/boyle.html

Boyle, T., Bradley, C., Chalk, P., Jones, R., Haynes, R., & Pickard, P. (2003). *Can learning objects contribute to pedagogical improvement in higher education: Lessons from a case study?* Paper based on presentation given at CAL '2003, April 2003. Retrieved August 13, 2010, from http://www.londonmet.ac.uk/ltri/learningobjects/papers_pres/CAL_Objects_paper.doc

Cole, T. W. (2002). Creating a framework of guidance for building good digital collections. *First Monday, 7*(5). Retrieved August 13, 2010, from http://firstmonday.org/htbin/cgiwrap/bin/ojs/index.php/fm/article/view/955/876

Downes, S. (2001). Learning objects: Resources for distance education worldwide. *International Review of Research in Open and Distance Learning, 2*(1). Retrieved August 13, 2010, from http://www.irrodl.org/index.php/irrodl/article/view/32/378

Ferran, N., Casadesús, J., Krakowska, M., & Minguillón, J. (2007). Enriching e-learning metadata through digital library usage analysis. *The Electronic Library, 25*(2), 148–165.

Friesen, N. (2004). Three objections to learning objects and e-learning standards. In R. McGreal (Ed.), *Online education using learning objects* (pp. 59–70). London: RoutledgeFalmer.

Gibbons, A. S., Nelson, J., & Richards, R. (2000). The nature and origin of instructional objects. In D. A. Wiley (Ed.), *The instructional use of learning objects: Online version.* Retrieved August 13, 2010, from http://reusability.org/read/chapters/gibbons.doc

IEEE. (2002). Draft standard for learning object metadata (proposed standard). Retrieved August 13, 2010, from http://ltsc.ieee.org/wg12/files/LOM_1484_12_1_v1_Final_Draft.pdf

Jonassen, D., & Churchill, D. (2004). Is there a learning orientation in learning objects? *International Journal on E-Learning, 3*(2), 32–41.

Jones, J., & McNaught, C. (2005). Using learning object evaluation: Challenges and lessons learned in the Hong Kong context. In G. Richards & P. Kommers (Eds.), *ED-MEDIA 2005* (pp. 3580–3585), Proceedings of the 17th annual World Conference on Educational Multimedia, Hypermedia & Telecommunications, Montreal, Canada, 27 June–2 July. Norfolk VA: Association for the Advancement of Computers in Education.

Kennedy, D. M. (1998). Software development teams in higher education: An educator's view. In R. Corderoy (Ed.), *FlexibiliTy: The next wave?* (pp. 373–385). Proceedings of the 15th annual Australian Society for Computers in Learning in Tertiary Education '98 conference, University of Wollongong, 14–16 December. Retrieved August 13, 2010, from http://www.ascilite.org.au/conferences/wollongong98/asc98-pdf/kennedyd.pdf

Kennedy, D. M. (2004). Continuous refinement of reusable learning objects: The case of the Interactive Graphing Object. In L. Cantoni & C. McLoughlin (Eds.), *ED-MEDIA 2004* (pp. 1398–1404). Proceedings of the 16th World Conference on Educational Multimedia and Hypermedia & World Conference on Educational Telecommunications, Lugano, Switzerland, 21–26 June. Norfolk VA: Association for the Advancement of Computing in Education.

Kennedy, D. M., & Fritze, P. (1998). An Interactive Graphing Tool for web-based courses. In T. Ottmann & I. Tomek (Eds.), *ED-MEDIA & ED-TELECOM 98* (Vol. 1, pp. 703–708). 10th World Conference on Educational Multimedia and Hypermedia and World Conference on Educational Telecommunications, Freiburg, Germany, 20–25 June. Charlottesville: Association for the Advancement of Computers in Education (AACE).

Kennedy, D. M., McNaught, C., & Fritze, P. (2004a). Conceptual tools for designing and learning. In P. Kommers (Ed.). *Cognitive support for learning: Imagining the unknown* (pp. 141–154). Amsterdam: IOS Press.

Kennedy, D. M., Vogel, D. R., & Xu, T. (2004b). Increasing opportunities for learning: Mobile graphing. In R. Atkinson, C. McBeath, D. Jonas-Dwyer & R. Phillips (Eds.), *Beyond the comfort zone* (pp. 493–502). Proceedings of the 21st annual Australian Society for Computers in Learning in Tertiary Education 2004 conference, University of Western Australia, 5–8 December. Retrieved August 13, 2010, from http://www.ascilite.org.au/conferences/perth04/procs/kennedy.html

Khan, J. (2005). A comprehensive e-learning model. *Journal of e-Learning and Knowledge Society, 1*(1). 33–43.

Khoo, M. (2001). Community design of DLESE's collections review policy: A technological frames analysis. *In Proceedings of the 1st ACM/IEEE-CS joint conference on digital libraries* (pp. 157–164). Roanoke, Virginia, US. New York: ACM Press. Retrieved August 13, 2010, via http://portal.acm.org/dl.cfm

Koppi, T. & Hodgson, L. (2001). Universitas 21 learning resource catalogue using IMS metadata and a new classification of learning objects. In C. Montgomerie & J. Viteli (Eds.), *ED-MEDIA 2001* (pp. 998–1001). Proceedings of the 13th Annual World Conference on Educational Multimedia, Hypermedia & Telecommunications, Tampere, Finland, 25–30 June. Norfolk, VA: Association for the Advancement of Computers in Education (AACE).

Koppi, T., Bogle, L. & Lavitt, N. (2004). Institutional use of learning objects: Lessons learned and future directions. Journal of Educational Multimedia and Hypermedia, 13(4), 449–463.

Lam, P., McNaught, & Cheng, K. F. (2008). Pragmatic meta-analytic studies: Learning the lessons from naturalistic evaluations of multiple cases. *Association of Learning Technologies Journal ALT-J, 16*(2), 61–79.

Laurillard, D., & McAndrew, P. (2003). Reuseable educational software: A basis for generic learning activities. In A. Littlejohn (Ed.), *Reusing online resources: A sustainable approach to e-learning* (pp. 81–93). London: Kogan Page.

Lefoe, G., Philip, R., O'Reilly, M., & Parrish, D. (2009). Sharing quality resources for teaching and learning: A peer review model for the ALTC Exchange in Australia. *Australasian Journal of Educational Technology*, 25(1), 45–59. Retrieved August 13, 2010, from http://www.ascilite.org.au/ajet/ajet25/lefoe.html

Levy, P. (2003). A methodological framework for practice-based research in networked learning. *Instructional Science, 31*, 787–109.

Mandinach, E. (2005). The development of effective evaluation methods for e-learning: A concept paper and action plan. *Teachers College Record, 107*(8), 1814–35. Retrieved August 13, 2010, from http://www.csupomona.edu/~dolce/pdf/mandinach.pdf

McKenzie, J., Alexander, S., Harper, C., & Anderson, S. (2005). *Dissemination, adoption & adaptation of project innovations in higher education.* Policy advice to the Carrick Institute. Canberra: Department of Education, Science and Training. Retrieved August 13, 2010, from http://www.altc.edu.au/resource-dissemination-adoption-uts-2005

McNaught, C. (2007). Developing criteria for successful learning repositories. In J. Filipe, J. Cordeiro & V. Pedrosa (Eds.), *Web Information Systems and Technologies* (pp. 8–18). Dordrecht: Springer.

McNaught, C., Phillips, P., Rossiter, D., & Winn, J. (2000). *Developing a framework for a usable and useful inventory of computer-facilitated learning and support materials in Australian universities.* Evaluations and Investigations Program report 99/11. Canberra: Higher Education Division Department of Employment, Education, Training and Youth Affairs. Retrieved August 13, 2010, from http://www.dest.gov.au/highered/eippubs1999.htm

McPherson, M. (2004). *Developing innovation in online learning: An Action research framework.* London: RoutledgeFalmer.

MERLOT (2010) MERLOT peer review process. Retrieved August 13, 2010, from http://taste.merlot.org/peerreviewprocess.html

Nesbit, J. C., & Li, J. (2004). Web-based tools for learning object evaluation. *International Conference on Education and Information Systems: Technologies and Applications*, Orlando, 21–25 July. Retrieved August 13, 2010, from http://www.sfu.ca/~jzli/publications/Nesbit_Li_2004.pdf

Oliver, M. (2000). An introduction to the evaluation of learning technology. *Educational Technology & Society, 3*(4). 20–30. Retrieved August 13, 2010, from http://www.ifets.info/journals/3_4/intro.html

Parrish, P. E. (2004). The trouble with learning objects. *Educational Technology, Research and Development*, 52(1), 49–67.

Phillips, R. (1997). *The developer's handbook to interactive multimedia: A practical guide for educational applications.* London: Kogan Page.

Reeves, T. C., & Hedberg, J. G. (2003). *Interactive learning systems evaluation.* Englewood Cliffs, N.J.: Educational Technology Publications.

Taylor, P. C., & Richardson, A. S. (2001). Validating scholarship in university teaching: Constructing a national scheme for external peer review of ICT-based teaching and learning resources. *Evaluations and Investigations Program report* 01/03. Canberra: Higher Education Division Department of Employment, Education, Training and Youth Affairs. Retrieved August 13, 2010, from http://www.dest.gov.au/archive/highered/eippubs/eip01_3/01_3.pdf

Tschirner, N., Muller, M., Pfeiffer, O., & Thomsen, C. (2006). Design and realization of multimedia-examinations for large numbers of participants in university education. iJET *International Journal of Emerging Technologies in Learning, 1*(2). Retrieved August 13, 2010, from http://eprints.physik.tu-berlin.de/89/01/iJet.pdf

Weller, M. (2004). Learning objects and the e-learning cost dilemma. *Open Learning, 19*(3), 293–302.

Wiley, D. A. (2002). Learning objects-a definition. In A. Kovalchick & K. Dawson (Eds.), *Education and technology: An encyclopedia*. Santa Barbara: ABC-CLIO.

Wiley, D. A. (2003). Learning objects: Difficulties and opportunities. *Academic ADL Co-Lab News Report*: No. 152-030406. Retrieved August 13, 2010, from http://opencontent.org//docs/lo_do.pdf

Williams, D. D. (2000). Evaluation of learning objects and instruction using learning objects. In D. A. Wiley (Ed.), *The instructional use of learning objects: Online version*. Retrieved August 13, 2010, from http://reusability.org/read/chapters/williams.doc

Chapter 10
Open Educational Resources: Motivations, Logistics and Sustainability

Niall Sclater

10.1   Introduction

On a cool summer's day in Paris in 2002 (UNESCO 2002) a group of 34 people from around the World gathered together to discuss a phenomenon that had been growing rapidly in importance: the availability of free educational content over the Internet. UNESCO and the William and Flora Hewlett Foundation had brought this eclectic mix of nationalities and professions together to look at how best to promote and develop the open content movement. Attention was centred on Anne Margulies as she introduced the Massachusetts Institute of Technology's (MIT) new OpenCourseWare (OCW) project, where much of the university's material was about to be given away freely to any learner or educator who wished to use it.

Alain Senteni from the University of Mauritius was quick to spot the potential of the OCW initiative and proposed that his university involve itself in repurposing the content for developing nations and translating it into French. The availability of such content could help to address the problem of the growing and largely unmet demand for higher education in places such as Cameroon, suggested Mr Emmanuel Tonye. It could also help to show educators pedagogical models, unfamiliar in Mohammed Dahbi's home country of Morocco. However, Abdoulaye Diakité from Guinea noted that to make effective use of the content, efforts would also have to be put into building the technical and support infrastructure. V.S. Prasad from India also mentioned the importance of translations and taking into account cultural sensitivities.

The opening comments of the meeting encapsulated many of the hopes and fears surrounding open content. In the following days the international group expanded on many of these issues and produced a definition for what they termed "open educational resources" (OERs), which would require at a minimum the provision of a course description, syllabus and calendar. The content itself could include lecture notes, demonstrations, simulations, illustrations, learning objects, reading

N. Sclater (✉)
Learning Innovation, Open University, Milton Keynes, United Kigndom
e-mail: N.L.Sclater@open.ac.uk

N. Ferran and J. Minguillón (eds.), *Content Management for E-Learning*,
DOI 10.1007/978-1-4419-6959-0_10, © Springer Science+Business Media, LLC 2011

materials, assessments and projects. The materials would need to be adaptable and the technology to access them freely available. OERs were defined as: "The open provision of educational resources, enabled by information and communication technologies, for consultation, use and adaptation by a community of users for non-commercial purposes."

At a subsequent UNESCO meeting in Paris (UNESCO 2004), the definition was broadened to include:

- Learning resources
- Courseware, content modules, learning objects, learner support and assessment tools, on-line learning communities
- Resources to support teachers
- Tools for teachers and support materials to enable them to create, adapt and use OERs; as well as training materials for teachers; and other teaching tools
- Resources to assure the quality of education and educational practices

Other commentators have since expanded the definition further to such an extent that Stephen Downes discusses whether other resources such as visiting lecturers or paper-based resources ought to be considered as OERs (Downes 2007). It seems clear though that a defining feature of an OER should be an ability to transport it over the Internet if it is to retain many of its supposed benefits. Downes reports that the Public Library of Science considers the concept of "open" to include free, immediate access online and unrestricted distribution and re-use, with the author retaining attribution rights and the materials deposited in a public archive.

Institutions providing OERs take different approaches to what they mean by the term. In the case of OCW, each course publication includes a syllabus and calendar, content such as a reading list or lecture notes and a learning activity such as an exam or project. While some resources such as PowerPoint presentations are of questionable value when disembodied from the lecture itself, OCW does not intend its materials to provide a full online educational experience (Stacey 2007). Complicating the picture many repositories of OERs do not abide fully by their most commonly accepted attributes such as free access, licenses for easy re-use and the ability to use open source software for accessing the content (Geser 2007). Given such diversity in the types of OERs being produced and the ways in which they are being used, perhaps the main benefit of the term is that it provides a rallying point for discussions and activities around the provision of educational content freely on the Internet.

10.2 Motivations and Benefits

The primary motivation for the OER movement is the "powerful idea that the World's knowledge is a public good." The Web provides unprecedented opportunities to share that knowledge (Smith and Casserly 2006) and reduces the costs of reproducing and distributing content to almost zero (Caswell et al. 2008).

This altruistic driver is continually in the minds of those involved in the growing numbers of OER projects; educators already generally believe that learning is beneficial for their students and can easily get caught up with the idea that these benefits should be extended as widely as possible. While there are potential commercial motivations too, as will be discussed later, the desire to give something back to society is arguably the strongest driver for the organisations and individuals in the OER movement. An analysis of the open content phenomenon is therefore heavily influenced by the wider socio-political agenda, as defined by representatives of developing nations as well as the charitable foundations who have driven and provided much of the funding for OER projects.

OERs could make it possible for far more people to study in countries where there are not enough places currently in universities and reach disadvantaged sectors such as rural communities and women who have not had adequate access to higher education. They could also demonstrate new forms of course structure and pedagogy. OERs are claimed to be able potentially to bridge the divide between universities and the public and to free learners from formalities such as admission criteria, prerequisites, tuition fees and examinations (Stacey 2007). Courses built around OERs certainly save students money by not having to buy books, and dramatically increase the variety of resources available to them, assuming they have access to the appropriate technology. They may also develop habits of independent self-regulated learning, autonomy and self-reliance (Stacey 2007).

OERs could also affect the developing syllabuses of institutions elsewhere in the World. For example, it has been suggested that the John Hopkins School of Public Health OERs could influence the development of public health initiatives in developing countries (Smith and Casserly 2006). They can also provide a useful conceptual framework for organisations to work together on the development of content, sharing costs and making better use of taxpayers' money (Geser 2007).

The growing OER movement itself has been a motivation for some institutions, including the Open University, which felt that it was naturally placed to be at the forefront of the open content revolution. It also felt that it could learn how to draw on other resources from around the World and try out new technologies and new ways of working, which could benefit mainstream provision. A "feel-good factor" has been identified by those institutions involving themselves in OER initiatives, which can extend right across the institution (McAndrew 2006). The profile of the institution is raised across the World and its teaching materials given much higher exposure (Johnstone 2005). The sharing of knowledge through OERs can be used to enhance the institution's branding.

In 2006, the UK Open University launched an OER initiative called OpenLearn with funding from the Hewlett Foundation. The University had always had a mission to extend educational provision as widely as possible by allowing students to sign up for courses without prior qualifications, by broadcasting lectures and television programmes to massive audiences on BBC TV, and by helping to set up other open universities throughout the World. It was therefore felt that an OER project fitted very well the aims of the University to spread the benefits of learning and higher education as widely as possible. In addition to pledging to provide considerable amounts of its distance learning materials as OERs, the Open University would provide tools to help learners manage their learning and would encourage the formation of learning communities around the content.

By viewing materials that colleagues have created there is potential for noticing overlaps in topics which they teach and for generating new collaborations between departments (Johnstone 2005). About 40% of faculty at MIT, for example, found OCW to be helpful for updating their courses, many also using the site for advising students (Caswell et al. 2008) At Tufts faculty use the OER website to plan their curricula, prepare for teaching or to learn themselves (Lee et al. 2008). In addition, OERs provide multiple perspectives on the same subject (Stacey 2007) for both educators and students, taking the learning beyond institutional or national boundaries. These are widely quoted as benefits of OER initiatives; however, such internal uses would also be possible with a learning management system, open to all staff but closed to external users.

Another supposed benefit of OERs is that individuals or institutions who make them available may receive them back enhanced. The OpenLearn initiative has seen many downloads of OERs from its LearningSpace site but relatively little reworked content uploaded back to its LabSpace by others. The reasons for this may be that educators are using the content without changing it significantly because of the lack of time, lack of technical skills or a feeling that they do not wish to interfere with the integrity of the materials. They may also be changing the content but do not feel confident or have the time to deposit them back in the LabSpace. Even if there are significant uploads of reversioned materials to OER repositories, there would be an expensive process in quality assuring the content and possibly a reluctance to do so by original authors who feel that their carefully crafted materials have been interfered with.

Knowing that your colleagues and indeed a worldwide audience are going to be viewing your content may lead to higher quality products (Smith and Casserly 2006) and greater recognition. In MIT, the OCW initiative has created peer pressure and competitive pride, which has led to significantly enhanced content (Geser 2007). All the Creative Commons licences require the creator of the materials to be attributed in any use or redistribution. However, in research-led institutions, professors are likely to prefer to put their efforts into research publications rather than develop their reputations for the production of OERs. This may be short-sighted. Surveys show that academic publications made freely available on the Internet receive considerably more citations than those in proprietary publications (Geser 2007).

The motivations for consumers of OERs are also strong. Knowledge gained in schools and in higher education becomes out of date after a few years and it is becoming essential to develop new skills and acquire new knowledge continuously (Brown and Adler 2008). In many countries there is a lack of educational resources and an escalating cost of books and journals (Stacey 2007). Some students use OERs to supplement materials on the courses they are enrolled in, to enhance their personal knowledge or for professional updating (Lee et al. 2008). About 71% of students at MIT used OCW during their studies, the vast majority of those reporting a positive impact on their student experience (Smith and Casserly 2006).

There is also a wider range of materials available to learners and the possibility to connect with other learners in networks based around the resources.

Whether OER initiatives can have a positive impact on student recruitment is a key question for institutions running them. MIT reports that 35% of newly enrolled students who were aware of OCW prior to attending MIT considered the initiative to be a significant or very significant influencing factor in choosing where to study. The Open University has noted that more than 7,000 people registered for a course in the same online session as being on the OpenLearn site. Those who had used both the LearningSpace and LabSpace sites were five times as likely to register (McAndrew and Santos 2008).

10.3 Risks and Objections

There are many obstacles for institutions engaging in large-scale OER initiatives; one of the major ones is resistance from faculty. Some suggest that OERs are not appropriate for their disciplines, particularly where practical skills are involved in areas such as medicine which require experiential learning and human interaction (Lee et al. 2008). Authors are concerned that their content may be altered in ways which reduce its accuracy or quality but is still attributed partially to them. They also fear that their ideas and content will be used by others without acknowledgement or remuneration to themselves or their institutions. There is a strong argument however that some developing countries are so far behind that charging for the materials is never going to be feasible and that rich nations have nothing to lose and much to gain by providing OERs freely (Stacey 2007).

There are worries too about the workload and costs involved in maintaining OERs (Smith and Casserly 2006) and that users might violate authors' privacy by attempting to contact them (Lee et al. 2008). Fortunately most of these concerns have proved to be unfounded and it has proved possible to involve large numbers of staff in OER projects. OCW reports that 70% of MIT faculty are participating in the initiative; however, some cynicism is reported as to what "participation" actually means with many faculty simply agreeing to having their lecture notes placed online by the central OCW team (Stacey 2007).

Publishers are also concerned about the threat to their business models posed by OERs and may have a significant influence on governments in their arguments that a fair, competitive and self-sustaining market must be maintained. However, countering this is a growing movement to make better use of public funding by promoting OER initiatives. There are also ongoing complaints from institutions of rising journal subscriptions and an unfair system where universities fund their staff to write, peer review and edit journals and then have to pay subscriptions to publish to receive those journals for their libraries (Geser 2007).

Many materials that may be suitable for conversion to OERs contain elements where the copyright is held by third parties. Copyright clearance is a particularly time consuming and expensive process, which often results in negative reactions from publishers. At Tufts University some faculty were concerned that having to exclude copyrighted materials impoverished their courses, made them seem basic and could affect their reputations. They felt that this could impact negatively on their academic credentials and affect their promotion prospects (Lee et al. 2008).

One major concern for educational institutions is that content which is delivered in an environment isolated from some of the key attributes of formal learning including a cohort of fellow learners, assessment and accreditation is likely to be less engaging and effective. Motivation is a key factor here; individuals with a strong interest in a subject or requirement to learn about a topic, together with well-developed study skills, may find OERs delivered in isolation are perfectly adequate for their immediate requirements. However, that is if they can access them in the first place. The digital divide remains a major obstacle to the adoption of OERs. In many parts of the World, particularly in Sub-Saharan Africa and South Asia, the infrastructure for electricity supplies and internet connectivity is unavailable, intermittent or simply too expensive for individuals or institutions to afford. Ironically these are precisely the areas which could benefit the most from free and OERs and therefore fulfil the humanitarian aims at the heart of the OER movement.

10.4 Running Institutional OER Initiatives

Initiating a successful OER initiative at an institution involves high levels of commitment from senior management and is likely to require significant start-up funding. A vision will be required for why the institution should be making its educational resources freely available. Funding from an external organisation can give added impetus to the venture and pilot projects to develop OERs can then be used to demonstrate the production processes required and the potential uses.

Systems such as eduCommons, funded by the Hewlett Foundation, assist with the processes of placing materials into a repository, tagging them with appropriate metadata, copyright clearance, quality assurance and publication. Technical staff who can convert materials into appropriate OER formats will be required to assist faculty whom, as was noted earlier, will inevitably be concerned about time commitments (Caswell et al. 2008). Addressing such concerns should be a priority for institutional OER ventures. It has been found necessary to emphasise the altruistic nature of the venture, reinforcing this and the project's links with the worldwide OER movement continually through a variety of communications. Showing statistics that demonstrate global uptake and providing examples of positive user feedback can be particularly effective (Lee et al. 2008).

There are a large number of issues that institutions need to address if OERs are to be produced on a large scale on a sustainable basis with maximum benefit to users. Andy Lane (Lane 2006) reports that OpenLearn had a particular challenge in taking material designed to be part of larger distance courses which assumed tuition, support and assessment, and repurposing it for learners who would not experience the wider context of formal learning. Another issue was the tension between making large amounts of existing, primarily text-based, materials available on the web while knowing that this was not the optimum medium for such content; it would be better to have less text, more images and more interactivity for on-screen delivery. The aim was to minimise scrolling by having no more than two screens' worth of text per web page, though it proved impossible to maintain the integrity of some of the original materials by dividing them up in this way and in the end there were some long pages requiring considerable scrolling.

Lane identifies five different characteristics of the content which may need to be tackled in the transfer from standard distance learning to OERs: type, medium, structure, language and pedagogy. The type of content will include activities, text and video. The medium is how it is rendered; video content might for example move from CD-ROM to streaming video. Structural changes such as breaking the content up into smaller chunks will be necessary. There is also the language of instruction, which is not changed by the OpenLearn team, although translations have been made by users abroad. Finally, there is the pedagogical model. Attempts to keep this as close to the original as possible were made, but the other changes frequently impact on the pedagogical approach.

One of OpenLearn's biggest challenges has been attempting to retain the essential nature of the learning content while transforming it into OERs appropriate for online delivery with smaller chunks of text, more interactivity and greater use of multimedia. The approach of placing mainly text-based materials on OpenLearn as the starting point drew criticism from some commentators but meant that large amounts of content could be uploaded quickly, maintaining consistency with the original content, but able to be transformed into more engaging OERs later.

OERs will achieve much greater penetration, particularly in less affluent regions where they may have the most benefits, if they depend only on free or open source software for their usage. Providing materials in simple web pages will guarantee the greatest visibility. The incorporation of flash animations or video may enhance the content and be visible using a freely-downloadable plug-in for the web browser. However, OER authors may not realise that such content is bandwidth-heavy and therefore difficult or costly for some users to download (Smith and Casserly 2006). It is also of course likely to be more expensive to produce and much more difficult to edit by other teachers than text. Moreover, it may be less accessible for users with some disabilities; there can be a trade-off between the engagement achieved with the use of multimedia in educational software and the accessibility of the materials.

The issues may be more acute with OERs than with educational software designed for distribution in affluent countries where more aspects of the supporting infrastructure such as bandwidth and the underlying software and hardware can be assured. A further issue with providing content such as video or flash files is that teachers may not have the skills to adapt more complex materials or access to the proprietary software required to do so. Alternative low bandwidth versions of content for areas with limited infrastructure may therefore be required.

The use of mobile phones is however growing massively in developing countries. Handheld devices can be charged from intermittent power supplies or solar power, and the supporting infrastructure is easier to maintain than a network of cables to individual houses. The implication for OERs is that in order to prove maximum benefit (in the developed world too) they will need to be accessible on devices with small screens and a variety of operating systems. This has major design implications and renders much of the content produced to date inaccessible without considerable re-engineering.

Deciding how big an OER module should be and whether there should be subdivisions is a challenge for all creators of content, and brings out many of the issues about granularity and dependencies which the learning object community has been debating over the past decade. In the case of OpenLearn (Lane 2006) it was decided that a "unit" should be between 3 and 15 hours of effort (including study time, "thinking" time), i.e. between an evening's worth of study and a week's worth of part-time study. Subdivisions into smaller sections of three hours' length would be possible but the unit would be self-contained with no references to other units and minimal hyperlinks to other websites. There could be several learning outcomes per three hours' study. The units would be put together into "groups" of between five and ten units in the same discipline area and level. Within these groups, learners would be free to study the units in any order they chose. In the end the expected study time for units was between four and thirty hours.

Determining the level of study is another complex issue. Most courses make assumptions about the capabilities of the learner and assume prior subject knowledge. With OpenLearn no assumptions are made about prior knowledge as the units do not lead from one to the next. However, OpenLearn classifies units in four levels: *introductory undergraduate* (the learner's qualifications would not guarantee entry to higher education), *intermediate undergraduate* (the learner has qualifications appropriate for starting higher education), *advanced undergraduate* (the learner has already studied at university level) and *masters* (the learner already has a degree).

OpenLearn took the decision to include self-assessment tasks covering every learning outcome in a unit – either an interactive quiz or a reflective activity that the learner writes up. Because of the limitations of the virtual learning environment used, not all forms of paper-based interaction such as filling in a table could be easily replicated online so sometimes these had to be left out. A forum was provided for each unit too, where learners could discuss the content or provide evaluations of the materials.

Determining the recommended study time for a unit was another issue which exercised the OpenLearn team greatly. It was assumed that English would be the learner's mother tongue and that study time would be likely to be longer if not. Learners studying units at *introductory undergraduate* level would be given more time to read than those at *masters* level, for example. It was also assumed that on-screen reading would take longer than reading from print. Further allowance was made for the fact that the materials might be delivered in isolation, thus taking learners longer to "tune-in" than those who were studying a lot of related modules on a formal course. These factors meant that an additional 35% of time was added to the recommended study hours for most content than when they were in their original form.

10.5   Translation and Localization

Learners are likely to be more motivated when the medium of instruction is in their mother tongue (Stacey 2007), but this can add considerably to costs. At the UNESCO meeting in Paris, Professor Dahbi reported that in Morocco "Multilingualism... functions as a limiting factor [since] institutions feel that it is inappropriate and improper to be present on the web only in French, so they spend a lot of energy and resources trying to have Arabic as well as French and sometimes English, which makes the whole effort much more costly or simply aborts the project" (UNESCO 2002).

Various organisations are involved in translating OCW, OpenLearn and other content into different languages. Pre-eminent among these is China Open Resources for Education (CORE) which incorporates a number of prestigious Chinese universities, and provides a mirror site for MIT content with much of it already translated into Chinese (Johnstone 2005). Translations in Spanish and Portuguese are also provided by Universias, a large consortium of institutions in Spain, Portugal and Latin America.

There are serious logistical issues in maintaining translations of OERs. When resources in the original language are updated, those in translation risk being outdated unless there are processes in place to ensure that new translations are made. Finding out which bits of an OER have been updated in order to update the translation could be a time-consuming process. In addition, there will always be questions as to the quality of the translation and whether the author's meanings have been interpreted correctly by the translator.

Allegations of cultural imperialism are also levelled at the OER movement and many would like to see a two-way flow of content and interaction between the developed and developing nations. OERs are built around a host culture, using a specific language, pedagogy and institutional philosophy, with literature generally originating from that culture. Such issues have led to discussions regarding the possibilities for local initiatives in developing countries themselves for the production and dissemination of OERs. Interestingly, Universias latterly changed its emphasis from translation to assisting their members in the creation of their own OERs. Carnegie Mellon's OLI initiative has partnerships with faculty and institutions in Chile, Columbia and Qatar in order to localize, translate and enhance the courses. Encouragingly, partners include instructional designers and learning scientists as well as subject experts (Stacey 2007). However, the predominant model is likely to remain the provision of OERs by developed nations with the developing countries lacking the financial and human resources to initiate and maintain significant repositories of OERs.

10.6   Sustainability

Although many institutions have recognised the benefits of OERs, there remain powerful incentives for institutions to protect their investments in educational resources. This may be particularly acute for institutions where distance education is prominent and a large amount of resource is devoted to the production of content. A valued part of the student experience at institutions such as the UK Open University is the receipt through the post of packages of learning materials at the start of a course. These materials are a physical manifestation of the investment a student has made in their studies and remain of value well after the end of the course. There are concerns that some students might not register for study if all the materials are available freely and this may be one reason why OERs on the UK OU's OpenLearn site generally represent only a proportion of the total content for individual courses.

There remain numerous opportunities for staff and universities to make money through the sale of educational content by deals with publishers or distance learning courses, and the OER movement undoubtedly presents a threat to the status quo. However, many institutions and even publishers may see that the benefits of providing OER "loss leaders" are worth forgoing other forms of income generation. The Open University has commissioned popular television programmes with the BBC since the 1970s, which cost a significant amount of money but generate positive publicity for the University and increased interest in studying there. One recent television series *Life in Cold Blood* inspired 83,054 potential students to enquire about Open University courses. If similar evidence of registration on OU courses after browsing courses on OpenLearn can be ascertained then there is more justification for sustaining the initiative. McAndrew (2006) quotes costs of €600 recruitment costs per student and suggests that the €9m costs of the OpenLearn project over two years would be covered if 15,000 new students were recruited as a result of the project. Given that the costs will be significantly lower in future years as the infrastructure has already been developed it begins to look as if maintaining OpenLearn could be almost justified solely on the grounds of student recruitment.

Repositories of OERs will require ongoing substantial investment to retain their usefulness. OERs themselves will become outdated and therefore need to be updated when necessary. New content should be added on a regular basis in order to add dynamism to the site and drive continued visits from users. The sites themselves incur costs in hosting, backing up and installing server upgrades. Stephen Downes examines various financial models for sustaining OER initiatives (Downes 2007) and these are worth analysing in some detail.

Many US institutions rely heavily for their funding from endowments, and Downes proposes that the *endowment model* might provide a mechanism for the ongoing funding of OER projects. However, with interest rates at unprecedented low levels and an uncertain outlook for other investments in the current global economic climate this is unlikely to be a viable option.

This downturn in the World economy may also negatively affect the viability of a *donations model* where a non-profit foundation requests and receives funds to maintain the OER initiative. Wikipedia is funded on this basis; however, it is able to run its operations with minimal staffing and relies on many thousands of volunteers to create and maintain a website which, though hugely comprehensive, is far less complex than the range of materials considered to be OERs.

A *membership model* is also proposed, where a consortium of institutions funds the OER initiative. There are successful examples of such groupings such as SAKAI, for building educational software, and IMS which coordinates the development of underlying specifications and standards for educational software. MERLOT (MERLOT, 2009) is an example of an OER initiative where member organisations contribute to the costs of maintaining and developing a repository of OERs. However, one of the major benefits of OERs as outlined earlier is the branding and reputational potential for the institution that may be lost if efforts are subsumed into a wider membership organisation. On the other hand, participation in organisations such as the Open Courseware Consortium is arguably a useful way for the visibility of individual university websites to be increased. (Lee et al. 2008)

In the *conversion model* consumers of free content are converted to paying customers. Many social software sites utilise this model so that the majority of users can use the system at no cost but those organisations and individuals who find the service vital to their business or lives are prepared to pay for additional services such as support or advanced features. Flickr is one example and Twitter is another site investigating commercialisation possibilities. Building commercial services around OERs to generate income may indeed be one of the only ways for institutions to justify the continuation of OER initiatives.

The *contributor-pay model* requires producers or commissioners of content to pay for the cost of making it freely available. Downes mentions that the Wellcome Trust, which spends £400m producing nearly 3,500 papers each year (Geser 2007), requires research funded by them to be made available freely and is prepared to pay considerable amounts of money to ensure that this happens. Meanwhile, the German and Austrian government-funded research councils have open publishing requirements, the Spanish Government is investigating a similar policy of open access to the results of all research funded with public monies (Ministerio de Ciencia e Innovation 2009) and there is a possibility that public bodies will follow suit around the World. This model may be appropriate for publications which require no maintenance however OERs, as has been stated earlier, cannot remain static and it is unlikely that funding OER projects in this way will be sustainable.

A *sponsorship model* where sponsoring institutions raise their profile through logos or advertising does have potential, though intrusive advertisements are likely to be resented by users of OERs. To maximise the usefulness of OERs they will need to be able to be remixed by educators elsewhere who may of course use the opportunity to remove commercial advertising.

The *institutional model* is the dominant current model for sustainability and includes all the major initiatives such as OCW, OpenLearn and Connexions. Here an institution assumes responsibility for the ongoing maintenance of the OERs after initial funding from an outside body is reduced or ceases. With this model the institution retains many of the benefits outlined earlier however it will require considerable ongoing funding and can only be justified if there is an acceptance that the costs are outweighed by the benefits. If OER development practices are viewed as a burdensome additional responsibility for faculty they are unlikely to be sustainable. They may therefore have to become an integral part of teaching responsibilities and the educational mission of institutions (Smith and Casserly 2006) with their production recognised in promotion and tenure processes (Stacey 2007). Embedding such practices in institutions combined with the development of volunteer networks to support and maintain content may a viable way forward.

Also listed is a *governmental model* where governments provide funding for OER developments. In the UK, Joint Information Systems Committee (JISC) is funding a programme for the creation of OERs (JISC 2009). However, this and other initiatives are often designed to fund the development of the resources with less thought given to their sustainability. Governments are less likely to commit resource to the ongoing maintenance and development of repositories of OERs. The Worldwide recession may provide the impetus though for this with funding for the development of teaching materials being withdrawn from individual institutions and pooled for the centralised or collaborative development of OERs, maximising the government's investment (though also making the materials freely available to competing nations).

Finally, Downes mentions *partnerships and exchanges* where institutions exchange their expertise in OER production and the OERs themselves. This is a pooling of resources in a similar way to the governmental model but arranged by the institutions themselves rather than being imposed from on high. This has the potential to increase the range and quality of OERs but still requires substantial ongoing financial commitment from the institutions themselves.

In reality, none of the nine funding models described above will be sufficient to maintain the majority of the current OER initiatives which are based in a single institution. Where organisations wish to maintain the momentum of their OER programmes, they may need both to draw on a range of external and internal funding sources and to weave the production and maintenance of OERs into their institutional fabric so that it is not seen as an additional burden. The Open University's strategy for sustaining OpenLearn includes embedding the development and use of OERs within all existing activities, continuing to seek grant funding from a range of sources and investigating new business models for educational services around OERs. Perhaps most importantly though procedures and systems are being put in place for formal course materials and OERs to be created simultaneously so that there is minimal additional overhead for the production of the open materials (McAndrew and Santos 2008).

10.7   Conclusions

The importance of the social aspect to learning is recognised throughout the OER movement and some of the projects have attempted to build learning communities around the content. When students interact in groups they can clarify their understanding by asking questions or listening to answers to other questions. By explaining difficult concepts to other students they are reinforcing their own understanding. Where learning activities involve web-based forums, wikis, blogging and commenting on blogs, opportunities for reflection and the deepening of understanding are likely to be greater than when OERs are provided in isolation.

In fact some argue that providing OERs in the context of teacher-led education will simply fail to provide learners with the skills they need. OLCOS believes the focus should be more on open educational practices which use constructivist and competency-focussed models of learning to promote collaboration and engagement. With technologies such as blogs students gather and interpret information, take a position and back it up with evidence and refer to the writings of others; wikis go a step further by encouraging the collaborative creation of knowledge (Geser 2007). Teachers, they say, should "change their roles from dispensers of knowledge to facilitators of open educational practices that emphasise learners' own activities in developing competences, knowledge and skills." The teachers themselves should be involved in communities of practice where they share content and experiences and encourage learner participation through the use of social software (Geser et al. 2007). OERs will only make a significant impact if a new mindset and culture in education can be developed to make the best of them, and repositories continue to see teachers and learners primarily as consumers rather than producers and adaptors of content (Geser 2007).

The social constructivist paradigm behind the OLCOS vision may be based on sound educational research but it is difficult to facilitate. Online forums for learners are more likely to be utilised where there is a subject expert involved and where participation is clearly linked to the assessment process. With educators, effective communities of practice are not easy to put in place either and are much more likely to succeed if they form spontaneously between people who have a genuine interest in making them work. Wenger (1998) believes communities of practice comprise three main attributes:

- Joint enterprise as understood and continually renegotiated by its members
- Mutual engagement that binds members together into a social entity
- The shared repertoire of communal resources that members have developed over time

While it may be possible to build communities of practice with teachers, none of these attributes is likely to be fostered among individual learners who are outside formal courses of learning unless a highly engaging and dynamic site can be built which draws them back continuously and provides them with direct benefits from engaging with other learners. The OpenLearn project demonstrates the difficulties of attempting to build communities: despite huge interest in the content there is relatively little discussion between learners in the online forums, and educators have not uploaded their own or reversioned content to the extent that was envisaged.

Learners are more likely to benefit from OERs where an associated learning community has been established. They are also more likely to return to repositories which offer the attractions of dynamically-updated interactive content, thus providing added incentives for institutions to foster such communities and maximise the returns on their investment. Perhaps formal education in order to drive usage of

OERs will ultimately prove to be necessary. One venture, the University of the People, proposed by Israeli entrepreneur, Shai Reshev, aims to build on free educational resources and peer to peer teaching networks. It would incorporate attributes of formal education such as registration, weekly discussions, assignments and exams but at a nominal fee for enrolment ($15-$50) and exams ($10 to $100) (Lewin, 2009)

There is little doubt that educational resources will continue to be made available freely on an ever greater scale and that the OERs are already being used by large numbers of learners and educators around the World. Unlike the open source movement and the social software phenomenon, however, the OER movement is much more organised, less spontaneous, and funded and nurtured to a large extent by organisations such as UNESCO and Hewlett with socio-political agendas. It is not therefore a grass roots movement and runs the risk of floundering if the funding is pulled from it. A key question for the charitable foundations who have spent many millions of dollars in attempting to develop the movement is: has the tipping point for OERs been reached? In the coming years many people will be watching closely whether universities and other educational providers are truly able to embed the production and maintenance of OERs into their institutional processes without reliance on external funding.

References

Brown, J. S., & Adler, R. P. (2008). Minds of fire: Open education, the long tail and learning 2.0. *EDUCAUSE Review*, 43(1), 16–32.

Caswell, T., Henson, S., Jensen, M., & Wiley, D. (2008). Open educational resources: Enabling universal education. *The International Review of Research in Open and Distance Learning*, 9 (1) http://www.irrodl.org/index.php/irrodl/article/view/637/1396, ISSN: 1492-3831.

Downes, S. (2007). Models for Sustainable Open Educational Resources. (A. Koohang, Ed.) *Interdisciplinary Journal of Knowledge and Learning Objects*, 3, 29–44. Retrieved from http://ijklo.org/Volume3/IJKLOv3p029-044Downes.pdf

Geser, G., Hornung-Prahauser, V., & Schaffert, S. (2007). Observing open e-learning content: A roadmap for educational policy and institutions and hands-on tips for practitioners. Villach, Austria.

Geser, G. (ed.) (2007). *Open educational practice and resources: OLCOS roadmap 2012*. Salzburg: OLCOS.

JISC. (2009). *Open educational resources programme*. Retrieved February 15, 2009 from JISC: http://www.jisc.ac.uk/whatwedo/programmes/oer.aspx.

Johnstone, S. M. (2005). Open educational resources serve the world. *Educause Quarterly* (3), 15–18.

Lane, A. (2006). *From pillar to post: Exploring the issues involved in re-purposing distance learning materials for use as Open Educational Resources*. Milton Keynes: Open University.

Lee, M. Y., Albright, S., O'Leary, L., Terkla, D. G., & Wilson, N. (2008). Expanding the reach of health sciences education and empowering others: The OpenCourseWare initiative at Tufts University. *Medical Teacher*, 30(2), 159–163.

Lewin, T. (2009). *Israeli Entrepreneur Plans a Free Global University That Will Be Online Only*. Retrieved February 15, 2009 from The New York Times: http://www.nytimes.com/2009/01/26/education/26university.html

McAndrew, P., & Santos, A. I. (2008). *Learning from OpenLearn: Research Report 2006–2008*. Milton Keynes: Open University.

McAndrew, P. (2006). Motivations for OpenLearn. *CERI–Second Closed Expert Meeting on Open Educational Resources*. Barcelona: OECD.

MERLOT. (2009). Retrieved February 15, 2009 from MERLOT: http://taste.merlot.org/

Ministerio de Ciencia e Innovation. (2009). *El Grupo de Trabajo ha entregado hoy al Ministerio de Ciencia e Innovación el borrador de anteproyecto de la nueva Ley de la Ciencia y la Tecnología*. Retrieved February 15, 2009 from Nueva Ley de la Ciencia y la Tecnología.

Smith, M. S., & Casserly, C. M. (2006). The promise of open educational resources. *Change*, 8–17.

Stacey, P. (2007). Open educational resources in a global context. *First Monday*, 12(4) Available online, retrieved September, 2010 from http://www.firstmonday.org/issues/issue12_4/stacey/index.html

UNESCO. (2002). *Forum on the Impact of Open Courseware for Higher Education in Developing Countries: Final Report*. Paris: UNESCO.

UNESCO. (2004). *Second Global Forum on International Quality Assurance, Accreditation and the Recognition of Qualifications in Higher Education: "Widening Access to Quality Higher Education": Background Document*. Paris: UNESCO.

Wenger, E. (1998). Communities of Practice: Learning as a Social System. *The Systems Thinker*. Pegasus Communications Inc.

Part III
Conclusion

Chapter 11
Content Management and E-Learning: A Strategic Perspective

A.W. (Tony) Bates

11.1 Introduction

Content management is not an issue most senior administrators in educational institutions will be familiar with. In this chapter, I want to take a strategic view of content management, especially for those institutions that have or are about to make a major commitment to the development and delivery of online teaching and learning materials, or what I will call digital learning materials.

Although content management is probably most likely to be implemented from the bottom up, through small projects initiated on a departmental or divisional basis, there will come a point at which the institution needs to look at content management as a whole. At this point, the senior management will need to start asking some strategic questions:

1. Why do we need content management? What goals do or can it serve?
2. Where are we at the moment with content management?
3. What still needs to be done?
4. What does it or will it cost?
5. What are the alternatives?
6. What is the best way to manage this?

This chapter will not provide definitive answers to these questions, because the answers will vary from institution to institution. However, the chapter will discuss some of these questions and suggest a process for dealing with the management of content.

A.W. (Tony) Bates (✉)
Tony Bates Associates Ltd., 2906 West Broadway, Suite #342, Vancouver, B.C.,
V6K 2G8, Canada
e-mail: tony.bates@ubc.ca

N. Ferran and J. Minguillón (eds.), *Content Management for E-Learning*,
DOI 10.1007/978-1-4419-6959-0_11, © Springer Science+Business Media, LLC 2011

11.2   Why the Senior Administration Needs to Understand Content Management

E-learning differs from face-to-face classroom teaching in many ways. E-learning results in the creation of digital content that can be reused or redesigned for multiple use. The creation of digital content, particularly high quality educational digital content, requires time, money, and skill. Digital content once created can be made easily accessible through the Internet to anyone else in the world who might be interested in using that content.

Digital content therefore has potential value that goes beyond its initial use in a specific act of teaching or learning. As Magee (2005) comments, "the considerable investment in [digital] materials requires an organization to receive fair compensation for their use and maintain control over their usage." Even if the institution decides to eschew commercial gain, and offer its digital learning materials as "open content" (a crucial strategic decision that needs to be made at the highest level), there will still be an essential need to manage the content so that it is easily accessible, its use tracked, and intellectual property issues properly managed. Perhaps of even greater importance is the need to ensure that digital learning materials are maximally used within the organization, to avoid duplication and to build a "bank" of high quality, peer-assessed digital learning materials that are associated with the institution.

There is a very large and expanding technical discussion of educational digital content in the form of learning objects and meta-data standards. A great deal of energy has currently been focused on the design of learning objects, the implications for teaching and learning, technical standards, and engineering issues. It should be noted though that learning objects are only one, specifically technical approach to the management of content. Other approaches to content management are also possible. Unfortunately though, little attention has been paid in educational institutions to the issue of the management of digital content from the strategic perspective of an institution.

Some of the strategic issues are as follows:

- What are the values that should drive the availability of and access to the institution's digital content?
- The business case for digital content management.
- How best to create digital content so it can be reused?
- How to identify, store, and make accessible digital content?
- Who owns the copyright for digital content once created?
- What uses are permitted of that content and who decides quality control?
- What is the best way to manage content once created?

Although the participation of the institution's IT department is essential in such decision-making, it can be seen from the above list that the implications of content management are not just technical. Content management raises issues of stakeholder analysis, decision-making processes, and institutional goals, policies and procedures that require the attention of senior administrators.

11.3 The External Context

One important factor in deciding policy on content management is the wider context in which the institution is located. Factors that can influence decisions on content management include government policy regarding sharing and ownership of digital learning materials, local consortia and partnerships, and possible vendors or sponsors.

A number of governments have implemented policies that impact directly on local content management. For instance, a government may require institutions to adopt an open source or open content policy, either by legislation or more often through financial incentives. For instance, the Generalitat (the provincial government) of Catalonia, and the Federal government of Brazil have policies that give preference to IT solutions for educational institutions based on open source software. Several governments, such as the provincial government of British Columbia in Canada, have policies that require all digital learning materials created through public funding to be available free of charge to students at any other publicly funded institution within the province.

The institution may be a partner in a consortium that is committed to sharing digital learning materials, or distance education programs. This may well provide an external stimulus for both content management and agreement on technical meta-data standards. Thus, in British Columbia the government created BC Campus (http://BCcampus.ca), which provides local institutions with a number of services with respect to online teaching. One is the sharing of online courses between the 2-year community colleges. Another is funding to support the creation of digital learning materials or learning objects that can be shared across the provincial institutions.

One of the British Columbian 2-year institutions, the College of the Rockies, is now offering 100 online courses in English and Maths free of charge to other institutions in developing countries through a partnership with the Commonwealth of Learning, a public not-for-profit organization that supports ICT-based education in 56 developing countries (see: http://www.cotr.bc.ca/press/fullhdLine.asp?IDnumber=311 and http://www.WikiEducator.org). Also in Canada, eCampus Alberta provides the opportunity for students throughout the province of Alberta to take online courses from other institutions (see http://www.ecampusalberta.ca/). The providing institution owns the copyright for the course, and recoups costs of course delivery through payment of student tuition fees to the institution that has "ownership" of the course, even if the student is registered with another institution.

Some vendors offer products that are based on open standards, enabling the linking of different software systems such as student registration, financial services, and online courses. The decision to opt for open source software does not necessarily imply a commitment to open content, but it is much easier to make content available to other institutions if they are using similar learning management systems. At least from a student perspective there is greater consistency, even though they may be taking courses from more than one institution, if the software standards and in particular the LMS interfaces are similar between institutions.

Any college or university entering a consortium based on the sharing of digital learning materials or whole online courses, or funded by governments that require funded materials to be freely available to other institutions within its jurisdiction, needs to have a content management strategy that is consistent with this wider context. Thus content management is an important tool for building partnerships, and for reaching out beyond the walls of the institution, with digital learning materials.

11.4 The Internal Context

11.4.1 Creation, Storage, and Access to Digital Learning Materials

For many institutions without a current content management system for digital learning materials, the first question that needs to be asked and answered is as follows: "What do we have and where is it?" Once digital material is created, it needs to be described, stored and be easily found and accessed by a variety of users. This can be done manually (e.g., classified by course coordinators, and the registry of materials stored by the Library) after creation, or through the use of digital tools such as tagging at the point of creation, or through a combination of both manual and digital procedures. Whatever method is used to describe and store materials, it will involve substantial additional costs to those of creating them.

Once untagged or unclassified digital learning materials already created have been identified, another question arises. "Do we tag 'old' digital material or do we leave it and only tag new material?" Unfortunately, to answer this question, another set of questions needs to be answered first.

It might seem obvious that all newly created digital learning materials should be digitally tagged following a common standard, and this standard should be compatible with the standards being used by other institutions within the same jurisdiction or family of institutions. However, this is a complex issue, and can result in substantial costs if the wrong decisions are made. For instance at what level should materials be tagged, using what software, and using what categories or descriptors? Who should decide this and who should do this?

What is needed to drive such decisions is a clear management policy and strategies regarding the reuse of educational digital materials. In other words, what is the business case for the reuse of materials? To give an example, materials developed for regular courses leading to accreditation could be reused or redesigned for use by industry or business for in-house training. However, what is the market for this? What types of content and digital materials can be sold or licensed to external clients? What level of revenue is such use likely to generate and will it justify the costs of classifying and storing the materials?

These questions cannot be answered at the moment by many educational institutions, because the market research has not been done, or because the internal knowledge of markets has not been sufficiently organized and coordinated to answer such questions. Thus, it is necessary for areas concerned with marketing of an institution's academic services, such as Corporate Training or Continuing Studies, and also to some extent the academic departments, to be able to define potential external markets and products for the use of digital materials created for use by an institution's own students. At the same time, academic departments must be able to describe accurately and locate material that might be of value to external clients that currently exists within the institution, and to identify other potential areas of content that might be of interest to external clients. This will help to some extent to identify the external market for existing and for new content.

For many institutions wishing to market or make available to external users digital learning materials, it will be important to create a central registry of all digital learning materials already created by the institution, and to develop a system by which all new digital learning materials are automatically added to the registry. This content could include digitally recorded lectures (video or podcasts), course outlines and objectives, assessment questions and marking rubrics, online digital resources such as collections of online readings and urls of resource sites, as well as specially created digital content, such as academic text, diagrams, animations, and simulations.

Initially, it might be too expensive to create all digital learning resources so that they can be electronically searched and located through meta-tagging. Location of existing digital learning materials might be done manually initially, using an online template or form to be completed by the curriculum coordinator responsible for each course. The data from this form should be stored in ways that enable it to be quickly searched, again, possibly online but not necessarily automatically.

Technologists may scoff at the idea of manually locating digital learning resources, but for marketing purposes, quick and immediate access now may be more important than a fully automated system in 5 years time. This point was emphasized by a conference speaker from the National Library of Scotland, which had converted quickly two million artefacts (poems, photographs, illustrations, etc.) into digital format (see http://www.nls.uk/digitallibrary/index.html). When asked at a conference what meta-tagging standard was used for searches, the librarian responded: "The LA standard." This confused the computer scientists, who had never heard of this standard. "'Excuse me,' one asked, but what is the LA standard?" "Library Assistant," responded the librarian. "When someone wants an artefact, they e-mail a library assistant who sends it to them as an e-mail attachment." His point was that it was quicker and more effective to do it this way than to retro-actively tag over two million artefacts, which had already been manually classified and could easily be found by a librarian.

It should be remembered that many institutions are not even in the position of the National Library of Scotland, which had already manually identified and classified the two million artefacts. Many institutions will need to identify and classify – and in many cases evaluate – existing digital learning materials, before they can make them available externally.

As it becomes clearer from market research what kinds of materials are in demand for external use, selected materials may be digitally tagged on creation.

In order to assess the additional costs involved in digital tagging, pilot projects should be established and costs (mainly in terms of staff time) carefully tracked.

Irrespective of the methods adopted, then, most educational institutions will need to investigate:

- A clear business case for the reuse of digital materials.
- Ways to identify, store, and access digital learning materials already created and/ or owned by the institution.
- Ways to create, identify, store, and access all new digital learning materials in a cost-effective, consistent manner for reuse.

11.4.2   Values and Principles in the Reuse of Digital Materials

Without a clear institutional position on the sale or reuse of digital material, it will be extremely difficult to decide how much to spend on, or how important it is, to have an efficient content management system.

An institution can position itself at a variety of points on a continuum of values or philosophy about the reuse of digital materials. At one extreme is the purely philanthropic or "public good" position. All digital learning materials created by an institution may be freely used by external users. This for instance is the position of MIT's OpenCourseware initiative (http://ocw.mit.edu/index.html). Even these initiatives though have some restrictions, such as not to permit commercial use without permission, and in MIT's case, it is at the discretion of each professor as to what material will be made available. At the other extreme, everything is for sale. In the middle are positions such as that in Alberta and British Columbia, where any publicly funded fully online course must be available to any student attending any public institution within the jurisdiction, whether or not they are a student at the institution offering the course. However, outside the jurisdiction, the government encourages institutions to market their materials.

One argument for the "public good" position is that there is not much money to be made in the reuse of material, so it might as well be offered free. It is certainly true that there is little hard evidence to date of profitable reuse of material on a large scale. It may also be possible for an institution to have a more complex philosophy, such as making materials available free of charge to public institutions and nonprofit organizations, but to charge for use of materials by private or commercial organizations. The "Creative Commons" (http://creativecommons.org/) provides a way for institutions to protect their copyright while at the same time offering free access to selected categories of users. Nevertheless, even free content needs to be identified, classified, organized, and made easy to find for external as well as internal users, and so even the offer of "free" content has a cost. (MIT's OpenCourseware initiative for instance is supported by multi-million dollar grants from the William and Flora Hewlett and the Andrew W. Mellon Foundations.)

One policy of course is not to require consistency across the institution but to devolve the decision to academic departments, for instance. Thus Arts may offer all its digital materials free, while Business Studies will only allow reuse for payment. However, once again this should be a conscious decision by the senior administration, and will increase considerably the complexity of content management.

Thus every institution needs to make a clear statement about its financial goals with respect to the reuse of digital learning materials and online courses. This may need to be discussed and agreed with the institution's Board of Governors or even with the appropriate funding agency (e.g., Ministry of Higher Education).

11.4.3 Rewards for Creating Content

What benefits can the institution offer to professors and instructors to encourage content development, or, more precisely, what benefits can be offered to encourage the development of high-quality digital learning materials? The rewards need not be in terms of money, as professors are often more interested in having their contributions recognized professionally, although royalties or revenue-sharing agreements are a definite monetary benefit, even if in the end the sums earned by an individual academic may not be very great. Other benefits could be training in developing digital learning materials, technical and instructional assistance, direct funding for research, and/or reduced face-to-face teaching loads.

One advantage of digital learning materials is that they are readily available for evaluation, and so some form of peer evaluation is possible. As well as tracking academic contributors of selected content, a content management system should provide records of academic contributions to digital content creation and how much this is used. This information could be used by an instructor when seeking appointment, tenure, or promotion. However, for benefits to be earned, there needs to be in place some means of measuring and rewarding quality of output, and ultimately for selection of materials for external distribution, and this should be considered as part of a content management strategy (and more importantly, as part of a faculty development strategy).

In the end, every institution needs a clear and fair system of rewards that recognizes the contribution of those staff who create digital learning materials that have commercial and/or academic value.

11.4.4 Intellectual Property and Copyright Issues

The way digital rights are managed can vary enormously not only between institutions, but sometimes even within an institution. It is not unusual in some institutions to negotiate each agreement for content usage and sharing on a case-by-case basis. Legal counsel reviews each agreement to ensure that relevant legal issues are properly addressed. This is clearly an unworkable policy when all professors across an institution are creating digital learning materials.

In countries such as Canada and the USA, professors, rightly or wrongly, usually believe that they own any academic digital materials that they create. There is case law in Canada (Dorsey 2004) that IP rights for material created as part of their employment cannot be negotiated away on an individual basis (between the university and an individual tenured professor), but must be negotiated through the bargaining process with the faculty union. (Nevertheless, professors are often willing to agree IP issues on an individual, case-by-case basis.) On the other hand, in 2-year colleges in North America, often the institution has a clear policy that states that the institution automatically owns all materials created by its employees, including instructors.

Another issue that needs to be addressed is moral rights and protecting the integrity of the materials. Many academics are more concerned about "their" materials being used without acknowledgement (i.e., plagiarism) or being reused for other purposes (such as for profit by an external organization) without their knowledge or agreement (moral rights), if the materials are made freely available. With respect to the integrity of the materials, it may not be safe for an external client, say a trainer in a company, to take a particular diagram or animation out of the context of the rest of the course (which might for instance require an animation to be supplemented with supervised hands-on experience). Indeed, if an accident should occur as a result of faulty training, the institution that supplied the digital learning materials may be liable, if it does not have in place procedures to protect against such use. Similarly, external clients who have accessed materials from another institution should be restrained from selling on or incorporating the materials in other products without permission. Facilities such as the Creative Commons (http://creativecommons.org/) allow for limited rights for third parties to use materials, but it may be necessary for an institution to develop its own generic wording for the use of its materials by external clients.

Content management therefore requires clear policies on the ownership of digital materials. Content management needs to track the IP agreements on each "chunk" of digital learning material, and also be able to track external use of such material. This requires not only suitable software, and IP ownership policies in place, but also people to do this work.

For content management to be financially and educationally justified, there must be clearly agreed policies about the ownership and use of digital learning materials, either through faculty union collective bargaining agreements, by institution policies or through government legislation, depending on the local context. Where there is legal or employee confusion or disputes about IP ownership, it must be an important priority for the institution's administration to resolve these issues; otherwise, content management becomes extremely difficult if not impossible.

11.4.5 Quality

If content is to be marketed, or even distributed free, by an institution, issues around quality arise. There has been a great deal of concern in the literature about the often poor quality of e-learning materials, especially when developed by individual professors working on their own ("Lone Rangers" – see Bates 2000, for a fuller discussion of this issue; also Zemsky and Massey 2004). What quality checks, if any, should be placed on digital learning materials that are to be made available beyond the boundaries of the institution?

Many professors and some institutional managers believe this is a nonissue. The institution has a number of procedures in place to ensure quality teaching, such as hiring procedures, qualifications of professors, curriculum development and approval processes, and this applies as much to the development of digital learning materials as to face-to-face teaching. Quality is ensured by the institution's reputation. Others argue that let the market judge. If the materials are "good," they will be used. If the materials are poor, the author, the individual professor, may lose some reputation, but no-one will blame the institution.

However, as Shakespeare noted, reputation is hard won and easily lost. There is no guarantee that even a well-respected research professor, especially one working on their own, will produce high quality digital learning materials that incorporate good use of the technology, such as clear graphics and animation, and sound educational principles, such as clear learning objectives, interaction, and feedback.

Once digital learning materials become public, and distributed under the aegis of an institution, that institution's reputation is inextricably bound to the quality of the materials. It should be noted that this can be a positive as well as a negative. The success of the British Open University when it was established in 1971 was due mainly to the perceived quality of its broadcast TV programs and printed course books, which were public. Many of the academic texts and broadcast programmes became used by academics in other universities in Britain. However, the Open University established rigorous quality assurance processes, such as multi-disciplinary course teams and external review of its materials, before these materials were published (Perry 1976).

Some institutions have shown an interest in a content review process such as exists in MERLOT, a learning object repository in the USA that uses peer review to assess the quality of a learning object before it is accepted (http://www.merlot.org/merlot/index.htm). However, the vast majority of MERLOT's learning objects are not evaluated, and some of the proposed evaluation methodologies are very expensive – see Nesbit et al. (2002).

Once again, an institution can take a variety of positions regarding the quality of the digital learning materials, but it will certainly need a clear set of policies and procedures regarding quality as part of its content management strategy. (Doing nothing is always a possible policy or procedure, but it should be arrived at deliberately rather than by accident.)

11.4.6   Stakeholder Analysis

Content management may be seen as a technical issue, but in fact it crosses many divisional or departmental boundaries. Traditionally, the management of academic content has been mainly the responsibility of the institutional library. It is the library that has traditionally classified, stored and distributed content, in the form of books and journals. For content management to be useful, digital content needs to be appropriately classified for semantic as well as technical aspects. As libraries have moved to the provision of online services, such as e-journals, e-books, and online ordering of printed materials, they have set up digital authentication systems to enforce the restricted access to e-books and e-journals, to track usage, and to ensure access is only by registered users. Many of the procedures currently carried out by trained librarians can be adapted and modified to assist with the management of digital learning materials. Thus the library, as well as technical and academic departments, clearly has an important role to play in content management.

The academic staff, professors, and instructors, also have a clear role to play in content management, because they provide the academic content. However, it is not always appreciated that with digital learning materials, academics may not be the only creative people contributing to content. Instructional designers, web programmers, and graphic designers may also be involved.

Students are also increasingly important contributors to e-content. New tools supporting social networking and personal learning environments, sometimes under the generic heading of Web 2.0 (see Downes 2006), enable learners also to create digital learning materials, such as blogs, e-portfolios, digital project work, and online discussions. When whole online courses are offered for sale, should student contributions be stripped out? (This is not always easy to do and can be very costly.) Technically, students own the copyright to their own work, particularly if it is original, unless those rights have been explicitly signed away. At the very least, student privacy needs to be respected. It will then become increasingly important to be able to identify and classify student contributions, and students should at least be consulted both individually and as a stakeholder group about how materials to which they have contributed should be reused.

The marketing division, or the corporate learning division, will also have strong interests in content management. Who should be responsible for the marketing of digital learning materials (if they are to be sold) or for agreements regarding free access to learning materials? Often such agreements are negotiated by individual deans or even individual professors. What is the institutional policy for making agreements regarding external or third-party use of digital learning materials? Who has authority to do this, and on what basis or principles?

It can be seen that there are numerous stake-holders involved in content management. An institution then needs to be clear about the line management of content management. Is this to be devolved to a particular department – e.g., IT Services or the Library or each academic department – with or without a mandate to consult with other interested parties, is it to be the responsibility of a vice-president or vice-rector, or is it to be the responsibility of a committee, and if so, who should be on it, and what is their mandate? (See "Making Decisions on Content Management" below for further discussion of these issues.)

11.4.7 Financial Issues

On a relatively small scale, content management is often a hidden cost, subsumed under various departmental budgets. Sometimes specific content management projects are grant- or project-funded, on a one-off basis, e.g., for the purchase and installation of a specific content management software. Neither of these methods of funding though is satisfactory when large amounts of digital content are being created.

One problem that all institutions considering content management face is the likely cost of putting in and operating a content management system. Although the software and technical operating costs are usually well-defined, the major costs lie outside these areas, in the creation of content, in the tagging of content, in the semantic classification of content, and in the marketing and sale of content. Some of these costs will be incurred, whether or not a content management system is installed, but in many cases, costs of existing operations such as course creation and library activities could increase dramatically to meet the needs of content management. In other areas, such as marketing, totally new marketing strategies may be necessary to lever the advantages of digital content management.

In other words, it is currently difficult to develop a business case for content management, and as a result costs tend to be spread around different departments on a hidden and unknown basis.

11.5 Making Decisions About Content Management

Content management is basically a tool, albeit an increasingly important tool as the stock of digital learning materials grows. Like any tool or service, its value will depend on how it is used. Although content management has a strong technology base, its use has implications across a large range of departments and organizational divisions. In this sense, it is not dissimilar to building maintenance or managing IT services. Thus decision-making about content management should be handled in similar ways.

The decision-making implications can be seen if we consider a critically important decision to be made with regard to managing digital learning materials. For instance, at what level of "granularity" should an institution's digital learning materials be tagged? Should the tagging be at just the level of a course, or a module (a self-contained chunk of study, perhaps a week's work, that contains all the materials or links needed for study), or individual components of teaching and learning, such as learning objectives, diagrams, assessment questions, and digital text? Who should make this decision? On what basis should this decision be made? What are the cost implications?

This question is often considered, understandably, from a purely educational perspective (see, for instance, Wiley 2002). Providing very granular components, such as an animation of the creation of a normal curve of distribution in statistics, may lead to greater use by other professors or instructors, if they can easily adapt the object to their own needs (for instance, by changing the text descriptors to fit the subject matter). However, context is often important in education, so providing an assessment question on its own, without linking it to the learning objectives it is supposed to be measuring, may not be helpful. Furthermore, the more granular the components, the more cost or work there is to be done by the academic, at least in educationally describing or classifying the components (semantic meaning).

However, if the main purpose of content management is to ensure internal sharing of materials between professors, to save them time in the long run in creating their own material from scratch, then very granular tagging may be worthwhile. If on the other hand, the purpose is to leverage the reputation of the institution to market whole courses, then tagging at the course level may be sufficient, particularly if the institution has many online courses.

In other words, the decision needs to be based on the goals and purposes for content management. In a large organization, of course, these goals may vary between the institution as a whole, between academic departments, and between individual professors. This is why it becomes a complex process to make decisions about content management (but no more complex than other decision areas in a large educational institution).

We therefore need to look at some of the most common components of decision-making in complex educational institutions.

11.5.1 Experts

Content management has a significant knowledge base, combining a specialized area of computer science with that of information or library sciences, and some understanding of the needs of teachers and researchers. In any organization creating large quantities of digital learning materials, there needs to be at least one person with expertise in the content management area. This is particularly important because it is still a rapidly evolving technology and there are few existing successful models of content management implementation at an institutional level in education. Someone needs to keep on top of these developments as they occur.

Of course, it is a good idea to have more than one person with expertise in this area, but there should certainly be one person with formal responsibility at an institutional level for content management at a manager level at least. This person could be someone from the Information Technology service area or someone from the Library with specialist IT knowledge. This person should be involved in all key decisions about content management. Also, especially where IT services are decentralized, this person should be responsible for training in content management and for liaison and information provision on content management to all those departments and units where content management is required.

11.5.2   Divisional Responsibilities

Each department or division that is impacted by decisions on content management needs to develop some expertise in content management. It is really important for instance not to be bamboozled by technology jargon around standards and the latest software developments. It is also important, especially with regard to content management, to distinguish between promises and possibilities, small scale pilots, and robust and tested large-scale solutions, of which there are currently very few in education.

Content management is a tool, and needs to be used in ways that are useful to a department. Thus within academic departments, for instance, someone, or more likely, some group, should be able to assess the academic requirements and possibilities while understanding the potential and limitations of content management.

Thus in institutions where IT and educational support services are decentralized, an academic department may need a small group consisting of at least one academic with online teaching experience, someone from the department's IT support unit, and someone such as an instructional designer from the department's educational support unit, to liaise with the institutional manager responsible for content management. This group incidentally may already exist for other purposes, such as providing guidance to the department on IT tools and services. It would be natural to incorporate content management as another responsibility.

11.5.3   Committees

It can be seen from the stakeholder analysis earlier in this chapter that a wide range of stakeholders are impacted by content management. A very common mechanism in educational institutions to manage issues that impact widely is to set up a committee with representatives from each of the key stakeholder groups. Again, it is likely that such an institutional-wide committee may already exist to discuss other IT-based matters, and again this committee could add content management to its responsibilities.

11.5.4   Task Force

In those institutions where there is no current system for content management, or where content management has developed haphazardly, it will make sense to create a task force with a mandate to provide recommendations to the institutional administration and relevant departments about content management. A task force would have a clear mandate, would consult widely, and would have a defined timescale for making recommendations. The task force would be disbanded once its report was submitted.

One advantage of developing an institution-wide approach to content management through a task force would be to identify in as realistic a way as possible the likely revenues or other benefits, such as savings in other areas, that a content management system could generate, recommend goals and priorities for content management, identify intellectual property and copyright issues that need to be resolved, identify the direct and indirect costs involved in implementing content management, identify where most of the work will fall, recommend how content management should be organized and managed, and develop a set of first steps for implementing the recommendations.

Such an approach may result in some proposed content management projects being abandoned altogether, but in the long run a focused and direct institutional-wide approach is more likely to lead to a sustainable and effective system of content management. Such a task force though will require strong support from the senior administration.

11.5.5 Institutional Leadership

Content management is one of a number of developments that need to be properly managed as an institution increasingly develops digital learning materials. Broader questions such as the balance of face-to-face vs. online learning, faculty development and rewards, intellectual property issues, and e-learning support staff require a broad institutional strategy or set of strategies. In many institutions, this broad institutional leadership falls within the purview of the Provost and Vice-President Academic, although other institutions still split some of these responsibilities between a CIO and VP Academic.

It is my view however that the management of digital learning materials is an area of responsibility that should fall primarily under the Vice-President Academic, although as always with technology, decisions are best made when the senior administration all share the same vision for the institution and its use of technology.

11.6 Summary

Content management is still primarily at the early stages with respect to digital learning materials. There are a small number of international learning object repositories, and the open educational resources (OER) movement is rapidly expanding, but still relatively few educational institutions have implemented a system for the content management of digital learning materials created within their own institution on any large scale (see Lane 2008 for one of the few published accounts of the management of open educational resources). However, as inventories rise, content management will become more important.

There are though a number of difficulties institutions face in making effective decisions about content management. The most pressing is lack of information of the true costs of implementation that include not only software and IT service components, but also the impact on professors' and administrators' time. Equally lacking are good data on potential revenues, savings, or other quantifiable benefits. In other words, the business case for content management has yet to be made.

Another challenge for educational institutions is the wide range of stakeholders that have an interest in how content is managed. This means that it should not be delegated to a back room in the IT department, although this may be the easiest way to implement it.

Although valuable experience can be gained from small content management projects, with increased volume of digital learning materials being created, it is useful to take a longer-term perspective to decide how best to manage at least academic content, and to determine how it could be reused. It is essential then that a coherent, systematic approach to content management is developed that ensures participative decision-making from the key stakeholders. This chapter suggests some ways in which this may be done.

Acknowledgements I would like to thank Dr. Michael Magee of the University of Calgary, and the Southern Alberta Institute of Technology for their assistance in providing content and examples for this chapter.

References

Bates, A. (2000). *Managing technological change: Strategies for College and University leaders.* San Francisco: Jossey-Bass.

Dorsey, J. E., Queen's Counsel (2004). *University of British Columbia Faculty Association Union vs The University of British Columbia Re: Dr. Mary Bryson and Master of Educational Technology.* Vancouver: Labour Relations Arbitration Board.

Downes, S. (2006). Web 2.0, e-learning 2.0 and personal learning environments: Podcast slides, from http://www.slideshare.net/Downes/web-20-elearning-20-and-personal-learning-environments.

Lane, A. (2008). Reflections on sustaining open educational resources: an institutional case study. *e-Learningpapers*, No. 10 (A paper by the U.K. Open University's Director of OpenLearn).

Nesbit, J. C., Belfer, K., & Vargo, J. (2002). A convergent participation model for evaluation of learning objects. *Canadian Journal of Learning and Technology, 28*(3), 105–120.

Perry, W. (1976). *Open University.* Milton Keynes, UK: The Open University Press.

Wiley, D. (Ed.) (2002). *The instructional use of learning objects.* Bloomington, IN: Agency for Instructional Technology.

Zemsky, R., & Massey, W. (2004). Why the e-learning boom went bust. *Chronicle of Higher Education, 50*(July 9), B6.

Index

Breinigsville, PA USA
04 November 2010
248632BV00003B/1/P